Rambles of a Pennine Way-ster

Richard Pulk

A journey from Edale in Derbyshire, England, to Kirk Yetholm in the Scottish Borders

With special thanks to Calum and Rory Macdonald at Runrig and to Chrysalis Music for their kind permission for reproduction of song lyrics, which are included as sub-titles for my chapter headings. Runrig stand high amongst the greatest songwriters and performers of the past thirty years, and it's an honour to affirm that recognition in my modest Rambles. Moran taing!

"All things remain, to ignore and outlive you, from the man on the moon to the green hills outside your door"

("Precious Years")

Cover photograph – Cross Fell
Rear cover – Just after Wessenden Farm

Touchline '99

First published in 2007 by Touchline '99

6 Brechin Close, Arnold, Nottingham, NG5 8GN

Copyright Richard Pulk 2007

ISBN 978 0 9536646 2 7
EAN 9780953664627

Typeset by Richard Pulk at Touchline '99

Printing and final formatting:
www.printondemand-worldwide.com
Graphic House, 1 First Drove,
Fengate, Peterborough PE1 5BJ
Tel. 01733 352333

Contents:

~

Introduction

On Monday July 3rd 2006 I took my first step from The Nag's Head in Edale, Derbyshire, England, on my journey of 280 miles – including off route detours for accommodation - to The Border Hotel, Kirk Yetholm, Scotland, which is a fairly impressive pub crawl by any standards. They are of course the official start and finish points – or vice versa if you're heading in the opposite direction – of The Pennine Way, Britain's definitive long distance footpath.

Ever since my first attempt ended in failure, a little over half way at Middleton-in-Teesdale, I'd been promising myself that I'd settle the score "this summer". Following a health scare and a career break, not to mention advancing age, the old adage "now or never" launched me into an ill advised solo attempt to scratch that 36 year itch.

Fitness concerns were always going to be an issue, but if I'd known that they were to coincide with the hottest July on record, with temperatures hovering around 30C, even in the North Pennines, my hiking boots might have stayed in the cupboard.

These rambles are my personal account, based on my daily jottings, but will hopefully be of interest to anyone who has already walked, or may be considering, The Pennine Way or similar adventures. They are not intended as an authoritative guide, but a subjective experience of 20 days, including one full rest day, walking the Pennine spine of England and across the desolate Cheviot Hills into the Scottish Borders.

With time and space to think, it also offered an opportunity to indulge in some Meldrew-esque rants, and a few anecdotes, and "Rambles" is incorporated in the title in its widest sense.

Please also bear in mind that it's my experience of The Pennine Way at the time I walked it, so if, for example, your recollection of the short climb approaching the Redesdale Forest is of a dry, well manicured, jungle free path with steps carefully hewn into the hillside, all I can say is that it certainly wasn't like that when I was there. The same comment applies where I've expressed an opinion about my en route accommodation.

I'd read beforehand – and my previous experience of rambling bore this out – that friends and companions would readily be found along the Way, and thus it proved. Thanks go to all, and particularly Janet and Keith, whose company at various stages, and especially over the closing days, was invaluable.

If anyone has a particular story to tell, or point of view – whether in agreement or otherwise – I'd be delighted to hear.

The Pennine Way remains an enduring challenge in our ever changing world, so whatever your personal motivation, get out and do it!

~

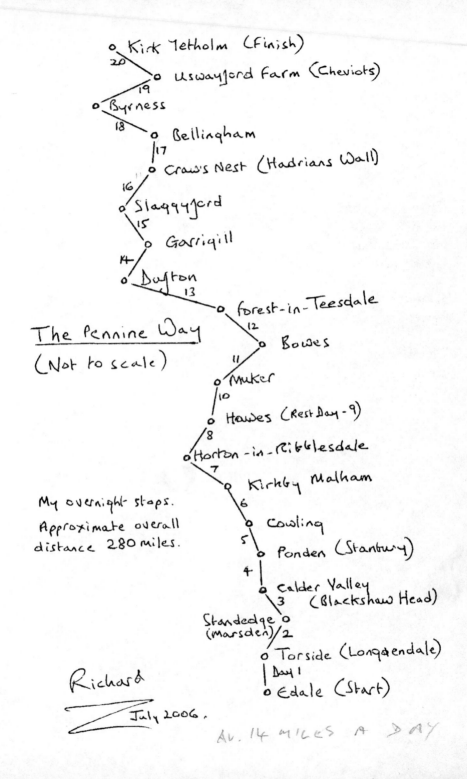

Kirk Yetholm (Finish)
20
Uswayford Farm (Cheviots)
19
Byrness
18
Bellingham
17
Craw's Nest (Hadrians Wall)
16
Slaggyford
15
Garrigill
14
Dufton
13
forest-in-Teesdale
12
Bowes
11
Muker
10
Hawes (Rest Day-9)
8
Horton-in-Ribblesdale
7
Kirkby Malham
6
Cowling
5
Ponden (Stanbury)
4
Calder Valley
3 (Blackshaw Head)
Standedge
(marsden)/2
Torside (Longdendale)
Day 1
Edale (Start)

The Pennine Way
(Not to scale)

My overnight stops.
Approximate overall
distance 280 miles.

Richard

July 2006.

AV. 14 MILES A DAY

Beginnings

"But memories are old ghosts, mountains of black and gold,
sunsets falling over the moor. Take me there"

Mid morning, late July 1970, Middleton-in-Teesdale. The blister under Steve Beer's foot is the size of a golf ball, and it's obvious that he can't continue. I've just slogged a panicky four miles back to a dry stone wall which we'd clambered over with difficulty late yesterday - after failing to find the alleged stile - and a relieved, but exhausting, four mile return, having re-claimed my wallet from the long wet grass.

On top of the twenty miles yesterday, which finished Steve off, my self inflicted solo eight miles first thing this morning, and with no breakfast, following a brain-racking night trying to remember where I might have dropped my life support system, hadn't helped my spirits. They were further dampened by the rain, falling steadily from a grey sky that shrouded the moors. Physically, my brother and me were fit enough to continue, but that would mean even more weight, as we'd have to shoulder the entire camping equipment between us. We could hardly manage our rucsacs as it was. Not only was outdoor equipment in the dark ages compared with today's state of the art gear, but our heavyweight tent and sleeping bags were obsolete even in 1970 terms. Each pack had to be lifted onto our shoulders by the other two walkers, and they were rotated so that we were only stuck with the crippling one, containing the tent, every third day.

Thus it was that with a mixture of relief and disappointment we found ourselves watching the scenery through the rain spattered windows of the local bus to Barnard Castle, before making our way to the sanctuary of my Uncle Harry's flat in Newcastle upon Tyne, only a modest walking distance from a desultory urban fragment of Hadrian's Wall, about which, unfortunately, more later. Harry commented, with admiration for Steve's fortitude, that in all his Army War Service he'd never seen a blister to compare.

That was it then, approximately 140 miles out of an official distance (per the 2006 website) of 268 - excluding diversions and off route

1

accommodation - apart from my insistent, nagging, feeling of "unfinished business", articulated by my regular, and less convincing, as the years turned into decades, response to the annual "What are you doing for your holidays?" question, "I fancy another crack at The Pennine Way". Nearly 36 years later and I was still offering the same clichéd reply, still imagining that I would have another "crack" as if somehow I was a passive bystander and it would just happen, based purely on wishful thinking. As with all dreams, if it's just mental escapism, fine, keep dreaming. If not, there comes a moment when you have to go for it, whether it's a new life in Australia, writing that book, or just a ride in a hot air balloon.

My moment came during my second stint in Insurance Broking, after more than thirty years in the Industry, when I decided that I could "buy" the time for a long summer break before seeking another direction. It suddenly hit me that now was the "window of opportunity", as they say on all the courses, to actually go for it. Notice given, and once I'd got my head into the maps I was on my way, metaphorically at least. I couldn't believe how easy it was – on paper. A sensibly paced 20 days, including a full rest day in Hawes, which was recommended as an ideal stopover, shouldn't be too much for my advancing years – 55 on July 18th – and lack of "match fitness". I'd survived a scarily over ambitious and pioneering charity trek in 2000 across uninhabited wilderness in Outer Mongolia, where even our accompanying team of native horsemen nearly came to grief in a swollen river, and one volunteer collapsed from exhaustion, and had a skirmish, a couple of years later, with the superb Atlas Mountains in Morocco, but nothing since, apart from local strolls around Epperstone, near my home town of Nottingham, and the occasional foray into Derbyshire.

It's reckoned, according to surveys of Pennine Way veterans, that the majority do it primarily as a physical challenge, with scenery, wildlife and rural tranquillity low on the agenda. Whether that's a representative assessment, I don't know, but in my case the physical aspect was essentially a vehicle for discovering whether I could regain an element of fitness and rehabilitation after illness by committing myself to a disciplined daily routine, with the hope and expectation that if I could survive the first couple of days then I'd gain the strength and confidence to enjoy my surroundings, and my prime motivation, the romance of propelling myself from Derbyshire to Scotland by my own two feet.

I'd been suddenly struck down, some 18 months previously, by Reactive Arthritis, and laid low, with three months off work, by excruciating joint and muscle pains that left me unable to lift my hands above shoulder height, turn on a tap, open a carton of orange juice, shower properly or, worst of all, sleep. My shoulders were racked with relentless, grinding, pain, finger and other joints agonisingly swollen, unmitigated by any combination of painkillers, prescribed or otherwise, or any posture, whether lying, sitting or standing. It's a ferocious and horrible condition, potentially triggered by one of a number of factors, including gastric infections, my likely cause, as initial symptoms arose shortly after my return from voluntary English teaching in rural Tamil Nadu, Southern India, where I had a nasty 24 hour stomach bug. The bug was alleviated, interestingly, by a diet of coconut water and whole oranges administered at regular intervals (i.e. when I was not asleep or on the toilet) by my female Indian carer. An unlikely remedy, but I felt fully recovered the following day.

The Reactive Arthritis left me debilitated and with the potential for recurring attacks, albeit usually much less severe, and residual problems, of which tendonitis (particularly the Achilles) and ancillary heel pain, are a recognised legacy, and were to almost curtail my walk. Numerous (and continuing) blood tests and monitoring, including on one occasion a Tony Hancock "armful" of eight phials taken by the nurse at my local GP, discounted every known condition, but had fortunately revealed a serious genetic auto-immune liver problem, which I have recently discovered to be shared by my Estonian niece. Doctor Steven Ryder of Nottingham's Queens Medical Centre brought things under control with immune suppressant medication, but suffice it to say, without wishing to labour the point, that my system wasn't exactly fully geared for my challenge, which I undertook against the advice of my local doctor.

3

Aside from seeking a health cure, I craved a spiritual lift, and the notion of a contemplative trek, at my own pace, up the Pennines and across the Cheviots into Scotland held the same excitement as it did back in 1970. I remember vividly my first ever, thrilling sight, two years earlier, of Mam Tor and the ridge to Lose Hill on the right, and the brooding bulk of Kinder Scout to the left as our train exited the tunnel from Chinley, next stop Edale, back in the days when rail access from Nottingham involved a circuitous route culminating in a final approach from the west, Manchester, side of the Pennines. By 1970 Sheffield was established as our logical transfer point for the local Edale service, where Britain's longest underground – as opposed to water – railway tunnel, The Dore and Totley, effects the equally dramatic transition from industrial hinterland and suburbia, in this case the elevated rural station at Grindleford, gateway to the High Peak.

Grindleford, Hathersage, Bamford, Hope, Edale. Consecutive village railway stations between the industrial giants of Sheffield and Manchester, protected and served at either end by huge tunnels bored through the intimidating moorland expanses, they punctuate one of Britain's most scenic and dramatic stretches of railway. Miraculously, they're still open today, although no longer visited by the Hikers' Specials that used to run on advertised weekends and Bank Holidays from Nottingham and other East Midlands towns. The trains invariably comprised bog-standard British Rail multiple units, usually of six carriages, although on high demand occasions an extra three coach set was added, making for an impressive sight as walkers poured out at their favoured station, often returning from further up the line, perhaps following a glorious ridge walk from Lose Hill towards Edale, or a gentler wooded excursion from Grindleford to Bamford.

Returning after a wet day, an overwhelming mustiness from mud-caked boots, rucsacs, damp or dripping clothes, sweaty hikers and a fair sprinkling of soggy-doggies (including our Golden Retriever Sally, although she stank even in a heatwave as she always found something unpleasant to roll in, whatever the conditions) turned the

4

atmosphere into something reminiscent of our local football changing rooms at Colwick Racecourse. I'd smear a clammy porthole and grab every last second of the passing scenery before we left Grindleford and plunged back into the Dore and Totley, to re-emerge a million miles away, back into suburbia.

I'd been addicted since I set foot for the first time on the platform at Edale – which is still, despite travels further afield, one of my most exciting places at which to alight – and gazed in awe at the forbidding mass of Kinder Scout to the north, and back across the valley to the sharply defined peak of Mam Tor. The Pennine Way had scarcely been open three years, although I was only vaguely aware of its existence, and hadn't the remotest concept that a couple of years, and a handful of visits to Edale, later, I'd be heading up the Grindsbrook, destination Scotland.

It's an adventure that pales into insignificance compared with climbing in the Himalayas, exploring the Amazon Basin, trekking to the Pole or even crossing Nottingham's Mansfield Road at its Shakespeare Street junction after our "planners" (a euphemism if there ever was) multi million pounds "Turning Point" traffic scheme/pedestrian annihilation programme, but even as I type these words, some three months after my second attempt (on the Pennine Way - I've yet to find the courage for another assault on Mansfield Road) it brings a renewed surge of excitement.

In 1968 Mam Tor was the immediate and obvious attraction, and no sooner had we pitched our tent in the campsite a mile or so up the road towards Barber Booth than we'd scrambled up to the top, where the views, on that glorious early evening summer's day, were spectacular. So, in its way, was Mam Tor. It's called "The Shivering Mountain", as it's permanently moving and a-shaking, with bits regularly falling off or subsiding. The old "A" road subsided, then a section disappeared off the edge of the hillside, and it was closed, never to re-open. I walked up recently from the Castleton side and it's quite eerie, following a broad, well surfaced road to the limit of current vehicular access, from where it becomes a shrub and sundry vegetation peppered stretch of decaying and crumbling tarmac, then

5

snakes and tilts like a scene from a San Francisco earthquake, before disappearing altogether along with a chunk of the collapsed mountain.

It put me in mind of a sad and thought provoking experience in Germany a few years before the fall of Communism. I was touring with my wife, and we stayed for a couple of nights in the attractive little town of Molln, not far from the East German border. Curious to witness at close hand the reality of the East/West ideological partition I followed what my map indicated to be an old trunk road, previously connecting large towns, but which now terminated abruptly at the frontier point, beyond which it was shown to resume its meaningless path. Once we'd left the last West German village behind us we had this once major highway entirely, and uneasily, to ourselves, as it pursued its pointless course, through fields and woodland, before a series of signs of the "Achtung!" variety brought us to a halt at a barrier, not unlike the approach to a railway crossing, but in this case permanently in the down position.

Behind it was a strip of "no man's land" with further warning signs, including graphics of guard dogs and mines, then another barrier, and above the trees in the forest beyond, a line of guard towers stretching across to their respective horizons. We stood, mesmerised. It was like something from "Smiley's People", the BBC Cold War TV drama - the tense border exchange scene for which was filmed at a mocked up set at Lady Bay Bridge, just downstream from Nottingham Forest's Trent End stand – except that this was for real. We watched the guards, in their lofty perches, and they undoubtedly watched us, except that they'd got machine guns.

It seemed surreal that people of a common nationality and kith and kin had been suddenly and arbitrarily separated on pain of death if they tried to make physical contact. Villages that were ten minutes apart were now effectively on opposing sides of the planet, worse, even. I mentioned our trip to the hotel manager on our return that evening and he recounted the story of his own family. His brother, who lived just a short distance over the border, was, to the manager's obvious disdain, now a confirmed and "good" East German

Communist, alienated from him politically and, it appeared, emotionally. Rare visits from the West were only available by special permission and via designated roads.

I wonder whether the subsequent political reconciliation led to a family one, or was the emotional damage permanent? Unlike Mam Tor, the road would be easily reinstated, and drivers no doubt now bat along that erstwhile stretch of no man's land with scarcely a thought that a historical blink of an eyelid ago, birch trees and buddleia (always the likeliest suspects where concrete is abandoned to nature) were defiantly sprouting.

A car drew up, and an elderly man joined us at the barrier, nodding a brief acknowledgement but otherwise staring in sad, lonely, silence towards those gaunt towers. Their occupants surely reciprocated, monitoring our every move, if nothing else out of sheer boredom. I wondered at the Wartime experiences and memories of the passing stranger, and what lay beyond the Cold War barrier that now partitioned his country and drew him to visit in melancholic contemplation. We suddenly felt like voyeuristic tourists intruding on personal, and national, trauma, and beat our retreat, but not without mishap.

I drove back for several miles along the deserted road, lost in thought, until we re-claimed the first village, where I was aware of an opposing van in the distance, on our side, clearly about to pull in to make a delivery. As we approached I noticed to my concern that he wasn't stopping, but was continuing to head towards me. The distance closed. As impact minus ten, and counting, loomed, the penny suddenly dropped. "Shit, I'm on the wrong side of the bloody road!" simultaneously wrenching the steering wheel, and the car, to the right. The oncoming driver hadn't even flashed his lights, and sped past, seemingly unconcerned. Given that it was a white van, he was probably ogling the Page 3 girl, filling in his delivery note, or searching for his fags (or all three) and hadn't even noticed me. It's the only time, in numerous overseas visits, that I've forgotten to drive on the right, and hopefully it's the last.

As for Mam Tor, I can't remember if its road was still open in 1968, before the dramatic collapses, but access for walkers was certainly less restricted, and we merely attacked it in one direct assault, fuelled by youthful exuberance. The Kinder Scout plateau squatted bleakly on the other side of the valley, behind Edale village, and this huge wedge of mysterious wilderness compelled exploration. It was the first time I'd seen a North Derbyshire moor close up and its impact was seismic (shades of Mam Tor!) 24 hours later we were sprawled, exhausted and chastened, outside our tent, having learnt the painful lesson that the High Peak is not to be trifled with, and that hiking boots and windproof anoraks weren't just the domain of poseurs or macho explorers but a pre-requisite for anyone tackling those exposed and rough uplands.

We'd hauled ourselves, breathless, up over the top of the Grindsbrook onto Kinder, to find a moonscape of dark peat, wiry stems of endless sweeps of heather, spiky grasses, oozing mud, pools of black, treacly liquid, lighter patches of wind dried crusty earth, barren outcrops of stones and rocks, and randomly scattered boulders of all shapes and sizes, one giant specimen of which perched precariously on top of another huge rock. That it had stood there for thousands of years, blasted by gales and attacked by rain, ice and snow, belied the impression that one good shove would send it hurtling hundreds of feet down into the valley, although we tried anyway, secure in the knowledge that thousands before us had done likewise, and also failed.

To our surprise, the plateau was anything but flat, deep groughs criss-crossing the moor, making navigation difficult and straight line walking impossible. (This was in the days before paved footpaths were prudently lain to protect the fragile peat from the ever increasing numbers of visitors from the surrounding conurbations, often using flagstones from old mills, dropped down by helicopter.) We were forever plunging down into gullies, wrenching our shoes from the deep, cloying, mud or squishing through unexpectedly boggy clumps of grasses before scrambling back onto the next vantage point. We stumbled across the ghostly wreck of an aircraft, one of several to come to grief over the decades, its skeleton sitting on a bare and stony outcrop. Others were simply swallowed up by the peat, as were our feet, to be released again only after a struggle as we ploughed erratically on, eager to reach the next horizon.

Several hours later we were giggling semi-hysterically as we endeavoured to re-trace our steps, with not a sole in view, and Kinder's rugged plateau throwing up no familiar landmarks, not even the aircraft which, not for the first time in its history, had disappeared without trace. Our unsupported ankles turned and twisted in our lightweight footwear as our silly laughter, borne of tiredness and nervous apprehension, gave way to exhausted silent plodding, weaving up and down, into and out of the featureless mire, until we somehow found the approach to the Grindsbrook and eventually staggered back to the sanctuary of our little canvas shelter.

Nevertheless, I was hooked, and celebrated by purchasing my first pair of hiking boots, Hawkins, size 11, following the then conventional advice to take one size above normal shoe, the slack to be taken up by two thick pairs of woollen hiking socks. They had a Vibram sole, with a steel plate running its length, and are virtually indestructible. Veterans of my 1970 attempt, I still have them, essentially for sentimental reasons, as each boot weighs the equivalent of several modern pairs and would use up my entire luggage allowance for any expeditions by plane. They were my first skirmish into "proper gear" but I reckon that, like most activities and hobbies, many folk are now in it primarily for the fashion statement and snob-value equipment, with a whole industry having arisen to provide an embarrassment of riches for today's disposable incomes and leisure time.

Back in my early days, when God was a lad, more or less everything "outdoors" was ex-army surplus, including our first tent. Gore-Tex was light years away and my waterproof top was a bright yellow oilskin cycling cape that would have looked the part on a North Sea trawlerman – although I have to say, with hindsight, that it did the job, apart from billowing up like a sail in strong winds, and allowing dribbles of water to trickle down from the neck area. Hiking boots were just that, but have metamorphasised, and a good thing too, into everyday wear, with any number of permutations and styles. I've yet to be convinced by trekking poles, which seem to have assumed the status of a "must have" accessory, even if it's only for a gentle walk along the canal bank, but I am passionate about my adjustable lightweight metal walking stick, with its proper (90 degree) handle, indispensable on the Pennine Way, and purchased specially from a disabled accessories shop in Nottingham. As well as having a more logical grip, intended for walking as opposed to mountaineering, it's got a broad rubberised "foot" instead of a sharp metal point - hopeless on rocky terrain - with a steel insert for strength, and is excellent for support and purchase on any ground, particularly when scrambling down rocks and stream beds. So, if you're looking for practicality ahead of "pose value", get yourself down to NHS supplies.

One of my earliest acquisitions, another essential, yet inexpensive, piece of equipment, was my first bush hat, a distinctive ex-Desert Army khaki camouflage, on which I sowed – as was often the custom at that time – a badge, in this case a Garibaldi Red tribute to Nottingham Forest. This led to a memorable experience involving the Grindsbrook and our dog. Sally was acquired shortly after our 1970 Pennine Way attempt, and accompanied me on many a slog onto Kinder, even Bleaklow on one occasion, when I under-estimated the return distance and we had to race back, following a direct compass bearing (or at least I was, Sal just followed me, and her nose) with minutes in hand when we arrived, puffing and panting – both of us – at Edale station. She finally popped her clogs, aged 16, and is still missed. She would have made excellent company on my 2006 challenge, being placid with animals – including sheep - and children, her only vice, which leads back to the tale of my bush hat, being an obsession with water and all things wet and muddy. A few random examples illustrate this watery fixation:

We were at the summit of Cader Idris, in mid-Wales one fine summer's day, when she suddenly plunged over the near vertical crag and disappeared down the scree. Panic stricken, I raced down the circuitous path to find her, oblivious to my screams and shouts, swimming in the tarn some 1,500 feet below, having spotted, or smelt, the water and taken the direct route. How she survived that drop, I'll never know.

In the Lake District, three of us hired a rowing boat on Derwent Water, taking advantage of the one decent day, when it was only drizzling steadily, and the precaution of keeping Sal tightly under control until she was safely aboard and we'd cast off. She sat quietly, sniffing the air, until we were a nice distance from land, then without warning she launched herself over the side with a mighty splosh, into the considerable depths of the icy water. Furthermore, she didn't want to come back, and when we did row close enough to grab her we had all on not to capsize whilst trying to haul her considerable, sodden, bulk on board. We ended up like the proverbial drowned rats, but no sooner had we towelled half of Derwent Water out of her thick, spongy coat – retrievers have an extra layer to insulate them from the cold water and aid buoyancy – than the little bugger jumped back overboard. We didn't know whether to laugh or cry, but having repeated the rescue exercise we headed quickly for dry-ish land, where she found some sheep droppings to roll in.

She even found trouble at my local Colwick gravel pits (now sadly desecrated by a hideous retail development and traffic generating loop road) which were at that time virtually unknown and had some good expanses of clean swimming water. Sal took off on a long distance swimming mission and disappeared into the reeds on the tiny island in the centre of the largest lake, whereby an almighty uproar, of the feathered variety, broke out. Ducks, geese and swans were going mental, with a cacophony of quacking, squawking, hissing and beating of wings, with me a helpless spectator from a hundred yards across the water, and Sal's fate looking grim – and serve her right, you might think.

To my relief and amazement she re-appeared from the fracas, seemingly in one piece, dog-paddling earnestly in my direction, as the racket died down and tranquillity returned. As she approached I noticed that she was huffing a bit, with her head held slightly above the water. She scrambled up the bank, and, clearly chuffed with herself, deposited into my hand a large egg, shell unbroken. Given the unlikely scenario of her swimming back and replacing it I carried

11

it home in my trouser pocket and attempted to hatch it in the airing cupboard in a makeshift towelling nest, but to no avail. Shame really, as it would have been interesting to see what kind of surrogate mum she would have made, with the patter of tiny webbed feet following her around.

Anyway, having set the scene, it goes without saying that we took separate routes on our excursions up the Grindsbrook, me following the path, Sal following the equally well defined stream. Those familiar with this original Pennine Way route from Edale will know that the brook varies from gentle stream to fierce torrent, sometimes close, sometimes well below the footpath, and that it is littered with stones, rocks and boulders, some of which enclose deep rock pools. On this particular occasion we were returning from Kinder, my treasured bush hat having gone missing, presumed dead, a couple of years earlier, following active service, most likely somewhere in Derbyshire. I always took it, but it was nowhere to be seen when I next packed my rucsac, so after a decent period of mourning I forgot all about it.

I was strolling back, with time in hand, towards the station. Sal, as always, couldn't walk quietly at my side, but was immersed in a particularly large pool. Typically, she was scrabbling about with her front paws on the stream bed, presumably looking for conveniently sized lumps of rock to excavate, so that I could chuck them back in and she could fetch them out again. Sounds pointless, but it was harmless, and we both enjoyed it. She always brought back the one I'd thrown, even if it meant totally submerging under the water, a stream of bubbles rising to the surface, often for what seemed an eternity, before she'd re-emerge, snorting and dripping. She didn't even bother to shake dry, desperate for the next underwater challenge.

On this occasion she'd been ferreting about in the same spot for ages, only reluctantly coming up for air before sticking her head back under, despite my shouts to "come on out of there!" and I became curious. (She also had selective hearing, and chose to ignore me at her discretion, but this example was obviously of above average canine interest.) As my impatience grew, so did her determination to extricate her prize, and after another stream of Jacques Cousteau-esque bubbles she emerged, triumphant, with something floppy in her mouth – my bush hat, to be precise.

Even now, over 25 years on, I'm amazed. First, she never retrieved anything "soft", even sticks – unless specifically thrown – preferring, strangely, rocks, stones, small boulders and bricks from the bottom. I hadn't a clue where I'd lost my hat, and it had almost certainly wedged there after being carried downstream, as it wasn't a place conducive to stopping for a break. I had walked past, and well above, the spot where Sal had plunged to reclaim it, so that ruled out the coincidence of a chance find whilst I was resting opposite the exact location. I can only conclude that despite its two years in a fast flowing stream, invisible a couple of feet below the surface, Sal had picked up a scent and dived underwater to investigate. If so, it's an amazing example of the canine sense of smell, and proof that it's not exclusive to Bloodhounds!

As for my hat, it appeared to have shrunk slightly, despite the "cold rinse" setting – or my head had grown – but was spotlessly clean, including my impressively colour-fast red badge. Unfortunately, it subsequently went AWOL again, and with no rescue-dog on hand, I've bid it a final goodbye.

Not so, my memories of the Grindsbrook, and Sal, and I prepared for my 2006 Pennine Way adventure with an acute attack of nostalgia.

~

Preparation

"I'm living on the borderline between the moment and the shining miles"

In 1970 it never occurred to us, albeit in part constrained by a lack of finances, to do other than use a tent for overnight accommodation. It also gave us the flexibility, given that we had no pre-booked sites, nor a finishing deadline, to pitch at whatever place and time suited us, subject always to an available spot with the permission of a friendly farmer. The downside to camping, and it's a considerable one, is that shower, toilet, washing, running water and eating facilities are a problem, as is the added weight and bulk, including sleeping bags and mats, although purists might argue that it's the real essence of an outdoor challenge.

In 2006 it never occurred to me to do other than book overnight accommodation, and only in part because I'd be walking solo. First and foremost, by pre-booking I'd got a fixed daily schedule and knew the distances I had to cover. I could vary my start times accordingly, and on the shorter days anticipate an early afternoon finish and a rehabilitating rest. In the event – which thankfully didn't happen – of being unable to make my next booking I could always telephone ahead. If I failed to do so for some unexpected reason then hopefully they would report their concern, thereby providing a degree of safety.

There was also the prospect of a guaranteed "Full English" (aka "Cholesterol Special") to start the day with suitable calorific and nutritional input, and no messing about with pre-packed – usually, in my experience, squashed, spilt, mixed up with something entirely incompatible, unappealing or simply inedible – "Boy Scout" rations, and the paraphernalia of preparation and cleaning up afterwards. Back in the Lake District, and an unfortunate colleague found himself deprived of his breakfast, having carelessly abandoned his plate temporarily, right in front of the dog. Other uninvited participants to outdoor food, most of them after human blood rather than the contents of the frying pan, include sundry midges, gnats, flies, clegs (of which, sadly, much more later) and mozzies, plus the

14

compulsory and revolting UFO that's just dropped in and is crawling across the plate as you're about to take your first mouthful, as in "Yuk, what's that?".

Not just breakfast, but the eagerly anticipated and morale boosting evening meal. The more remote B & B's, almost invariably farms, will provide one automatically unless declined, others will recommend the local village pub, and on some occasions your accommodation will be the pub, or hotel. No wrestling with the tent in a gale or pouring rain (or even worse, de-hydrated and sweat soaked in an unprecedented heatwave) before trudging, still grimy and unwashed, to the nearest inn, if there is one, and stumbling back across suddenly unfamiliar fields in the darkness, or the alternative of heating some congealed stuff outside in a pan, whatever the elements, followed by rudimentary "washing", of self and utensils, usually courtesy of the trickle of a nearby stream. I'd done all that, and whilst I'm sure things have improved upon my grim picture, it nevertheless remained firmly off the agenda.

I set off for each successive B & B comforted by the near guarantee (other than what proved to be just a couple of minor hiccups) on arrival of: a) shower, with water temperature to suit; b) fill available time prior to evening meal by dozing on soft, clean bed; c) evening meal, washed down by preferred beverage; d) retire for the night to soft, clean bed; e) re-visit hot water and fluffy bath towel during pre-breakfast ablutions; f) follow nose to Cholesterol Special, served at agreed time to fit the day's schedule.

To this end I utilised the excellent and free Pennine Way Accommodation and Public Transport Guide (tel., assuming it's still available, 0113 246 9222) which I'd acquired casually a full year earlier and which, in truth, was the catalyst for my final decision. I rediscovered it by chance whilst clearing out some drawers, and was hit by the simplicity of it all – hand in notice, which I'd been contemplating in a vague "Then what?" sort of way – make the bookings and walk the walk – after 36 years of talking the talk. As easy and final as that. The guide comprises 19 mapped sections, including a final one for possible accommodation at Kirk Yetholm, each one more or less equating to a reasonable daily itinerary, and coincidentally close to matching mine. It doesn't claim or intend to be definitive, and of course sections can be missed or duplicated for longer or shorter schedules.

I chose to follow it in numbered sequence, one stop per section, other than two nights at Hawes, which gave me a full rest day. With the longest day, 21st June, already behind me, thanks to an intervening "commercial" visit to Estonia to inspect my recently purchased little plot of land, I determined to start and finish within July, whilst plenty of daylight remained, and hopefully avoid the worst excesses of the notoriously fickle Pennine weather. Allowing for commitments the preceding weekend, that meant Monday 3rd July, with a final, hopefully celebratory, night in Kirk Yetholm on Saturday 22nd.

I assumed that I could simply pick out my chosen B & B's, make a call and confirm the booking, which was somewhat naïve, to put it mildly, given the short notice and the fact that, for example, the popular tourist attraction of Malham, coinciding as it did with my intended Saturday night, was full of weekenders, forcing Hobson's Choice, after a dozen increasingly desperate calls, of Kirkby Malham, and a longer walk than I'd anticipated the following day. Equally stupid, I booked in sequence from Section One, where listed availability, given the Pennine Way's proximity to higher population centres, was much higher, although even then I was never successful first time, and often had to pursue recommendations for unlisted places, with a sequence of "Have you tried Mrs …?", until finally securing my bed for the night.

North of Middleton-in-Teesdale availability is particularly limited and often remote, none more so than the isolated Uswayford Farm (pronounced something like "Oozyfud") which, although necessitating a round hike of almost four miles from the Pennine Way, is the only realistic and listed possibility to break what would otherwise be a gruelling 29 mile trek over the exposed and desolate Cheviot Hills to the finish line. Following a brow mopping and surprisingly time consuming exercise – two days of phone calls, sending of deposit cheques and careful listing of directions and other

16

information on the relevant pages of my accommodation "bible" – with severe difficulties in pinning down, as options ran out, digs at a couple of northern outposts near Hadrian's Wall, I made my call to Uswayford with some trepidation.

Nancy Buglass confirmed, to my expressed relief, that she had a room, simultaneously advising me that "You'll be wanting an evening meal", which, given that it's officially England's remotest B & B, (21 miles to the nearest shop, down a rough track for several miles before even a sniff of a minor lane) wasn't my most difficult decision. Pennine Way walkers excepted, I can't imagine other than the hardiest and most curious of visitors "dropping in" off the moors and through the forest, but I'd have been in some trouble, having secured and confirmed all my other bookings (bar my final call, to Kirk Yetholm) if a party had beaten me to it.

That left a week to sort out maps and additional equipment, boosted by a generous and thoughtful leaving present of Outdoor retail vouchers by my work colleagues at Alexander Forbes. My 25 litre day-rucsac was clearly too small, so following best advice from a helpful assistant I opted for a blue 45 litre jobby, theoretically big enough to lug everything for a B & B trek, but not recommended for camping. Given that I wasn't sure if and when I'd ever be using it again, or even if I'd finish the Pennine Way, I'd asked for "best value", and plumped for the first – and cheapest – option, based on it feeling comfortable, lightweight (as it would, being stuffed for demonstration purposes with nothing heavier than tissue paper) and possessing, as far as I could judge, all the right pockets, flaps – including foldaway waterproof cover – and straps. Its papoose shape rode high on my back and despite the lack of a "designer" label, and the threefold price hike (apologies for pun) to match, it looked well made.

Experience and common sense teach that, like a new pair of boots, a rucsac should be broken in, fully loaded, before engaging long distance duties, to avoid back or shoulder problems, be it aches, strains, bruising, friction sores, or general incompatibility, but my first test, due to time constraints, would be the half mile walk to

Hucknall Railway Station on day one, en route to Edale and the trek across Kinder and Bleaklow. In the meantime I merely lifted it a few inches from the floor, as I packed and re-packed, just one day before departure, following my initial "Bloody hell, it weighs a ton". I was fortunate to discover that apart from some chafing on my back, just above my waistband – exacerbated, and in all probability caused by the heat – it was just the job.

Next priority was a compass, a reluctant purchase as I had a perfectly good one somewhere, but hadn't a clue where, having last seen it some ten years previously. As an old work colleague always used to say, annoyingly, when a file went missing, "It'll be the last place you look", which of course is true – provided that you find it. I followed the compass with a couple of pairs of pricey, but "Guaranteed 1,000 miles blister free" socks, to supplement the half dozen other pairs I was taking.

I'm fastidious concerning foot protection and hygiene, which of course should be a pre-requisite for any walker, but have the added incentive that my big toe joints are fused by metal pins following surgery for a localised arthritic condition, not helped by years of pounding, including a round six miles daily walk to school and back, hiking, tennis and football. I was told that surgery was the only option if I wasn't to end up crippled, and almost twenty years on it still feels like a miracle cure, thanks to the expertise of orthopaedic surgeon Mr Brian Holdsworth.

A lightweight, quick-dry, non iron long sleeve top also found its way into my bag. I was seduced by the claim on the label that it was impregnated with a non-toxic (to humans) insect repellent, accompanied by a convincing, at least to me, who wanted to be convinced, statistical table on the lines of "kills 99% of all household germs", relative to its efficacy in two categories, a) the large percentage that were dissuaded from alighting in the first place, and b) of those that did, the small percentage that would still summon up the determination, presumably through clenched teeth and streaming eyes, to bite or sting. How they tested the product to produce those compelling statistics, I don't know, but I have to report that following (unsolicited) trials involving a particularly vicious specimen of the insect world I took to rinsing it out nightly for repeated wear and can claim 100% protection.

I've already mentioned my stick, and that left the minor afterthought of a decent set of maps. There are various possibilities, including definitive Ordnance ones, but for convenience and weight I opted, taking the advice of a veteran Pennine Way colleague, for the two Companion Footprint foldaway maps, the Pennine Way South, from Edale to Teesdale, and the Pennine Way North, from Teesdale to Kirk Yetholm. Less detailed than some, including the Ordnance publications, and confined solely to the narrow strip of the Pennine Way (impractical if you intend to stray far from the route or seek broader orientation) they proved the ideal compromise for my purpose, apart from an occasional wish for greater detail.

So, a good morning's catch from my trawl around Nottingham's city centre, enhanced by a bonus that evening at my local supermarket. Having decided to carry water, that most precious of en-route supplies, in a couple of large plastic mineral water bottles, as was my wont in the Derbyshire Dales, I alighted fortuitously on some lightweight 0.75 litre picnic accessory containers, insulated by thermal jackets like miniature central heating boilers. I snapped up a couple and they fitted snugly into the side pockets of my new rucsac. I also bought a floppy, folding, Velcro-strip wallet, with pockets, zip-up compartment and plastic map reading window, three fabric draw string bags for not sure what yet, and a zip-up toiletries bag for first aid, to complement my existing one for toiletries.

All set then, but with only the weekend now separating me from that 36 year dream I was suddenly hit by serious doubts as to whether I'd been kidding myself all that time. I'd scheduled that final Friday to sort out everything I needed, by working through my itemised list, then packing and re-packing to get things shipshape, before enjoying the weekend, but my second thoughts, borne of the scary reality that my appointment with my Pennine Way destiny was here, with no more comfort zone that I'd do it "next year", brought on a kind of depressed inertia.

It was a combination of a natural apprehension of the physical task ahead, concern regarding my Reactive Arthritis legacy and that I'd be skipping part of a designated programme of blood tests to check that my immune suppressant medication for my liver wasn't affecting my blood count, my age and lack of fitness, the frantic last minute rush, and not least, that I'd be doing it solo. I suddenly felt vulnerable and alone, not in terms essentially of safety, or my ability to navigate across the moors, but companionship. Despite the many words of support and encouragement there was no escaping the stone cold fact that I wasn't with a mate to share the planning, packing and the banter, and to take the sting out of any last minute doubts. If and when I do my next expedition – and the seeds are already sown – I'll try to persuade some other poor sod to accompany me!

The final blow was the weather forecast for the week ahead. I'd hoped for some warm July sunshine during the trek, maybe even the low 20s on the hills if I was lucky, interspersed with showers or a few rainy days, even longer cold and windy spells if I was unlucky. What I got was a forecast of 30C for Monday, my first day, and getting progressively hotter through the week. There were repeated warnings that in view of the imminent heatwave old people, young people, middle aged people, people with medical conditions, people without medical conditions, people planning sports or other outdoor activities, or walking to the shops or bus stop, cats, dogs, other household pets and farm animals should all stay indoors with their heads in the fridge – or words to that effect. The warning went on to imply that any persons contemplating walking the Pennine Way should be locked up for their own safety.

I'm paraphrasing, you'll be surprised to know, but the "don't go out in it unless there's no alternative" message was loud and clear, repeated in sensationalist Tabloid headlines. What I didn't know, and would have really made me think twice, was that next week would be just the pre-cursor, that we were about to experience the hottest July on record, and that even the Pennines of Northern England would scorch in unprecedented temperatures. As it was, the forecast for week one, on top of my other misgivings, left me asking myself whether I was being a complete prat and attempting too much, and whether I should just forget it, cancel the B & B's, stick my head in the fridge and enjoy a long, self pitying, depressive sulk.

On Sunday evening, having done absolutely nothing to advance my preparations over the weekend, I stood looking at the scattered clusters of assorted essentials I'd carefully ticked off from my inventory – undies and socks in one group, tops and fleece in another, cag, waterproof trousers, light cotton jeans, toiletries, first aid, water containers, various bags, brolly, towel, navigational stuff, food supplies, contingency money and plastic cards – all of it to be packed into my untested rucsac, its 45 litre capacity shrinking and ever more inadequate as I stood, forlorn and mentally paralysed. I just couldn't face the effort of working out the jigsaw of which pile to stuff in first, or in which pocket, and only broke free from my torpor when I remembered my boots.

They'd still to be re-proofed, so I turned my back on the debris-strewn floor and table and spent the next thirty minutes kneading in half a tin of thick, waxy, water repellent that was, according to the tin, "suitable for Gore-Tex". I felt better after that, as is usually the case when a meaningful physical activity interrupts and reverses depressive stagnation, although it's one thing knowing it, it's quite another identifying a therapeutic task and having the will and sense to do it.

It was still a logistical battle, first putting all the fiddly things – razors, toiletries, tablets, first aid, films, spare laces, scissors, tissues, wet wipes, etc. – in their respective bags, then deciding what to cram in, where. I started with the towel, flat at the bottom of the main compartment, then the cag, not looking a likely early requirement given the forecast, spare jeans, tops (in separate plastic carrier), pants and socks (ditto), blue drawstring and toiletries bags, then towards the top for possible en route access, fleece (bulky, but essential for breezy hilltops – except that, other than two stormy days, there weren't any!), first aid bag, and right at the very top, day rations bag. The water containers, duly filled, would sit snugly in the side pockets, and the broad front one, almost un-useable due to the volume of stuff in the main compartment, was prised open to cram in four packets of Dextrose energy sweets, more or less unchanged in wrapper or content, as far as I could recall, since they provided supplementary rations on our 1970 expedition. The brolly fitted neatly into the trekking pole straps on the outside, and I decided to carry my camera and foldaway wallet, containing maps, compass and B & B itineraries in a hand held carrier for easy access en route.

Whilst my camera and wallet had adjustable neck straps, and also waist clips, brief trials convinced me that their swaying and banging against my body would drive me mad, hence the carrier bag, which evolved, from day one as the only viable option to accommodate extra food and drink, including a huge and surprisingly heavy packet of dried apricots, to become an essential accessory. I was to be gently teased by other walkers, but can report that it suited me perfectly, and I also used to drop in en route consumables, e.g. extra plastic bottles of water, Lucozade Energy drinks – two bottles per day after half way, subject to local availability – bananas, etc. I can advise that the Pennine Way, using medium-duty supermarket issue, is a six carrier bag route, and torn or damaged ones can be replaced at all good B & B's.

My emergency whistle remained on my key ring, in my trouser pocket. My walking stick occupied my left hand, balancing and supporting my potentially injury prone right ankle, legacy of torn ligaments, once playing football, then, to my incredulous despair, on Eyam Moor, Derbyshire, when a large stone gave way unexpectedly on my final fitness training prior to my Mongolian epic, resulting in me in agony on the ground, followed by a left footed drive home, 12 hours in bed, a hugely swollen ankle and, as the healing began, multi-coloured bruising from my knee to the end of my toes. I somehow limped the trek thanks to strapping, Ibuprofen Gel, and a borrowed NHS stick (the moment of my conversion!), which was soon, in shades of déjà vu, to become a familiar Pennine Way experience.

That I didn't seek medical help in 2000, with only six days to go prior to flights to Moscow and on to Ulan Bator, was because, having been signed off work for a week – albeit that I only took one day - last time I'd done my ankle, less seriously and ten years younger, my local doctor was hardly likely to sanction my trip to an unexplored and inaccessible wilderness, and that would therefore invalidate my Travel insurance. Given that I'd raised £3,500 in sponsorships I was going, whatever, and achieved my mission thanks to the invaluable advice – a lengthy telephone consultation – of my old schoolfriend Richard Skinner, a practising GP in southern Sweden. It proved then, and was motivation for my 2006 adventure, that it's not always in the patient's best interests, not least psychologically, to err on the side of caution or "best medical practice". To quote a profound line from a Moody Blues song – "It's easier to try, than to prove it can't be done".

Having tested my rucsac by the simple expedient of lifting it a few inches off the floor, I subsequently emptied and re-packed it three times, on each occasion abandoning more bulk and weight, including a couple of tops, some of my underwear and socks (en route laundry was to mean that I still finished with some unworn) and my lightweight "evening wear" shoes due to their inflexible shape, making do, reluctantly, with boots only, and stockinged feet on most indoor occasions. The dry weather and lack of mud – bar one or two days – was to be a bonus, but I'd always take extra footwear, space permitting, in future.

By the time I'd finished, my final inventory was as follows:

Inventory

Rucsac – 45 litre capacity

Multi-section foldaway Velcro wallet, containing:
Compass
Pen
Maps (folded and displayed daily in plastic window at relevant section)
Pennine Way Guide – my "bible", within which I'd marked up every B & B, date, contact name, details of booking arrangements and telephone number.
Also used for en-route storage of B & B receipts, literature, etc.

Plastic zip-up Toiletries bag (black), containing:
Toothbrush
Toothpaste
Disposable razors – 5
Scissors – small
Half a toilet roll (fortunately, never needed)
Wet wipes
Tissues
Shampoo sachets – several
Soap – small
Plastic hairbrush
Underarm deodorant – Old Spice, as always, 'cos it smells nice and never causes a rash

Drawstring bag (blue), containing:
Replacement films for camera
Exposed films
Notebook
Another Pen
Spare glasses
Spare bootlaces
Bank card wallet

Extra cash
Mobile phone charger
Cheque-book

Drawstring bag (black), containing:
Lightweight supplementary rations, e.g.:
Cereal bars (minimum 2/3 days contingency supply)
Mars Bars or similar as purchased daily
Sweets, mints, etc.
Any other compact food, including Complan bars on day one

Plastic zip-up Toiletries bag (blue) for First Aid, containing:
Crossover ankle support bandage
Knee support bandage
Tubi-grip bandage
Animal wool – 1 box
Plasters – assorted, plus broad strip
Antiseptic multi-use cream
"Plix" – Estonian bought Mozzie cream
Nurofen
Paracetemol
Ibuprofen Gel
Daily medication – Azathioprine tablets
Diarrhoea sachets
Indigestion tablets

Socks – 6 pairs
Pants – 6 pairs
Shorts (never worn) – 1 pair
Lightweight jeans (for evening wear) – 1 pair
Lightweight non-iron easy dry long-sleeved top – 1
As above, but insect proofed, and consequently worn almost daily –
1
Nottingham Forest "Away" shirt, long-sleeved, Brazilian Yellow,
worn for 2 hours in the Langdon Beck Hotel and for the last 20 yards
of the Pennine Way - 1

Small towel – 1

Lightweight wind and waterproof (allegedly) cagoule – 1

Lightweight Waterproof trousers (never worn) – 1 pair

Hooded black fleece – 1

0.75 litre water containers – 2

Dextrose Energy sweets – 4 packets

Car and house keys fob with emergency whistle attached

Cash – carried in pocket, in addition to supply in drawstring bag

Mobile phone, in waterproof soft plastic Velcro case

Yashica "Point and Shoot" pre-digital camera

Umbrella

Dried apricots - 1 x Family size pack

Spare plastic carriers for dirty clothing etc.

Adjustable lightweight metal walking stick

Worn on departure:

Underpants

Hiking socks – 2 pairs

Hooped rugby shirt, long sleeved

Heavy duty black jeans (too heavy, in hindsight)

Hiking boots, veteran, comfort assured

Bush hat

~

Day One. Edale to Torside, Longdendale.

"The sun is melting over the hills, all our roads are waiting to be revealed"

Monday July 3rd dawned, as forecast, hot and sultry, and even as I stumbled into the bathroom at the unearthly (for me) hour of 5.30 I knew that I wouldn't be needing my fleece, even on the High Peak.

I'd decided to get the train, or rather, trains – three of them in total – from Hucknall, just north of Nottingham, to Edale, some sixty miles away, which meant catching the 6.40 Robin Hood Line train to Nottingham for the Sheffield train, then change again for Edale, arriving 9.47, at an average overall speed, including a considerable time waiting around, of just under twenty miles per hour. I'd explored the logical, geographically speaking, option of heading from Hucknall to the line's northern terminus at Worksop, and a Sheffield service from there, but the timings reduced the average speed to little above my intended daily walking schedule, so that was a non-starter.

At 6.20 I hoisted my fully loaded rucsac onto my shoulders, literally for the first time, mindful of the extra weight generated by the vital expedient of carrying my 1.5 litres of water, a quantity that would prove totally inadequate in the exceptional heat, but was more than ample on the handful of wet or cooler days. I thought I'd legislated prudently, but had to rely on stream water, a commodity that proved almost non-existent in the North Pennines and the notoriously dry and remote Cheviots, with no access to hostelries or farms. In an endeavour to compensate, I would over-indulge on tap-water at my B & B prior to breakfast, followed by orange juice – prudently refusing the coffee – then another full pint of water, before setting off, but the heat soon drained it out of me, and by the end of the first sweat-soaked climb I was already making alarming inroads into my supply and keeping an eye open for clear, bubbling streams to replenish my containers.

All that was to come, although past experience, and the fact that my system has always run higher than average on water intake, pre-warned me, and had been a trigger for the depression when I heard

27

that distressing weather forecast and the repeated "stay indoors" warnings. They hadn't specifically mentioned slogging for miles over rugged and exposed moors with a heavy pack, but I intelligently drew that conclusion.

At 6.21 I was striding across a deserted Hucknall Market Place, already, after just fifty yards, reassured that my rucsac, as I'd predicted when I tried it on in the shop, would be both comfortable and practical. I was perhaps foolish not to have made time to give it a test run, but in any case I was stuck with it, one way or another, so might as well leave it until the real thing rather than risk another worry. "It'll be alright on the night" was my maxim, and so, fortunately, it proved.

I had my stick in my left hand and a Tesco (if memory serves me) carrier bag in my other, containing my camera, foldaway wallet and my giant size "special offer" re-sealable pack of dried apricots from Sainsbury's. The apricots were gone by day three, but the carrier, or at least its successive replacements, went from strength to strength in the indispensability stakes. A cautionary note, though – if you worry about Street Cred, take my advice – trekking poles are "cool", carrier bags aren't (yet!)

By 6.41, having safely negotiated (never guaranteed, especially on a Friday night, when screaming piss-heads infest the pavements and the Police are conspicuous by their total absence) the half mile walk to Hucknall Rail/Tram station, I was already on board Central Train's elderly two coach DMU, which was Sod's Law, given that they're often late. I wouldn't have minded a sleepy ten minutes on the platform bench, eating into my long wait at Nottingham. The Sheffield train, ultimate destination Liverpool Lime Street, used to pass my work-day train in the opposite direction, just outside Nottingham, hence my having to take the 6.40 one, nearly a full hour earlier. Impeccable scheduling.

The Liverpool service normally comprised a modern three car set, usually full, but on this baking Monday morning it pulled into Midland Station's platform 1a with a miserable two carriages, witness, it seemed to me, of Central Train's permanent juggling of inadequate rolling stock resources, evidenced by several farces on the Robin Hood Line. One recent peak hour "train" comprised just one coach instead of the usual crowded three, with scores of passengers (sorry, "Customers") stranded on the platform, with insulting announcements asking for any Bulwell or Hucknall bound occupants to leave the train and get the tram instead. Still, as long as any unscrupulous Franchise Directors have a framework in which to extort their guaranteed rake-offs, subsided by the "legal" (albeit morally nauseating, the more so when it's encouraged and applauded by Blair and his Spoof Labour clique) pick-pocketing of the taxpayers' pocket, then that's OK. The three car unit was probably needed more urgently elsewhere.

By the time we reached Alfreton we were packed like sardines, with luggage – always bad following a weekend – piled up in every conceivable nook and cranny, and people standing the length of the train. Despite being mainly geriatric and noisy, the Hucknall units do have the advantage of a controllable air supply, courtesy of the opening windows above every seat, whereas this fully air conditioned set didn't, and the system had failed. The guard (sorry, "Revenue Protection Officer") somehow forced his way through to check that we'd all bought a ticket, and in response to the plea from the young lady next to me that she was about to faint, directed her, pleasantly and sympathetically, through the jam to the other carriage where, he reported, it was "about minus ten" due to the perversity of the mechanical problem. She opted for the Arctic, rather than pass out on the floor, and the rest of us sweated it out.

Sheffield thankfully arrived before the oxygen ran out, and I managed, with difficulty, to extricate my rucsac from behind and below the morass of assorted baggage piled under, on, and all around the inadequate luggage stand, then push and shove my way through the door and out onto the relative comfort of the platform, where the early morning temperature had just a few modest degrees to climb to reach the forecast 31C, the graphic for which had been ominously writ large on yesterday's weather map right on top of the erstwhile Steel City. I dumped my bag and sat on a shaded bench, pitying those poor souls replacing, and more besides, which scarcely seemed possible, those who'd just escaped. There should have been a porter (sorry, "Customer Logistics Facilitator") on hand to direct passengers – "Sardine Class only, today, Heatstroke coach on the left, Hypothermia to the right".

My rather quaint Dinky-style toytown train waited in the bay platform at the south end of the station and had the dual benefit of opening windows and only a relative sprinkling of passengers. Two of them, an older couple of fellow walkers, engaged me in conversation and it transpired that they were from Conisborough, off on a day's ramble from Hathersage. We sat together and talked hiking, and travel, and the Pennine Way, and the little train soon clattered and rocked into the black hole that is the Dore and Totley Tunnel, finally re-appearing, just when it seemed that we really had descended into the bowels of the earth, into the painfully harsh brilliance of the sun-scorched Grindleford Station, and another universe.

To my great joy, I was instantly hit by that familiar, but no less diminished, surge of excited anticipation, and the surreal limbo of the past few weeks, preceded by the trauma and agonies in deciding whether to resign from my job, instantly evaporated. I was on my way, fully focused and finally enjoying the undiluted prospect of striding out over those bleak moors, now coming gloriously into view to my right, destination Scotland. I bade farewell to my new friends – as undoubtedly they were, kindred spirits united on a brief train journey – and watched Kinder Scout appear as the little train rattled on beyond Hathersage, Bamford and Hope into Edale, 9.47 on the dot, just like it said in the timetable.

Water was already my first priority, and suspecting from vague recollection that there was a tap in the Pay and Display car park I exited right from the station, instead of left into Edale village, where lay the official start of the Pennine Way, with the intention of making significant inroads into one of my containers before re-filling it. After a few yards I changed my mind and opted instead to call in at the village shop, where I could buy a bottle.

30

Ordinarily I detest paying hundreds of times more for stuff that isn't up to tap water standards of either taste or hygiene, and comes, often after transportation over huge distances, in a pretentiously labelled bottle and bulk packaging that will take thousands of years to disintegrate. It's an insane – literally – "fashion statement" gone bonkers (I'm convinced it's possible to travel two stops on the bus without resorting to swigging from a plastic container) that's an environmental and profiteering scandal and should be urgently curtailed, maybe by a combination of education and swingeing taxes. Nevertheless, needs must, and somewhat hypocritically, given that I'd abandoned my half-hearted quest for the Edale tap, I bought the cheapest one litre bottle, the contents of which were demolished by the time I'd ascended Kinder Scout.

The benefit of my indecision was that I met Mike, who had half followed me from the station, instead of going the correct way and disappearing without trace. Having pointed him in the right direction, we strolled into the village and he waited whilst I bought my water, our having by that short time agreed to walk together to Crowden, in the Longdendale valley, our scheduled overnight stop. This was despite my expressed reservations that my lack of fitness might hold him back, as I was committed to pacing myself sensibly for the first few days. I also told him that if I really struggled, especially given the heat, I would reluctantly abandon ship, knowing that I'd given it my best shot. He was unconcerned, and for his part welcomed a companion who knew the area and the route.

From first sighting I'd realised, by his lean and wiry physique, that Mike was fitter, and no doubt faster, (although in my younger days I once hammered a measured twenty five miles in five hours on a midnight charity walk, followed by another two miles home) and I could be committing to a stranger with an incompatible expectation of realistic progress. I discovered that he was a couple of years my senior, a keen runner and fitness enthusiast, and had just taken early retirement from his career as a Social Worker. His wife was still employed as a Teacher, back in their locality down on the Hampshire coast, and Mike was taking time out ahead of the Summer holidays for a solo seven day dash up the first part of the Pennine Way as preparation for a pre-booked trek with friends in late Summer around Mont Blanc. My early impression, that he was a nice bloke and wouldn't have any ego problems if he had to keep waiting for his slower companion to catch up, proved to be correct, although I'm pleased to say that once I'd endured and overcome the first couple of hours of slog, especially the lung-bursting ascents onto the moors, we were fairly evenly paced.

Using my newly developed easy-access camera-in-a-carrier-bag rapid-photo-shoot system I pointed my Yashica Auto-focus at the "Official Start of the Pennine Way" sign on the wall of The Nag's Head, pressed the shutter release, and we were off, but not, this time, up the Grindsbrook. That nostalgia trip was denied me by the re-routing of this first section to the Kinder Scout plateau via Upper Booth and then along a track and up Jacob's Ladder, an initially more gentle, but longer, introduction than the climb alongside the stream, with the steep, rocky scramble at the top. The "V" shaped valley of the Grindsbrook is still an alternative option, but not one that seriously crossed my mind, given the extreme conditions.

The gently undulating opening stages, with a fine panorama unfolding over the Edale valley, allowed me to settle into a comfortable stride that seemed equally suited to Mike. We exchanged pleasantries and backgrounds, then brief introductions to Janet and John (eponymous reminders, whenever our paths subsequently crossed, of learning to read in my early school days!) who were sheltering from the heat whilst adjusting their packs in the little National Park unmanned stone built information hut at Upper Booth. Like us, they'd just set off from Edale, and were tackling the Pennine Way with the same scheduled finish day to mine.

I was to see a fair bit of them during the coming days, and to learn that they were also making a second attempt, having failed due to John's health breaking down early on in their venture a couple of years back. Aged in their sixties, they were experienced walkers, and Janet was a veteran of a number of solo treks, including the Coast to Coast. They lived in Wigan, evidenced by John's regional Lancashire burr, with his wife a southern incomer. We were mutually supportive whenever our paths crossed, but never exchanged contact details as their finish didn't ultimately coincide with mine, with news, courtesy of my B & B farmhouse on the penultimate stage over the Cheviots, that Janet had telephoned to cancel their booking due to Heatstroke. Hopefully, they were merely delayed, and perhaps able to continue after recovering, but regardless, I would love to hear from, or of, them.

We walked on, and I was gratified to learn, courtesy of a quick glance at my newly developed waterproof map-in-a-wallet-in-a-carrier-bag rapid-navigational-information-assimilation system that we'd already covered more than a whole mile, leaving (as it transpired) a modest 279 remaining. My floppy bush hat, bought from M & S specifically for my Mongolian trek, was already proving invaluable, and without this simple accessory there's no doubt that the fierce sun would have finished me off. Mike, Janet and John, incidentally, were similarly attired. Nevertheless, and as anticipated, the ascent to Kinder up Jacob's Ladder was purgatory. Gasping for breath, sweating profusely, and already making worrying inroads into my shop-bought extra water, I had to stop at ever shortening intervals, for ever lengthening periods, whilst Mike patiently waited on each occasion, clearly more than capable of making the ridge in one fell swoop (couldn't resist the pun), and scarcely drawing breath.

I'd known from the moment when I decided to re-visit the Pennine Way that I'd struggle on the first couple of days, especially on steep ascents, but hoped and anticipated that I'd walk myself into fitness. I couldn't realistically legislate for the debilitating affect of the heatwave, nor the embarrassment factor of accompanying a bloke who ran miles every day. I regularly reminded Mike during those early stages that I was happy for him to press on, but he graciously declined, and I accepted that he was content to clip his wings to my pace, reminding me in turn that he appreciated my company and knowledge of the terrain.

At least I was psychologically prepared, and whilst no-one could have expected the hottest July on record, perversely extending to the normally cooler Pennine uplands, past years of experience had preconditioned me mentally. Sometimes it's best not to know what lies in store, but the old motto "Fore-warned is fore-armed" stood me in good stead and I was largely attuned to the forthcoming demands of Britain's premier long distance footpath. I was also curious to experience again, at least as far as our previous demise at Middleton-in-Teesdale, any familiar sights and places from our 1970 effort.

Casting my mind back I could recall with total clarity the hoisting onto our backs of overweight rucsacs at Sheffield station, cotton grass on Kinder and Bleaklow, camping at a gloomy Crowden, and behind the pub, accompanied by more rain, at Standedge, glorious views over the Calder Valley on a beautiful evening from our impromptu pitch in a field temporarily donated by a kindly farmer, sweeping vistas over the Yorkshire Dales above Hawes, a grey and rain-swept Malham Tarn, our tramp over the featureless moors behind Tan Hill Inn, and that dismal finish, in dismal weather, at Middleton.

Huge chunks in between were a fog, and I was hoping to clear the mists of time and re-kindle old memories so as to re-experience much of that distant and hazy adventure. Disappointingly, even the images I'd held seemed different or unrecognisable, and those missing chunks refused to materialise as I re-traced my steps, those at any rate that hadn't been lost forever by 36 years of footpath tinkering, diverting, re-aligning and paving, not to mention changes in scenery brought about by forestry or agricultural practice.

We skirted Kinder Downfall, which was reduced to a predictable trickle, and began the long, gentle descent towards the Snake Pass and the aptly named Bleaklow. Of the cotton grass, of which I vividly recall large expanses of white fluffy tufts waving in the breeze, there was almost none, possibly due to the dry state of the moors, a consequence of longer term drought, although Bleaklow, which seemed to retain more of its bogs and black pools, offered greater reward. Of the North Derbyshire Pennine breeze, a euphemistic term for "perishing wind", (as is "bracing", in the context of "Skegness is so bracing" - but it's still one of my favourite seaside resorts, regardless) and a familiar feature of my hikes over the high moors, not a whisper. Zilch. Not even the odd helpful puff. And so it was to remain, with the exception of a few contrasting days.

The flagstone path dropped us down from Kinder, and we could see the sharp glints of sunlight reflected from the traffic moving silently below. Without a map, I would have taken it for a modest twenty minutes to the road, but a quick glance showed, amazingly, that we had nearly three miles to cover. Thus are distances so deceptive, usually under-estimated, as in "it's just across the valley and over that ridge", which at the end of a long tiring day with daylight fading and bad weather closing in can lead to disaster. Even in recent days, as I currently type, in mid October, a party of half a dozen Duke of Edinburgh Award seekers had to be rescued from one of the less severe and remote areas of the Derbyshire Peak District. In my experience (the endless approach to Stoodley Pike was to prove another example) it's always further than it looks, and despite stepping out briskly along the weaving path it took us nearly an hour to reach the A57.

Some purists contend that paved paths are a form of "cheating" and are entirely against the spirit of open access and exploration of the countryside, and they may have a point, but the modern causeways, usually utilising traditional pavings, have an essential function to protect the fragile peat and wildlife areas and are an obvious – again, some would suggest molly-coddling – aid to navigation. One downside is that their inconsistent sizes, textures and heights mitigate against a relaxed stride pattern, but ploughing erratically through the groughs, gullies, water holes, marshes, bogs and uneven tufted grasslands of the peat moorlands is infinitely more demanding, exhausting even, especially in wet and heavy conditions.

In 1970 there were no paved paths and I can only stand back from a distance and admire our achievements in crossing, not long out of school, and with ridiculously heavy packs, an undefined and dangerous Kinder Scout and Bleaklow, in deteriorating weather and light, with me successfully using the compass to plot, in 100 yard fixes, the demanding traverse to the approaches to Torside Reservoir, and our descent to Crowden. Army units on exercise have come to

35

grief on that wilderness, so it's a feat that we can reflect upon with pride.

Mike and myself were guaranteed (one subsequent hiccup excepted) no such difficulties, crossing the Snake Pass to find, as stated in my Footprint Pennine Way Guide, that there was indeed now a paved path leading up and onto Bleaklow, but not before, thirsty and with only half a bottle of water remaining, I'd cheekily replenished my supplies. Two large vans were awaiting an outward bound party in the lay-by and a multi- gallon water container, with tap, was on duty on the open tailgate of one of the vehicles. My polite enquiry of the lady in attendance was greeted with the response that they had more than they needed and she insisted that I exhaust my supply before filling both containers. Blessed relief!

Suitably re-hydrated, and with the knowledge that only six miles now remained, most of it, once we'd completed the shallow ascent ahead, flat-ish or downhill, I felt confident and capable for the first time. We walked well, catching an older walker, a recurring feature. Why aren't more youngsters up for the challenge? Are they too occupied for their entire twelve months Gap Year – we slotted our 1970 effort into a "Gap Three Weeks!" – jetting off all around the world to find a derisory month on a magnificent challenge that's right on their own doorstep? Or am I mistaken, drawing an erroneous conclusion from my narrow experience of one scorching July?

The chap ahead was a Geordie in his sixties, accompanied by a Black Labrador, already, despite its youth, and plentiful exercise, doing what Labradors do (they're a poverty stricken man's Golden Retriever, in truth), i.e. running to fat, chunkily plodding just ahead of him – although that was to change the following day when it charged after some sheep. They were fellow Pennine Way-sters, veterans of a previous success on Scotland's West Highland Way (which is beginning to sneak into my reckoning as a possible future challenge), and he told us that he was now taking the dog on a "proper walk". Support was provided by Mrs Geordie, who met them at the end of each day for a lift to their overnight accommodation. As with Janet and John, I would see him intermittently, but I then lost track after the first few days, although word came via others that he was still well on course.

Bleaklow, despite my earlier optimism and its helpful flagstones and cairns, was more difficult than expected, as it simply extended ever onwards in the relentless heat, a shimmering, amorphous, rolling mass of exposed and disorientating upland, unlike Kinder with its recognisable plateau and defined edges and views. The path wound upwards following deep gullies cutting through the moor, views often curtailed entirely by the peaty parapet. It was steeper than I'd remembered, and as we rested briefly, and I surveyed that wild and beautiful expanse, I wondered how we'd ever crossed it in 1970, in poor weather and visibility, and not a single flagstone to guide us. We'd simply followed the compass, with youthful exuberance and naivety, over whatever the terrain threw up, with no cosseting by "sanitised" footpaths, nor, despite being aware of the dangers, undo concern about getting lost or stranded.

My concern was that Torside and the Longdendale Valley remained stubbornly elusive, still hidden beyond more hillocks and ridges, but I was comforted by Mike's agreement that the view from Bleaklow's northern perimeter seemed long overdue and he was also ready for a good rest at his B & B. After trudging across another rise, the valley and its reservoir suddenly lay enticingly ahead, some 1,300 feet below, but as with our approach to the Snake Pass, a deceptively long haul still lay ahead. The path initially ran parallel to a steeply dropping gully to our right that clearly wound its way into Longdendale, but then threw its spanner into the works as we crossed the stream that is Torside Clough. It became almost non-existent, undefined and unsigned, possibly, but not obviously, climbing very steeply and sharply back up the moor and above us along a narrow and difficult ledge to the left, which seemed illogical, as we had a lengthy descent ahead.

After much deliberation and consulting of respective maps, soon joined in discussion by the re-appearing Geordie (the dog opted out, preferring to drink 2 gallons of stream water whilst we debated) we incorrectly concluded that our route must proceed down to the right, alongside the stream. Fifteen minutes later, having descended a couple of hundred feet down what became an increasingly steep and difficult descent, funnelling into the stream itself, we were back, breathless, up onto that ledge, from where a narrow but well defined path suddenly revealed itself, as did, from our lofty vantage point, the further progress of the stream, cutting an ever narrower path before dropping and tumbling, at times vertically, and always inaccessibly, hundreds of feet over rocks and boulders.

The Pennine Way is not for clueless idiots who've no idea how to read a map or a compass, but this was the first of thankfully just a handful of occasions when a clear way-marker – be it a cairn, arrow painted on a rock, or fully fledged sign-post – was necessary, to point us back up the hillside after we'd descended near the head of the clough. An exhausted walker, or walkers, in bad conditions might have continued to follow the stream, with potentially disastrous consequences, and maybe something similar had happened to that recently rescued group, albeit in a different part of the Peak District. Once a psychological point of no return is passed – "We can't go back now" - every advancing step compounds the danger. As if to prove my point concerning Torside Clough, Janet and John, and Janet and Keith (who I was soon to meet at my first B & B) also got confused and temporarily lost at this location. It's also the case that if numbers are going wrong in the same place then boot-prints and worn ground – as happened with us – can prove to be another pointer in the wrong direction.

Having reclaimed the straight and narrow – except that it wasn't particularly straight – we were disappointed that the path refused to commence its descent into the valley ahead, stubbornly gripping and meandering along the extreme edge of Bleaklow and forbidding escape, whilst Torside Clough dropped ever more abruptly away on our right, as did the shoulder of the moor. I was suddenly tired, and discouraged by the fact that my only prospect of an evening meal, confirmed verbally when I booked my accommodation, was a lift by the farmer at 7.00 to the pub, sharing a taxi back with two other pre-booked Way-sters (Janet and Keith, as it transpired). It was already

5.30 and if, at a push, I made it for 6.30, with another hour's heat and fatigue under my belt, I'd have thirty minutes to shower and rest before dragging myself out again, yet I knew that I had to eat well – better than average – or I was doomed.

Even Mike was getting weary as Bleaklow hung on, only losing its hold at the very last when we suddenly descended steeply, and gratefully, down the hillside towards the track and paved road from Reaps Farm. My hard working stick, not for the first, and far from the last time, especially so on the severe inclines which were often encountered late in the day due to most villages and farm accommodation sheltering down in the valleys, came well and truly into its own, and shared with my bush hat my accolade for indispensable accessory. As we met the track a lady came towards us, announcing that she was awaiting her husband, who was visible on the ridge, along with their black Labrador, picking his way carefully towards that final descent.

Mrs Geordie (I apologise that I didn't register their names, or even the dog's for that matter) kindly offered her mobile as mine didn't have a signal – as was often the case, and if walking in a group I'd suggest varying networks for optimum coverage – enabling me to report my position and e.t.a. to my digs. To my surprise and relief my host offered to pick me up, which wasn't cheating as I'd be rejoining at almost the same spot tomorrow. I bade farewell to Mike, who was still two miles short of his overnight, the Youth Hostel at Crowden, and his intended crack of dawn start next day for his mammoth trek – heat allowing – to Hebden Bridge, and a farewell by proxy to the Geordie and his dog via his wife before, a few minutes later, my lift to The Old House, Torside, arrived.

Mr Crook, my chauffeur for the half mile journey, and Mrs Crook, who met me on arrival, afforded a friendly welcome, and after abandoning my boots in the hallway alongside another two pairs, property of my fellow guests, I was introduced to my downstairs room, gloriously cool thanks to its thick stone walls and shaded aspect, and well appointed, with modern en-suite facilities. As I was to discover, many farmhouse B & B's, even in remote areas, provide smashing, friendly, accommodation in beautiful surroundings, and with facilities and ambience better than many "brochure" hotels I've stayed in. I had maybe forty minutes to shower and put up my feet, but not before I'd demolished the cold drink provided on arrival, plus another three or four glasses from the bathroom tap, an essential re-hydration that became my daily priority, the odd cooler days excepted.

Torside Reservoir sparkled in the hot evening sunshine through the windows of the spacious lounge/cum breakfast room, where I met Janet and Keith for our 7 p.m. lift to the pub in Padfield. There was no way I could face a late night, and I was relieved to find my new colleagues of like mind. Mr. Crook informed me that most Pennine Way walkers, after this first, and demanding, stage are back in bed by 9 p.m. It's a feature of the challenge that the initial two days, in either direction, whether the High Peak moorlands from the south, or the remote Cheviot Hills from the north, are considered the most difficult, the more so that body and mind are often unused to these sudden rigours, and they account, no doubt accentuated by lack of preparation, both physical and mental, for the fairly high incidence of early drop-outs.

Unlike the younger guests (late thirties/early forties, I'd tentatively speculate, terrified, as always with that sensitive issue of age, of causing any offence!), who'd prudently brought evening wear shoes, I had to prise my feet back into my sweaty boots, and with hindsight I'd have gone for a slightly higher capacity rucsac with space for lightweight footwear. I was otherwise pleased to discover that my packing list was just about spot on, given that I couldn't have legislated, for example, for my fleece remaining redundant due to the unprecedented weather conditions.

Over an enjoyable and filling meal at The Peels Arms I learnt that Janet was a G.P. and Keith a self employed Agricultural Advisor to farmers in their resident town of Bury St Edmunds (which unfailingly evokes in my childish mind that corny line, "I come to bury St Edmunds, not praise him) and that they'd opted for one of the "luggage in advance" services, only carrying their day to day essentials. The downside of such facilities is that they don't cover the more remote, northern, sections, it's expensive, and there's always the risk – as they were to find on one occasion – of arriving at overnight accommodation to find that the bags are still en route.

In truth it had never crossed my mind, but in any case I'd pared my weight down to a sensible minimum (I was surprised to find that my rucsac was considerably lighter than Mike's seven day bag) and even assuming the luxury of baling out my spare clothes, toiletries and a few other bits for onward transportation I'd still have my cag. and fleece (however hot, if I came to grief anywhere I might need protective clothing, and also my brolly as shelter), navigational stuff, first aid, daily rations and, not least, water, which of course is by far the heaviest commodity by volume. So, on balance, I was happy with my arrangements.

I also learnt that Keith had studied in Nottingham, and had lived in my old stamping ground of Carlton, Westdale Lane if I remember correctly, partaking of local refreshments at such haunts as The Punchbowl and The Plainsman. It was another illustration that the more I've travelled, the smaller the world seems to be. He'd spent the odd Saturday afternoon at The City Ground, in a halcyon period when Forest provided decent entertainment at realistic prices. That position, throughout Football, has been more or less reversed, and my true comments concerning the "earnings" of Premiership "stars" are unprintable. Suffice it to say, and remembering that they also get obscene sponsorship deals and huge payments for auto-biographies (almost invariably ghost written) when they're scarcely into adult-hood, plus all the other sycophantic trimmings, that a cap, on 2007 average UK earnings levels, at £2,000 per week would be more than generous, and I'm including Chelsea's mercenaries in that category.

As predicted, we were back for 9-ish, having shared a taxi summoned by the barman (it's obviously a regular arrangement) and as I creaked into my comfy bed I knew that tomorrow, with aching, tired, body, and the intensifying heatwave, would be an ordeal. I'd always known that the second and third days would be defining ones as my system came to terms – or not – with its gruelling regime and I reckoned that provided I'd no injuries or strains by Wednesday night my stamina would be improving. I've always been a slow starter anyway, even at football as a kid, when I'd be gasping for breath first thing, but wanting to carry on under the streetlights until midnight when everybody else had had enough, and all being well the worst should be over by the end of day three, just after the Calder Valley.

If I'd known what day two held in store I'd probably have had a lie-in at The Old House and caught the train back from Edale.

~

Day Two. Longdendale to Standedge.

"Nothing but the sun"

I opened the curtains to find a horse's head hard up against my window. I'm pleased to report that it was nothing to do with a dire Mafiosi warning, as it was connected to the remainder of this large and thick-set beastie, an equine lawnmower intent on razing every last blade of grass, even if it meant dropping alarmingly down the slope that ran up from my side of the farmhouse, almost, it seemed to my bleary eyes, about to drop in and introduce itself. Chickens were scrabbling about above and behind in the farmyard grit, and a variety of doves, most of them unusually distinctive, with attractive colourings and fans, were hovering and perching in and around their artificial roosts in the outbuildings. I learnt from Mrs Crook that they were indeed uncommon varieties, but as they were her husband's exclusive passion her knowledge otherwise extended no further than mine.

Breakfast had been agreed for 8-ish, which was to be my usual preference, allowing for a start by 9, often 8.30, yet a not unreasonable 7.15 clamber out of bed. That gave me time to sort out my day's provisions, re-pack my rucsac, which I'd empty every evening, transferring dirty clothing into a plastic carrier for stuffing next morning into the bottom and subsequent laundering when the build-up demanded, fill my water containers and generally get everything organised and planned so that I could march off straight after breakfast. Hopefully there'd be ten or fifteen minutes spare before my "Cholesterol Special" to enjoy the luxury of a horizontal sprawl on the bed, casually perusing the map of the day's section ahead.

Mrs Crook didn't disappoint in the brekky stakes, serving up the archetypal, and very nice too, "Full English" (the Scottish version of which, from my experience, concedes even less to healthy eating!) comprising options from all or some of fried eggs, bacon, sausages, mushrooms, beans, black pudding, bread – fried, toasted or as it came – tea, coffee, orange juice and fruit, with choice of cereal for starters. I indulged heavily during the earlier stages, but as the walk progressed I got "Full English Fatigue" and reached the point where the thought of another traditional fry-up, for all its calorific merits ahead of a long day, was no more savoury than the prospect of a season ticket for Notts County.

Instead, I went for cornflakes, two boiled eggs (thus maintaining my cholesterol intake!), toast and orange juice, plus fruit, even bananas, which I love, but had long since given up as they cause a catarrhal reaction. Bugger the snot, I needed the slow release energy, and the walking, plus hot sunshine, reduced my usual runny nose to a few derisory drips. Not forgetting my Azathioprine tablets – "take with food" – and having skipped the prescribed blood tests to tackle the Pennine Way I was relieved that there were no noticeable side-effects and that my immune system (as has been subsequently confirmed) remained fully functional.

Also at breakfast was a man, now with his wife, who Mike and myself had spotted acting strangely on the approach to Bleaklow. Crouching down secretively in the heather, he was obviously watching something, and presuming it to be a rare bird, or maybe an unusual animal sighting, I enquired, to find that he was an observer in respect of an outward bound group taking their Gold award, which doubtless explained the roadside vans where I got my water. His wife, although I'd not recognised her, was presumably the ladler.

He was judging a group of late teenage, supposedly experienced, girls taking their orientation and self sufficiency final exam and was in despair as they were "absolutely hopeless". Apparently, amongst other disasters, they'd even failed, in clear visibility, to find Torside Reservoir from the edge of Bleaklow, and he and his wife were about to break the news that the exercise was to be immediately abandoned as they were nowhere near the required standard. He was puzzled and disillusioned that the girls had been put forward in the first place and implied that they'd have been more suited to a beginners' course. Still, and following my earlier complaint, they were youngsters, and were at least trying – extremely so, in his head-shaking opinion.

Janet and Keith set off ahead of me after breakfast as Keith was on a mission to launch an early attack on Black Hill before the sun got its act fully together. Mike, with a two miles start at Crowden Youth Hostel and his first-light departure, was probably already ten miles into his charge to Hebden Bridge. My first mile, across the fields and over the dam at Torside Reservoir, was something of a geriatric crawl as my legs re-acquainted themselves stiffly with the idea of another day's tramp over the moors, in this case to the A62 Oldham – Marsden road, just south of Standedge, where I was to telephone my B & B host Diane Hawkins for transport to her Manchester Road, Marsden, accommodation some three miles east. That is, unless I failed to get a signal, in which case, she advised me – no doubt borne of previous difficulties – that I should get one down the road at the pub. Similar accommodation exercises were carried out by the two Janets and respective partners, as there are no B & B's in that immediate vicinity, and in their case public transport along the A62 provided partial assistance.

Despite walking for long periods – frequently entire days – on my own, I didn't lapse into sad conversations with myself, although at a confusing point I might exclaim "Now where?" or let out the occasional expletive if circumstances dictated, perhaps after scrutinising the map - "Shit, is that all I've done?" - so it was an unfortunate and embarrassing coincidence that shortly after I'd crossed the dam and spotted the slightly overgrown path that cuts through the trees to cross the A628 I gave myself an audible and self congratulatory pat of "Well done Richard, that's the way up there" just as a walker appeared through the canopy in the opposite direction. It wasn't even particularly "well done", as the village idiot would have spotted the clear Pennine Way sign.

We exchanged "Mornings", and I felt foolish whilst he looked around to see where "Richard" had gone to, before he revealed, in a Scottish accent, that the Pennine Way was just an incidental section of his epic hike from Cape Wrath to Dover. Edinburgh based, early retired, and a Mike clone in the lean and fit stakes, he told me that his worst part of the walk so far had been Cross Fell, where he'd had to divert along the roads owing to storm force winds and poor visibility, but as he wasn't a purist it didn't particularly concern him. I wished him well for his final Pennine Way stage over Bleaklow and Kinder, and the few remaining miles to Dover, and he did likewise for my northern journey with my imaginary friend.

At least I wasn't, as I did occasionally, partly to amuse myself and partly as a mildly irritated response to their incessant bleating, responding with a loud "Baaaah!" to a group of sheep, sometimes, it has to be reported, with definite reciprocation. Nor did he witness me singing "Three wheels on my wagon, but I'm still rolling along", which came to me, rather appropriately, out of the blue after a few days and stuck, off and on, and driving me mad in the process, for the remainder of the walk. "Those Cherokees are after me, they look mad, things look bad, but I'm singing a happy song …….."

Crowden, rather than a hidden cave, lay about a mile up the road, and whilst I thought I recognised the camp site location where we'd pitched on that gloomy, drizzly, summer evening, the Pennine Way headed sharply north, to the left of the Crowden Great Brook. My 1970 recollection, which may well be a false one, is that after de-camping in the morning we'd followed the gentle ascent immediately alongside the brook, before the final climb towards Black Hill, up and through the narrowing valley, whereas the route now follows a fairly severe and more immediate climb on the left, high onto the ridge at Laddow Rocks (bringing back memories of a childhood Nottingham greeting of "Ey-up me laddo!") and one that had my lungs bursting again, sweat pouring off me as the temperature rose.

I spotted Janet and John up ahead, resting several hundred feet higher on a large rocky outcrop, and vowed to do likewise, worryingly consuming over half a bottle of water when I got there. They'd already pushed on, although we were to meet up on Black Hill, and I took my turn on the shelf (not for the first time!), waiting until one man and his dog, visible in the distance below as they in turn slowly ascended from Crowden, were within range, before waving a greeting and resuming my trudge. The staccato nature of the steep climbs – at least early on, until, as I'd hoped, my improved stamina eliminated most of the oxygen breaks – had of course a damaging affect on progress, with the result that I took only very short lunch breaks to compensate, and also to prevent aching joints and limbs from ceasing up, a problem that became acute in the later stages.

I drenched my bush hat at every available opportunity, the water running down my face and neck for a couple of minutes before the heat dried it out again, but those regular cold dousings and its permanent shade were undoubtedly fundamental in my battle against heat stroke or exhaustion. There was, to my unbounded relief, plenty of available water approaching Black Hill, and with my supplies already half finished, but only a fraction of the day's walking under my belt, I threw caution to the wind (or I would have done if there was any) and made the decision to refill from streams. There was no realistic alternative as I couldn't see me making the daily distances otherwise.

In "average" weather my 1.5 litres plus my substantial pre-departure intake and Lucozade or similar en-route extras would be more than adequate – as proved on the cooler days – but in temperatures consistently hovering around 30C, with no cooling breeze and the sun scorching down relentlessly on the exposed, tree-less, uplands three or four litres was a realistic en route minimum for someone of my high consumption. The "dead sheep upstream" syndrome didn't bother me as a) I'd never seen a dead sheep in a stream, b) I selected only juvenile, babbling, little chappies with relatively little "upstream", and certainly not enough for a sheep to fall into, and c) even if – and statistically I reckon it's thousands to one – there was a dead sheep in my carefully vetted supply, what I didn't know would hopefully not harm me, as the dilution by endlessly running water would surely have dissipated most harmful germs by the time it got to me.

That last argument's a bit dodgy, I know, and isn't necessarily borne out by Medical Science, but I understand that the greatest – and admittedly, potentially nasty – risk is Giardia, but it's relatively uncommon and caused or spread, I believe, by human contamination – e.g. faeces – and prudent selection of a source high up on a desolate hillside, suitably above or away from the path, and farmland, seemed relatively safe. Regardless, needs must, and having decided at the planning stage not to buy any water purification tablets as they render the taste disgusting – and, I believe, are no remedy against Giardia either – I sunk the remainder of my rations on Featherbed Moss and re-filled from the local free and ready chilled supply, and continued to do so, without so much as a dickey tummy, for the ensuing 264 miles. Water consumption was also a consideration in my decision to step back from my morning fry-ups, salty bacon most definitely included.

Fully re-hydrated and with that gruelling assault behind me I anticipated an easy walk above Laddow Rocks, only to find that the narrow, unpaved, footpath hung at the very edge of the precipitous ridge. Instead of the confident, steady, progress expected, I was nervously shuffling and picking my way gingerly along the crumbling path, in places over or around huge boulders or slabs that overhung the dizzying drop. Accepted, I'm not a great lover of heights, and I'm sure that the Fred Dibnahs of this world would have marched blithely on, scarcely breaking stride. I'm capable of doing likewise when I'm walking along the pavement, veering around fellow pedestrians to within a few dramatic inches of the road, secure in the knowledge that I won't stumble off the edge of the kerb, simply because it won't matter if I do.

It's all in the mind, and whilst I've nonchalantly taken photos looking straight down the Empire State Building from behind the protective barrier and can sit glued for hours at an aircraft window at 35,000 feet I turn to jelly near an unprotected harbour wall or cliff edge. My sense of balance is, I reckon, as good as most – I used to show off by riding my bike for miles "no hands", until the inevitable pot-hole exacted retribution – but my brain, unlike the late lamented Fred's, is programmed to continually remind me that if I'm at the edge of a bloody great drop one false step guarantees death or serious injury. Fred's would presumably have told him that walking along that ridge was a piece of cake.

Not for me it wasn't, as I concentrated fiercely on every step, averting my eyes from the otherwise compelling panorama to the right. As a result I was consciously leaning to my left, thrusting my stick down for re-assurance at every stride, and frequently stumbling, occasionally falling, with a cry of "Shit!" into the safety of the clumps of heather as the path disintegrated barely a couple of feet from the brink. I was consoled by the indistinct threads that intermittently deviated for a few yards parallel to the defined route through the difficult tangle of vegetation, illustrative that I wasn't the only one to struggle with heights. For once, I was grateful that there was no wind.

The path finally fell away gently and safely to the right, meeting the higher reaches of the Crowden Brook, a bit squishy in places, before a tolerably shallow climb on flagstones led across the desolate moor up to the trig point on Black Hill. I enjoyed my steady progress and the gloriously bleak emptiness surrounding me, the silence broken only by startled birds suddenly launching themselves out of the heather for a short ground hugging flight before disappearing again into the undergrowth.

One particular variety, approximately Blackbird size, and with a white rump and black tail, had been identified on Kinder by Mike as a Wheatear, and they were a regular and entertaining feature of the North Derbyshire and Lancashire/Yorkshire moors. In contrast, a large and extremely noisy species would often frighten me half to death by crashing out of its invisible hide, where it could have safely remained undetected for years, at least as far as I was concerned, in a frantic, panic stricken beating of wings, screeching its familiar alarm call of "I'm here, shoot me, I'm here, shoot me!" It's a wonder there are any Pheasants left.

I think I just about recognised the trig point from my last visit, and Black Hill's peaty mass seemed vaguely familiar, although more sanitised courtesy of the pavings, and consequently, although fewer people are, sadly, now walking the Pennine Way (partly due to greater choice of alternative footpaths, both in length and locality) less "pioneering". Janet and John were resting there and I needed no encouragement to join them for a few minutes before they set off again and quickly disappeared as they fell away on the descent to cross the A635 Oldham-Holmfirth road at Wessenden Head. I waited

49

for one man and his dog to arrive, partly so as to discreetly check that the Labrador was under control and up to no mischief.

It had forged some way ahead of its owner after Laddow Rocks and semi attached itself to me, before dramatically tearing off down the hillside and across Crowden Brook where, to my horror, it made for two sheep that it had obviously spotted from afar. The sheep bolted, hotly pursued, until thankfully my screams of "Come here!" succeeded in calling the dog off. Its owner was so far back that he hadn't realised until I enlightened him, and I knew from his actions on Bleaklow that he always had the lead to hand when sheep were nearby, but there'd been none visible immediately prior to that isolated pair.

I suspect that, like me, he'd been watching his footholds on that ridge whilst his four- pawed-drive canine friend had pressed assuredly on, with me its original goal. Regardless, neither a savaged sheep, nor a shot dog (or both) would have made a pretty sight. They turned up together, drama over and hopefully never to be repeated, and after a pleasant chat it was my turn to disappear down the path, but not before, somewhat ungratefully, and despite previously displaying friendliness, the dog snapped at me when I bent to stroke it. Maybe it still had frustrated visions of lamb chops.

It was that next stage, a modest couple of miles of apparently easy descent on a flagstone causeway towards the A635, that hit me for six. As the path fell away I could see the sunlight shimmering on the distant cars traversing the open moorland, but didn't much relish the effort of getting there, especially as the approach to Snake Pass reminded me that it would be a much longer slog than it appeared. I'd enjoyed the climb onto Black Hill, but the rushed preparation for my expedition, stress of resigning my job, lack of sleep and fitness, illness and hospital visits, and today's traumas, compounded by the blistering heat, suddenly caught up with me, with no prior physical or mental warning, literally within a few seconds of hauling myself back onto my feet after my brief rest. "I don't fancy this".

The pavings snaked unevenly and surprisingly steeply down towards a deep gully that my map revealed to be Dean Clough (no doubt also one of Brian's many relatives dotted about the Notts/Derbys borders) and I realised, with sinking spirits, that the Pennine Way, despite approaching initially from a much higher elevation, dropped down well below the level of the main road to cross the Clough before climbing steeply back up. If I'd studied the contours I'd have been fore-warned, but none the cheerier for knowing. Janet and John were sprawled out way below me, taking early lunch in an idyllic spot alongside the cooling stream.

I scrambled down the dusty zig-zag path, devoid of its mill slabs on this steep section, to join them, only too aware that every jarring step, every missed foothold, stick thrust down urgently to stop me sliding onto my backside, would be countered by its equivalent uphill torture, muscles aching, stick now used for propulsion rather than braking, and worst of all, the sweat and the thirst, under that baking sun. Every serious ascent, even the shorter ones, had me gasping for a drink. I dunked my bush hat, exchanged pleasantries, then commenced my assault on the other side. If I'd rested, tempted as I was, I reckon I'd never have got going again, and in any case I had a rule of never stopping for a break at the foot of a climb. I somehow hauled myself up, in short bursts, back above the clough, and plodded on uphill to finally meet tarmac at Wessenden Head.

The road surface oozed dribbling black ribbons under my boots. Traffic squished by, tyre noise more reminiscent of a damp, drizzly day. I always disliked my skirmishes with asphalt, and this one entailed a short eastbound stretch along the "A" road, then a left for a few hundred yards up a minor one before, thankfully, another left onto a track that led to Wessenden Reservoir, before I cut across the desolate Black Moss to my pick-up on the A62 at Standedge Cutting. It was that easy on the map! I'd intended to stop for lunch when I met the road, but the passing vehicles and the shimmering heat, intensified by the melting surface, persuaded me to slog on for another punishing mile and down the stony track where I sprawled on a grassy bank, with fine views down towards the reservoir and Wessenden Farm, my next objective.

A study of the map revealed that a modest three miles remained, the first one along the easy, gently descending, track to the farm, then a final couple, with scarcely a contour line in sight, across the moor. Fresh, and in tolerable weather, it would have been a doddle, but in those conditions – and in my condition – it became one of the longest walks of my life. I guzzled most of my remaining water, relieved to find, as indicated by the blue lines on my map, replenishment later from a kindly stream, and demolished all but my emergency food rations. Eating en route was always a bit of a chore, through necessity rather than perceived hunger, as the debilitating heat and thirst suppressed my appetite. Nevertheless I duly persevered, knowing that to do otherwise would be foolish, potentially dangerous, as tiredness set in.

Duly refreshed, I relaxed and enjoyed the remainder of my thirty minute break, my back to the sun, hat protecting my head and neck, legs outstretched, next target visible an "easy mile" ahead, or so it seemed. I rose reluctantly, with an audible "Ouch!" as aching legs testified that, as anticipated, day two would be critical, and hobbled painfully into some semblance of a respectable stroll, gradually regaining a rhythm as I crunched along the gravelly surface. No navigational considerations to concern me, but the constant glare – despite my darkened photo-chromic glasses – and waves of heat reflected from the light coloured aggregate were murder. The clichéd maxim "It's a long road that has no turning" was never truer, as I measured my agonising progress by fixing on minor landmarks a hundred or so yards ahead, such as a grazing sheep. In sad fashion, I even exchanged the occasional "Baaaah" as I passed by.

To my relief and surprise, Wessenden Farm, and the inviting clump of trees that cast the only available shade that I'd seen for miles, eventually came into range, as did a couple who'd taken refuge from the mid afternoon furnace on a sheltered stone ledge. I estimated them to be in their early twenties and learnt that they were fellow Way-sters, also on their second day, and had previously done the Hadrian's Wall Walk, the Pennine Way section of which was to give me considerable grief on another blistering afternoon. Speaking of blisters, the woman was suffering badly, and they were both, despite being fit, properly equipped and experienced, struggling with the heat. I discovered that Janet and Keith had sheltered with them briefly, and given that they hadn't been within my range of vision when I stopped for lunch I reckon that the young couple must have been there for maybe an hour or more.

Even so, I was up and off again ahead of them, mindful that my body was not attuned to a re-start if I made myself too comfortable. I was also well aware, which was a slightly scary thought, that I had no alternative but to crack on across that sun-baked and isolated moor if I was to reach the sanctuary of my B & B. They followed on a few minutes later but to my surprise – I'd taken it for granted that with age and fitness on their side they'd soon overhaul me – they remained some distance behind, which was a minor crumb of comfort over those gruelling final miles. I was to learn the following day that they'd dropped out reluctantly at Standedge, unable to continue, which perversely encouraged me in my efforts. The conditions clearly were as extreme as I believed, (it wasn't just me!) my age and experience counted for something, my stamina was better than I thought, and my mental toughness, based on prior knowledge of how difficult it might be, was proving invaluable.

Of Janet and John, still somewhere to the rear, and one man and his sheep-worrying dog, there was no further sign. Nor was there, either today or most of the days to come, a single soul walking in the opposite direction. I got the impression that on any given day there was only a handful of thinly scattered northbound Way-sters, remembering also that our Monday start day from Edale is a relatively "busy" one, and a derisory one or two heading south. Throw in a handful of trans-Pennine folk on other designated footpaths, and a few local day ramblers and that was just about it, apart from skirmishers out of Edale, Malham, Hawes and the like. I felt a mixture of surprise, disappointment – that Britain's best known and most evocative long distance footpath is less popular in an age when people have more leisure time and the means to enjoy it – and relief, that there are still huge swathes of glorious open countryside and wilderness where it's possible to roam, alone and quiet.

I was certainly alone and quiet in my exhausting tramp over Black Moss, having negotiated another of day two's unexpected and disappointing – to put it mildly – little obstacles. Just past the farm the Pennine Way took a sharp left off the glare of the track, as I knew it would, in relieved anticipation of some soft, cooler, moorland peat under my boots, and respite for my eyes, but not before it crossed another gully, Blakeley Clough. The narrow path cut sharply down all the way to the stream and the little bridge where I'd cross, and could be seen winding its way equally sharply back up the other side onto the moor. I could have wept. It took twenty sweat soaked minutes and half a bottle of water to drop wearily down and then grind my way back up, stop-start, including drowning my bush hat for the umpteenth time. I'd covered about 200 yards horizontally on my map, that's maybe ten seconds for a Wheatear, even an elderly and asthmatic one, but at least I'd done it, unlike the young couple way below, who were just commencing their painstaking ascent.

The sun beat down relentlessly, and I beat my way equally relentlessly over the wild hilltop, fixed on my pick-up rendezvous "only" two miles ahead. Black Moss Reservoir, roughly half way, came into view as, unusually, did some people, a family it seemed, doing something at the water's edge, doubtless following refreshing drinks and a gentle thirty minute stroll from their car parked at the roadside. Childishly, I found their distant presence somewhat intrusive – this was the Pennine Way, for genuine walkers, not picnickers from the nearest lay-by. Nonsense, of course, but I think the sun was getting to me. My thirty minute "stroll" to said lay-by was pre-empted by the agreed phone call to my landlady, courtesy of a surprisingly excellent signal, thanks no doubt to the altitude - the valleys proved to be the problem, the more so as they usually coincided with my overnight accommodation.

Erring on the side of caution I suggested she meet me in forty five minutes, and thirty minutes later, totally, utterly, spent, I prised my rucsac from my shoulders and collapsed onto a large boulder at the spot where The Pennine Way crosses the Standedge Cutting on the A62. For once, it was familiar from 1970, when we'd camped directly behind the pub a quarter mile up the road in the Marsden direction and I'd amazed the landlord by demolishing two consecutive mixed grills, followed by pudding. It siled it down (with thanks to Mike Bini for his reminder of that evocative expression) that night, fortunately just after we'd pitched our tent – a wonderful elemental cocoon with the rain beating down on the canvass – but the weather was perfect by morning and I remember my face burning red in the warm breeze. Strange, that I have such a distinctive and absolutely certain recall of that meal, the rain and the sunburn, yet practically nothing of the route itself next day until Stoodley Pike appeared.

The fifteen minute wait for my lift was horrible. Not only was the invasive sight and sound of the passing traffic an unwelcome contrast to the solitude of the lonely moors, but I was frying in the blazing sun, literally a sitting target. I knew it was hot, but hadn't appreciated the true ferocity until I sat unwillingly basking in the reflected intensity from the dusty gravel of the sun-soaked pull-in. "For Christ's sake hurry up" I muttered, as another minute ticked excruciatingly by on my watch. "She should be here in five". She was. Spot on. Never in the history of the 20th Century Motor Industry has a vehicle been a more welcome sight than that old blue Ford Sierra, my whole body – and spirit – having practically seized with the day's exertions and my final fifteen minutes of roasting in that enclosed, heat reflecting, oven. I could barely hobble to the car to drop my rucsac, carrier and stick into the boot, before lowering myself, like a struggling old man, into the front passenger seat.

In ten minutes we were outside her house, a traditional semi, having learnt to my amusement that the cattle grid just up the road had been filled in because the sheep had taught themselves to cross it by rolling over, and less amusingly, and for that matter not much of a surprise, that it was expected to be the hottest July day on record in Marsden. Whoopee! And tomorrow might be even hotter. Well, whoop-de-do! I had all on to clamber up the steep stairs to my room, having first demolished two glasses of water provided by my host, followed by another couple of pints as soon as I reached the bathroom, and reckoned that I must be suffering from a degree of heat exhaustion.

I struggled to undress for the shower, hobble into it, stand in it, and towel myself dry, before flopping back down onto the bed, caressed by a gentle breath of air through the open window of another thankfully cool and shaded room. What an oasis. It even had a telly, and despite my only prospect of an evening meal being a fifty yard walk to the local pub I knew that in my condition it was fifty yards too far. I was shattered, ached everywhere, and only after another huge intake of water and an hour on the bed could I bring myself to forage in my rucsac for the two Complan bars – each of them allegedly packed with vitamins, and the equivalent of a light meal – that I'd saved for an emergency. This was an emergency. I followed up my gooey main course with a couple of Jordan's cereal bars and some dried apricots and declined my landlady's advice re the pub, staying on that bed, toilet breaks excepted, from early evening until 7.15 the following morning.

Never in my entire life, other than the Reactive Arthritis attack, has moving been so painful and difficult. I ached from head to toe, and had clearly over-heated in the extreme conditions. Getting to the bathroom, once I'd gingerly levered myself out of bed, was an embarrassing, pain-racked, shuffle. I made a half-hearted attempt to watch Germany v. Italy in the World Cup, gave up at the end of the normal time stalemate, and found out next morning to my dismay that Italy had won.

They're just about my least favourite International team, having introduced the cynical "catenaccio" defensive system to the game decades ago and have seemingly followed just about every unsavoury aspect of Football since, although in an abysmal World Cup that was a cheats charter I ended up indifferent to whoever won, save maybe Australia who were robbed at the death when an opponent "fell over" in the last minute of normal time and the ref was fooled into giving a penalty.

The recipients of the award indulged in a nauseating self-congratulatory display that added the final grotesque insult and is outrageous testimony that successful sleight of hand is now an equally esteemed contribution to legitimate goalscoring. A few embarrassed looks wouldn't have gone amiss, but there's little shame left in the once "beautiful game". Australia's opponents, coincidentally, were Italy, the eventual "winners" of the devalued competition, but in all honesty it could have been any one of a contemptible, pathetic, bunch, England included.

As I switched the footie off I knew that my Pennine Way adventure was in the balance. It was over if I awoke on day three in anything remotely like the state I was in as I drifted into blessed sleep.

~

Day Three. Standedge to The Calder Valley.

"The Summer Walkers"

"A decent night's sleep will do you the world of good." Oft repeated, seldom so miraculously proven. I knew before I even roused myself for my visit to the bathroom, as I rolled over to check the time, that I'd recovered. My legs ached, and the back of my right ankle was sore (the first hint of the severe tendonitis that would develop as the days progressed) but that was to be expected after the two gruelling opening days. The rest of my system felt fine, no reaction to the heat fatigue, no other aches, including my shoulders and back, which bore the unaccustomed weight of the rucsac throughout the walk with not so much as a twinge. My feet were fine too. I seldom get blisters anyway, but had ample protection in the first aid just in case, including the plasters and animal wool.

The relief was orgasmic. With a bit of luck, the worst was over (it wasn't – that would come later) and I could concentrate on enjoying the scenery, acquiring a healthy, outdoor-type, tan and feeling the benefits of my daily fitness top-up. Game on again. Scotland, here I come! My main concern, the heat, would surely, and despite today's forecast, become tolerable, at least at altitude and further north (wrong!), couldn't possibly last the whole month (wrong, apart from a couple of contrasting interludes, one of them ridiculously so), and regardless, if all else failed I'd become acclimatised (wrong again!)

I had a Cholesterol Special but left the beans, which tasted a bit funny to me and certainly weren't Heinz, downed my usual copious quantities of tap water and was kindly dropped back at the pull-in before 9.00, next stop Hebden Bridge, or more specifically my B & B just the other side of the Calder Valley. I'd only covered a few yards, chuffed that my legs were already stretching themselves beyond stiff and aching into a tolerably comfortable obedience – "you've got another eighteen days of this, so you'd better settle down and get used to it" – when I alighted upon John, Keith and the two Janets, who'd coincidentally been evicted from their B & B's to arrive at the start line at an identical time. I'm not sure who won, as

58

we separated again to our respective digs somewhere near Stoodley Pike, but we got off to a cracking collective start. In fact, after yesterday's traumas it was a morning to lift the spirits.

We walked together, following the well defined way along the ridge at a steady pace, past Standedge, with fine views to the west towards the Manchester conurbation, and a warm, but not yet oppressive, sun at our backs. It's a point to bear in mind if you're thinking of walking south, that the sun will usually be in your face, which in those conditions would have been horrific, and that it also inhibits views and obvious photo opportunities. We made excellent progress on level ground and an easy path, for once starting the day on the ridge, with no thirst inducing early climb, and so far I'd scarcely needed a sip of water. This was a perfect morning. The A640 came and went, then up Rapes Hill, over White Hill and its trig point, and down towards the M62, first negotiating the A672 Halifax - Oldham road, which then crosses the motorway a few yards east at Junction 22.

There's a large off-road standing for trucks, serviced from an excellent, squeaky-clean, catering van, and I joined the queue of regulars, following Janet and Keith's lead, to indulge myself with an ice-cold can of coke and a bottle of water, given an ominous rise in the temperature. My purchase was interrupted by an angry exclamation from one of the HGV drivers "That bloody idiot's going to kill someone soon!", as a car roared past a slow moving lorry in the Oldham direction, right on the blind brow of the hill. There would have been carnage if anything was coming the other way, and I shared his anger. It's a particular issue of mine, accepting that we all make genuine, non-malicious, mistakes, that those criminally reckless morons who endanger fellow citizens whenever they get behind the wheel only receive appropriate punishment after they've inflicted their tragedy, never before.

If punishment should fit the crime, not the totally random consequence, then that pillock, assuming for the sake of my argument that his insanity had been recorded on a camera, should have been charged with "Constructive Manslaughter" (were there such an offence), and upon inevitable conviction received a substantial fine, lengthy ban, suspended prison sentence and compulsory extended re-test. "Justice" is applied, ludicrously, on the chance outcome, not the actual crime, which is quite literally a lottery. I would like criminals such as that, aggressive, impatient idiot to know that they'll be punished for their behaviour, not the consequence, which they've chosen to abandon to arrogant, reckless, life-threatening chance.

Musing on that passionately felt and indisputably logical argument I strolled on, crossing the manic M62 on the pedestrian bridge, which was strewn with stones, small rocks and other debris washed down from the hillside. It was the consequence of heavy localised thunderstorms a few days earlier that had sent floodwater surging several feet deep down the valleys and through those towns and villages unlucky to be in its path. Grateful to leave the roar of the traffic and "civilisation" behind I climbed the moor towards Slippery Moss, Janet and Keith setting a lively pace ahead, Janet and John somewhere behind. I'd picked out a group of distinctive boulders atop the first summit where I'd pause for a brief rest and enjoy my much craved, politically – and doubtless, medically – incorrect fizzy drink before it lost its chill.

The sun was unfortunately getting its act together but not, despite the forecast, at anything yet like yesterday's intolerable level, and my fifteen minutes relaxed on the purpose-designed rocky outcrop, with sweeping moorland vistas, was perfection. My legs were getting the message too, only that niggle above my right heel causing minor, but persistent, discomfort which for now at least was a negligible inconvenience that I elected to ignore. Janet and Keith had chosen the same spot, and with Janet and John approaching we were in tandem again as we passed Blackstone Edge, crossing the cobbled Roman Road that traversed east-west.

In addition to its more recent Industrial heritage, The Pennine Way is riddled with Roman and earlier remnants. The ancient roadways and drovers tracks, once busy with merchants, vendors, farmers, blacksmiths and sundry roadside services, soldiers, footpads and other criminal opportunists, horsemen, hand and donkey carts and villagers en route to markets, fairs and similar gatherings are a fascinating reminder of bygone eras, superficially an alien world, but in reality identical to the demands and needs of today's travellers. That Roman Road, running parallel to the M62 just a few miles north was the equivalent in its day, and if there's any mystery in wondering what those people were like, I suspect that the answer is "just like us, really".

We descended to cross the A58 and, in the case of Janet, Keith and me, dive into the White House Inn. Janet and John, having dropped slightly behind again, surprised us by pushing on, and that was our last contact that day. Of Geordie plus Labrador, no more sign, although that positive sighting, reported several days later, was hopefully an indicator that they made it, but I'd be pleased to receive confirmation. I enjoyed my leisurely Ploughman's, plus two pints of orange and lemonade, with ice, a drink that for some possibly metabolistic reason due to the exertions of the walk, I would crave as each day progressed, even after ample water intake, and which was usually my first order on arriving at a suitable hostelry. Keith had a similar tendency for Sticky Toffee Pudding.

We'd made cracking progress, seven miles already and scarcely lunchtime. Nine left, and with the remaining terrain if anything getting easier I was daring, for the first time since Edale, to feel quietly confident. The first three miles after the pub were a doddle, albeit a fairly boring one, as the Pennine Way took the broad, well surfaced Water Board track alongside and past a cluster of interestingly named reservoirs, Blackstone Edge, White Holme, Light Hazzles and Warland, with the weather, thanks to a breeze from the water and some light cloud cover, refreshingly cooler.

Janet and Keith were visible maybe half a mile ahead, having opted for drinks only, saving a later lunch for their packed rations, and I passed them further on as they enjoyed their waterside picnic. I found the support and friendship of my four fellow travellers to be a great comfort, typical of almost every encounter along the way, and we enjoyed a relaxed, unspoken understanding that enabled us to follow our own schedules and walking pace, alone or in the group, whenever our paths crossed.

61

Shortly after the track terminated at the extreme corner of Warland Reservoir, flagstone pavings defined the dedicated Pennine Way and my first view, across the open expanse of Withens Moor, to my next objective, Stoodley Pike. It's a massive monument commemorating victory over Napoleon, and his abdication, a compelling sight from afar as it dominates the skyline from its lofty perch on the hillside overlooking the Calder Valley. At closer hand it's revealed as a grim, blackened, and to my mind downright ugly structure in need of renovation. It put me in mind of a thick-set factory chimney – quite appropriate given the history of the mill towns thickly populating the valley below. Nevertheless it's an unforgettable landmark, to such an extent that it even brought back a clear memory of my 1970 sighting.

What I had forgotten, as my map reminded me, was that it was nearly three snaking miles away, up and down, up and down, over the featureless moor, in other words a good hour's unbroken walking. Like those miniature cars it looked tantalisingly close, only, paradoxically, revealing its true distance as I got closer, and it got further away as I fully appreciated its size and scale within its empty surroundings. Janet and Keith had overtaken me when I stopped for ten minutes, and I eventually caught them, fully extended on the grass in the shaded lee of the building, with time in hand, thanks to the day's excellent progress, to admire the view and have a doze before seeking their accommodation.

Mine was a little further on, Badgerfields Farm, Blackshaw Head, to be precise, at a similar lofty elevation on the other side of the valley, which proved to be a struggle in the suddenly intensifying mid-afternoon heat, but a blessing when I hadn't got to face that climb the next morning. Janet and John were headed, I believe, for the youth hostel down below at Mankinholes and would start tomorrow, (assuming that they re-claimed The Pennine Way where I presumed they'd left it, about one mile short of Stoodley Pike), a hefty six miles, plus a couple of taxing ascents, behind me.

I left Janet and Keith to their siesta and descended towards the narrow ribbon of communications, where road, railway and canal are crammed in to serve the Calder Valley's tightly packed industrial towns and hamlets that are, along with hundreds like them, the very fabric that once made Britain, with its huge Colonial empire, the World's "super-power", fuelled by Dickensian factories fed from cramped, disease-riddled slums. Whatever your views on this period in our history it's a gripping, scarcely credible, story of the rise to pre-eminence of a tiny island nation with the merest fragment of the world's population and land mass, and inspired by my Pennine Way flirtation I enjoyed a full day exploring Hebden Bridge and its surroundings a couple of weeks after my return.

Back in 1970 we were tramping down from Stoodley Pike, anxious to find somewhere to pitch our tent for the night. A kindly farmer offered us a secure – as in, cattle-free – field in a glorious setting and we made camp, enjoying the view and the early evening sunshine ahead of an unwelcome traipse down to Hebden Bridge for a pub meal. The farmer then re-appeared, to present us with a huge spread of sandwiches, cakes and coffee, all gratis and unsolicited, and I was keen to re-visit that farm and introduce myself to the present incumbents, hopefully the same family, and to recount my story. Unfortunately, and despite frequent stops, I couldn't for the life of me identify which one of half a dozen possibles it had been, and my nostalgic quest ended in disappointed failure. In an uplifting coincidence, 36 years on, just across the valley, another friendly Samaritan was to provide hospitality to a Way-ster in distress.

I dropped down the hillside, spotting a basking lizard, my only sighting on the walk, but disappointingly, and despite keeping my eyes peeled as I crossed many a sun-baked moor, not one solitary snake. There was little likelihood of any wildlife on the tedious one mile slog down the twisting metalled lane – although I was grateful for the shade as it cut through woodland – to join the busy, noisy, A646 on its Todmorden - Hebden Bridge stretch at the village of Mytholm, which clings in tiers to the steep hillside immediately north of the road. A narrow boat – what else for these cramped natural surroundings – chugged along the canal, then a train rattled by, all to the irritating backdrop of the relentless traffic.

Two passers-by gave me a cursory glance before heading down from the pavement to a dusty canal-side enclosure where a number of less than pristine caravans were collected. I had to remind myself, as a lady with a shopping bag went about her business, that I was suddenly, and dramatically, in the middle of a busy urbanised community and that passing strangers don't automatically exchange greetings. I waited for a suitable gap in the stream of vehicles, then crossed over, keen to re-capture the peace and quiet of the Pennine Way, which was clearly signed up a narrow roadway between the houses.

It didn't say "Bloody great hill ahead, not suitable for motor vehicles or pedestrians", with a blue sign depicting a mountain goat, but it didn't need to. Another vague, no doubt sub-consciously suppressed, memory from 1970 reluctantly surfaced, that the first bit after the valley had been difficult, although I do recall that we'd at least had the comfort on our trudge of a cooling early morning drizzle and fresh legs. No chance today, and having finished my water, with no available natural re-fills (I didn't fancy the canal) or inclination to walk down the claustrophobic and grimy main road in search of a shop, a difficult final mile or so lay ahead. The brief scribble written up that evening in my pocket memo book simply records:

"Stoodley Pike came. Easy descent into valley. Suddenly shattered, horrible climb up narrow paved pathway – very quaint, but not in my state. Raging thirst. Path split. Confused. Which way? Met lady at cottage."

The intimidating climb, up, through and above Mytholm, which is somehow exacerbated by the unlikely residential surroundings – half-hidden stone built cottages hanging defiantly onto the partly wooded hillside – is, over its relatively short distance, one of the steepest of the whole walk, albeit up a rustic cobbled causeway that would be quaintly attractive in other circumstances. I had visions of inhabitants lazily sprawled on comfortable settees in cool rooms, drink in hand, whilst I struggled on with a heavy pack and a heavy heart, a sweaty refugee from another world.

Even worse, when I left the first cluster of houses behind me and came to the graveyard – an appropriately macabre touch – the Pennine Way suddenly split into two signed options, which was news

64

to me, as my map gave no such indication, nor detailed clues as to my best choice. Concerned that by the time the two routes re-joined, which may have been a mile or so ahead, I could have by-passed the approach to my B & B, verbally explained when I booked and carefully recorded in my "bible", I decided to phone for instructions. No signal. "Shit." And no-one around to ask.

I opted, after lengthy agonising, for the right hand route over a stile and into a field, but the path soon became overgrown and indistinct, forcing me into another halt, and a one man council of war. Somewhat pissed off by now, and literally hot under the collar, and most other places too, I decided to push on, sweating and overheating in the hot sunshine as the temperature hovered in the high 20s and a thunderstorm rumbled away in the distance, adding to the increasing humidity.

The Way took me above a farmhouse and traversed a field full of sun-bathing rabbits on a steep bank, pock-marked by numerous burrows into which they scattered and disappeared at my approach. Finally, just as I was losing hope, I was brought to some ancient stone steps at the side of a deep ravine with a stream following its bed, and climbed up, ducking under tree branches, to emerge, to my surprise, onto a narrow road with a couple of cottages either side.

I was in a leafy labyrinth of tiny lanes and tiny cottages with tiny windows, but whilst I'd lost all sense of direction I was confident, in the absence of any logical deviation from the route that I'd followed, that I must be still on The Pennine Way, whether "Official" or "Alternative". No sign-post, but no choice but to walk on up the hill, following the road through a narrow, steep, left-hand bend. Then, miracle of miracles, and the last thing I thought I'd ever be pleased to hear, the sound of a car slowly negotiating the tight angle behind me.

I shouted an "Excuse me" through the open window as she pulled alongside. "Do you know where Badgerfields Farm is?" The response was good news and bad. She did, I was on the right road, but it was "a good mile" further on, "up this road, then right where the sign points across the field, then right at the junction with the main road, and it's up ahead on your left". Thanking her, and trying not to show my acute disappointment that having already walked more than a mile of my final mile I still had over a mile to go, I stood aside to let her past. She didn't move. I stood, waiting. "Excuse me, you're blocking my driveway." "Sorry." I hadn't realised, but seizing the moment I ventured "Any chance of filling my water bottle?" "Of course."

She parked the car, and I offered the bottle as she alighted, but she insisted, despite my initial declinature, on inviting me in for a proper drink first, from a glass. There was no-one else in the house, and I was surprised and pleased by her trust – a lone, attractive woman, maybe late thirties, inviting a scruffy, sweat-soaked stranger into her property. I asked how long she'd lived there and she revealed that she'd moved in some years back and originally came from Derby. "Oh, I am sorry" I responded, adding that I was from Nottingham. "You're not getting your drink now" she smiled, before inviting me to stay for a coffee and something to eat. Anxious to get showered and settled in at my accommodation, I declined, but I did wonder, as I plodded that last half mile (somewhat less, I was gratified to realise, than her estimate) whether I should have asked if she did B & B.

I wrenched my boots off at Badgerfields, depositing them, along with my stick, in the porch, and sat outside waiting for my cool drink, an introduction to my room and a therapeutic shower. Thirty minutes later I was back in their beautiful garden anticipating the call for my evening meal and rocking gently on the suspended padded bench, another drink in hand, my plate, containing a few tiny crumbs of chocolate cake, on the grass beside me. Stoodley Pike still dominated the view towards the horizon, but now some four or five arduous miles behind. The storm continued to rumble away in the distance, lightning forking from the purple sky across the purple moors, but to my disappointment it never reached us and the air remained sultry, the unbroken evening sunshine hot.

Two older guests were relaxing on comfy chairs on the terrace of the wooden summerhouse, a pot of tea on the table along with a couple of empty plates and two larger ones displaying two freshly baked scones and the last piece of a large chocolate cake. I learnt that the couple were from Staffordshire, visiting their daughter to help with some house renovations (hence their need for separate local accommodation) and that the man, now too old for cricket, had become a keen indoor bowler. When I mentioned my local bowls centre, the Richard Harrod at the Carlton Forum Sports Centre, near Nottingham, he revealed that he'd played there on several occasions, and without a doubt he must have been in opposition against a couple of my ex-work colleagues who were fixtures in the team. As I said before, it's a small world.

The couple were off for a surprise meal somewhere at a venue booked by their daughter, so I eat alone. My hostess, Miriam Whitaker, served up a delicious meat pie, new potatoes and tender veg and I reckoned that eating in was an excellent option. I ventured back outside afterwards and explored the garden, taking care, in my socks, not to tread on any of the bees foraging busily for nectar in the clover on the lawn - which would have been an unfortunate way to end my Pennine Way challenge, and none too healthy for the bee either – and began searching for frogs and fish in the wildlife pond.

Mrs Whitaker told me that the garden was featureless grassland when they first moved in and, exactly as I did when I first started a garden, she basically "made it up as I went along", planting a few things here and there, courtesy of garden centres and donated specimens and cuttings from friends, gradually expanding her interest and knowledge. Whilst she professed it not to be the finished article, it looked magnificent. I sat out till quite late, (for a Way-ster - well past nine, nearer to ten!) enjoying the balmy air and the continued lightning flashes in the darkening sky, before reluctantly retiring for the night.

When I'd booked I'd been allocated single occupancy of a double or twin, but on arrival, and with my landlady's apologies, plus confirmation of relevant price reduction, I found that I'd been re-allocated the small single room due to a late booking – two ladies with a little dog, I think. It wasn't a problem, as I only needed a comfy bed and bathroom facilities for the one night, but when I lay down in readiness for the land of nod I found, not for the first time in a B & B or hotel, that I didn't quite fit, even by wedging my pillow tight against the headboard and lying diagonally. I'm a scarcely freakish, officially measured (per Nottingham's QMC) six feet one and a half inches, and there's many a sixteen year old nowadays who's taller.

Air travel can be a nightmare, and it's an added insult that many airlines now charge extra for additional legroom, when they should be compelled to provide it automatically for six footers. As it was, the tailboard on the bed refused to detach and after an hour or so of a frustrated and dispiriting effort to wedge myself sufficiently comfortably so that I could drift into sleep I gave up in despair and hauled the duvet, mattress and its cover off the bed and onto the floor, plonked the pillows at one end against the wall, and got a semi-decent kip, albeit a couple of hours less than I'd expected and needed. Furthermore, I had to re-assemble the bed in the morning, which was a bit of a pain and messed up my pre-breakfast routine.

So, my message to anyone licensed for overnight accommodation is "Headboard, yes, tailboard, no!"

~

On your marks....

Only 280 miles to go

Mike, near Edale

Kinder Scout

Bleaklow

About to exchange greetings,
approaching Laddow Rocks

Black Hill (including John's
trekking pole

Looking back 20 minutes after leaving the glare of the track, in ferocious heat, just after Wessenden Farm

The Summer Walkers at Standedge - Keith, Janet, John, Janet

M62, looking West

Locals, Blackstone Edge

Stoodley Pike

Looking back to where I met the berry pickers, shortly after Badgerfields

Just after Heptonstall Moor

Bronte Country, approaching Top Withens (inset - plaque on ruin)

Stanbury, near Ponden. The original carriage mount steps are still intact alongside the road

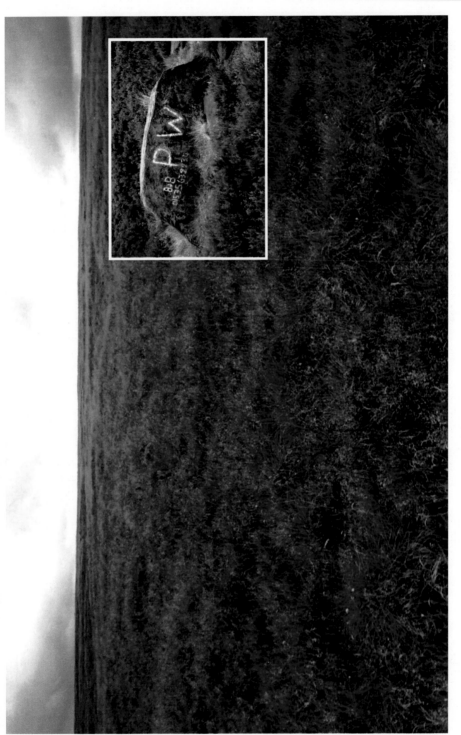

Ickornshaw Moor. The B&B number is of my accommodation in Cowling

Cowling

Lothersdale

Pinhaw Beacon

The Leeds and Liverpool Canal near Thornton

Gargrave

My B&B, Kirkby Malham

Approaching Fountains Fell as the weather closes in (picture by Ivan)

From my room at the Golden Lion, Horton - Pen-y-Ghent invisible as I arrive, drenched

...and starkly outlined as I head for bed

My digs at Horton

The Golden Girls, from the USA, approaching Hawes en route from
Arnside to the Yorkshire Coast

Hawes (Two haweses in fact!)

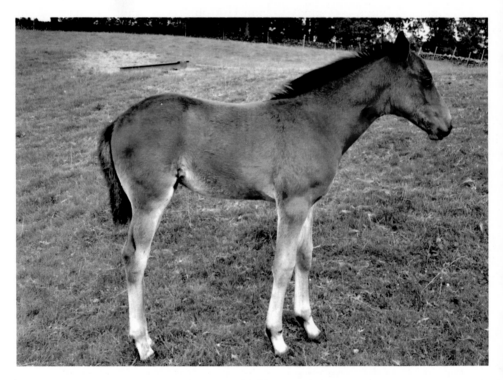

Unimpressed, after nibbling my hand

My accommodation in Hawes

The five mile ascent of Great Shunner Fell in thickening fog and a freezing gale

Descent towards Thwaite after the clouds lift

Thwaite

Looking back over Thwaite, en route to Muker

From my room, Bridge House, Muker

Day Four. The Calder Valley to Ponden.

"So resurrect the bards, liberate the word inspired"

Breakfast was a bit more formal than I'd expected, some half a dozen of us around the table, although it was nice to be the youngest for once! My Pennine Way agenda was a talking point and I set off with the best wishes of all concerned, trying, but failing, not to limp as I creaked into action down the long, ranch-like, driveway between the open fields that led down onto the road. It was hard work early on as I followed a narrow flagged path, slippery and uneven, down the side of a field, then dropped through an overgrown section, hemmed in on both sides, unexpected evidence that The Pennine Way, as I'd discovered around Mytholm, is lightly used even in high season, and I had to force my way through, nettling my hand in the process.

That took me back to my childhood, when nettle stings and their remedy, rubbing the affected area with a dock leaf, were a daily occurrence. Most of today's children, with just about every available urban space now "developed" (I reckon it's about 95% in my old stamping ground) and the remaining bits off limits due to the paedophile that allegedly lurks around every corner, wouldn't know a dock leaf from a cabbage, or have any reason to, for that matter, which is the real tragedy. In all the current tax-levying scam citing "Global Warming" there's absolutely no move, not even the crocodile-teared rhetoric that epitomises Blair's Spoof Labour, (assuming they're still of any relevance by the time you read this) to halt or moderate their stated intent on concreting over much of the increasingly drought-threatened South East, and more besides, and expanding major airports, let alone mention of the single most vital issue, depressingly absent from every agenda, population control.

Using my rapidly developing tracking skills I found navigational re-assurance in some flattened grass and a boot print, and spotted the Bury St Edmunds Two, way ahead of me towards the brow of the next hill. We were to meet up during the day, but of Janet and John there would be no trace. Nor, for that matter, of anyone much before Bronte Country save a couple of locals picking berries and

69

exchanging cheery greetings as I crossed the little stream on the rustic stone bridge in a delightful sun-dappled wooded glade that magically appeared a couple of hundred yards on.

Also making an appearance was that curse of the walkers, the stile. Almost absent on the high open moorlands they began to pop up in increasing numbers in the lower farmland stretches, where they guided me through a patchwork of enclosed fields. I reckon there are about a hundred varieties, some presenting an almost military barrier to progress, and that's on The Pennine Way alone. The worst examples, and I'm sure it's illegal, have barbed wire fences attaching to the stile post, as opposed to a fixture offset a safe distance to one side, and I caught my rucsac on one occasion whilst dismounting, dragging me backwards and potentially – although fortunately I survived unscathed, apart from a temper tantrum – to disaster.

It's so easy to sustain a serious injury when you're off your guard, as happened when I tore my ankle ligaments on that loose rock on Eyam Moor, and I was always mindful of the possibility, particularly as I was walking alone. The last thing I needed was to come a cropper because a local farmer, whether maliciously or through indifference, had tangled his vicious fence around my legitimate access way. It wasn't a unique example, but at least I was on alert after that warning.

Emerging at the edge of open countryside again, Heptonstall Moor to be specific, on the minor road running through the village of Colden, I found that for some reason there was no familiar acorn logo or "Pennine Way" (or simply "P W") pointer to be seen. As with Mytholm – although I'd always been on the correct route there, just disorientated – I'd picked my way around a cluster of houses, but in this case erroneously followed a local cut-through to finish a hundred yards east of where I should have been. It didn't really matter, and only cost me a few minutes and some brief embarrassment until I realised that there was no-one about to witness my confusion, but it reinforced my view that it's surprisingly easy to get lost in a residential area, and a compass bearing's not much use if it points you directly through someone's back garden. The approach to and exit from Thornton-in-Craven would be another such example.

I climbed up onto Heptonstall Moor, and an obvious, easy, path with fine views across endless expanses of heather-clad peat. A derelict farm cottage hung on starkly to my right and further below, in the middle distance, the Pack Horse Inn, with its whitewashed walls, stood out in splendid isolation on the minor road to Colne. Beyond the pub the moors rolled on to the horizon, where they were to assume "Bronte Country" status, and people came to look and wonder. The only people that I saw for three hours after I'd left the berry pickers behind were Janet and Keith, and after I caught them taking a breather we walked together for much of the day, only separating for respective breaks. I'd stop for ten, they'd push on, stop some way ahead, wait for me to re-appear, and off we'd go.

Progress was good for the second day running, the early heat and humidity – legacy of yesterday's unfulfilled storm – replaced by a dull and cooler interlude, with rain threatening but not materialising, before bright sunshine re-appeared in the afternoon, and the heat returned by evening. The Pennine Way wound gently down off the moor to within "Pint of orange and lemonade with ice, please" distance, as my map promised it would, of the Pack Horse, but we weren't tempted. It was too early for lunch, there was no need, for a change, to shelter from the searing heat, and no raging thirst to quench, so we continued on our way, up the Colne road for a quarter of a mile then a right along the Water Board track to Walshaw Dean Reservoirs, three stretches of water separated only by two narrow dams.

Curiously, and to my disappointment, I couldn't recollect one tiny image from our 1970 walk, maybe, at least as far as Water Board tracks and reservoirs are concerned, because they're pretty boring and seem to take forever to slog past. So it proved, the first expanse of water only appearing after a country mile along the featureless, could be easier on the feet, tarmac-ed approach road followed by nearly two miles of counting ducks, before the Pennine Way sign thankfully slewed us to the right and a taxing climb back onto desolate, but scenic, moorland. Less desolate, it proved, once we'd

71

begun to descend beyond Withins (or Withens? – I've seen both spellings) Height, where respective lunches were taken, mine deferred until I reckoned that I'd reached the last of the day's uphill, a nice thought with only three or four miles remaining.

An easy day, an early finish, and I was feeling stronger, as I sat amongst the clumps of heather and sheep droppings, never tiring of another glorious view over empty wilderness. I love these bleak places, in any season. (The moorlands are carefully managed, of course, but they still come across as wilderness when you can walk over them for days and see only half a dozen people, with practically no-one coming from the opposite direction if you're heading north)

Withins Height fell away on winding flagstones and brightening skies to Top Withins, another of the many abandoned stone farm buildings that litter the Way, crumbling reminders of families and communities that once eked out their survival on the harsh Pennine uplands. Top Withins has a unique place compared with the other deserted ruins in that, according to the plaque on the wall, it is thought to be the setting of "Wuthering Heights" despite – maybe deliberately so in order to protect its anonymity - bearing no resemblance to the isolated farmhouse described in Emily Bronte's novel. Regardless, it attracts visitors from far and wide (and my chapter sub-title) and is a particular crusade for the Japanese, a couple of whom were in evidence, cameras at the ready, along with a spattering of other tourists who'd made the pilgrimage up the track from the tarmac road at Ponden Reservoir.

There wasn't much to see, not even a roof, but the view over the valley was smashing. The sheep were friendly too, in fact a bit too pushy, always a dead giveaway that you're in a tourist spot. Having been used to them scattering at my approach, often in blind panic when they hadn't noticed me until the last moment, I was surprised to find, as I sat down to demolish my remaining rations and stare at the sandal and flip-flop shod Bronte-philes, that one of them had its nose in my rucsac and another was trying to snatch my cereal bar from my hand whilst I was distracted shoo-ing its mate away.

A third one arrived and they stood and waited in a half-circle, heads barely inches from mine, fixing me with a blank yet slightly intimidating expression. I responded by rapidly finishing my snap, albeit with a sheep-induced twinge of guilt, grabbing the rucsac forager by its horns and pushing it away with a simultaneous "No, that's it, all gone, so bugger off". After a brief interlude whilst they convinced themselves that I was telling the truth they wandered off, still expression-less, to pester the Japanese duo.

It put me in mind of a similar incident, many moons ago, involving our dog. As I've already written, she was fully trustworthy with sheep and other domestic and farm animals, and even made a friend of next door's cat, a vicious thing that had bloodied the noses – literally – of most of the neighbourhood canines, but used to visit our garden and curl up with Sal for a snooze on the lawn. Soft as grease then, but a bit touchy, to put it mildly, where her food was concerned. Perfectly safe with humans, but not, despite my attempts to "socialise" her, ever likely to share her bowl with other animals (or people, for that matter – I'll drink stream water, but there is a limit).

It was a similar scenario – we'd stopped for a picnic on our hike somewhere in a touristy bit of Derbyshire when along came an opportunistic sheep. We both ignored it, as it stood, staring blankly, unperturbed by Sal, who was equally disinterested in the gormless animal, provided that she remained the exclusive recipient of any spare offerings. My unthinking mistake was to offer a tiny piece of my sandwich to our new "friend", which provoked an uncharacteristic and spontaneous explosion of what I can best describe as "dog rage".

It only lasted a few seconds, but it terrified me, and I wasn't even the object of the outburst. She hurled herself right up to its face, teeth bared, saliva flying, hackles raised, snarling and snapping like a cornered wildcat, and the startled sheep dropped the remnants of its patiently acquired snack and scampered back down the hill. Sal devoured the soggy remains (proof, if it were needed, that dogs aren't fussy eaters) in one greedy snatch, and peace was restored. She had no further interest in the woolly scavenger, never moved an inch to follow it and would, I'm certain, have happily co-existed, even sharing a sleeping place, but not, ever, "her" sandwich, and I made sure that the situation was never repeated. Such was her jealous rage that she'd have responded in exactly the same way if a Mountain Lion - not that I've ever seen any in the Peak District - had snaffled her tit-bit.

I was back in sync. with Janet and Keith for the last mile or so, past Upper Heights Farm and along the track before a final short descent towards Ponden Reservoir. The sun had got his hat on, playing sparklers on the water, but I was looking forward to the shade, and my orange and lemonade, at The Silent Inn, Stanbury, as the temperature climbed. First, I had to find it. I'd originally tried to book Janet and Keith's destination, Ponden House, which overlooks the reservoir and stands directly on The Pennine Way, but "Sorry, full up", as were the other listed places, led, via a recommendation, to the pub. It was followed a day later by a call from Ponden House to say that they now had a room, and as I watched my colleagues disappear I wished that I'd snapped it up.

In reality it wasn't much of an issue, particularly as, due to being unable to find better placed digs, I'd only got a seven mile tiddler of a day tomorrow, but I disliked the fact that I'd got to plod on in the opposite direction, then re-trace my steps next morning, on the unforgiving tarmac of the narrow road towards Stanbury, stepping aside as traffic whizzed by on the blind, hilly bends. Ponden Mill, well known to those – mainly of female persuasion – in search of towels, bed linen and similar things domestic, appeared in the dip on my right, then, as I wearily tramped on, up to the brow of the hill, The Silent Inn suddenly announced itself.

A traditional coaching inn, evidenced by the high stone step opposite a now bricked-up entrance, which used to be the dismount point for carriage passengers, it provided relief in the shape of my usual choice of welcoming drink, and an old fashioned but spacious and pleasantly cool room, with TV and en-suite. My phone wouldn't work, but I was advised that if I stood in the top corner of the car park I might get a signal, and thus it proved, provided that I didn't deviate more than a yard from where the little bars on my mobile suddenly burst onto the display.

After my shower and a restful slouch on the bed I descended for an early evening meal, then, strangely, given the state I was in only a couple of days earlier, went for a little walk, for once relishing the hot evening sunshine. I found a comfortable spot, seated on a stile in the corner of a field, where I was at blissful peace with the world, until a soggy slap suddenly hit me on the back of the neck. I leapt up and turned, to find that I'd been licked by an inquisitive cow from the next field that had moo-ched (no apologies for the pun!) quietly over to investigate. It pushed its head appealingly through the stile and I reached instinctively for my camera before remembering that I'd left it, along with my other clutter, back in my room.

David Bailey would have been ashamed of me.

~

Day Five. Ponden to Cowling.

"A rising choir of birdsong, your fields of summer green"

During my Cholesterol Special the next morning I learnt that The Silent Inn derives its name not from the sneaky local cattle but the fact that when the fleeing Bonnie Prince Charlie was in the area – he seems to have visited more places than Alan Whicker – the locals had a pact of silence. He still had to leave in a hurry though.

My departure was far more dignified, on a surprisingly grey, overcast and much cooler day and, as it turned out, the easiest walking conditions on what perversely was my shortest stretch. I wish I could have deferred that benign weather for Hadrians Wall. With only seven Pennine Way miles to negotiate I strolled at a leisurely pace past Ponden Mill, somehow resisting, despite having plenty of time in hand, the urge to call in and hunt out a bargain in fluffy towels, before re-capturing the Way half a mile on.

A convoluted but well signed combination of, respectively, track, footpath, public road and track led me the one and a half miles (according to my map) above and beyond the reservoir, to a footpath up and over Ickornshaw Moor and down to my next accommodation, Winterhouse Barn, Cowling. For the first time, my bush hat proved its versatility, keeping me protected for once from a cool breeze instead of the blazing sun. Even my lightweight cag made its debut as I felt the chill, and my water remained untouched. Maybe it was the fresh weather, but I enjoyed every step of the climb over Bare Hill and on past the Wolf Stones trig point to my left, wondering if the name was an echo of their historic territory or, like so many rock features, someone's idea of a likeness, which, as with the named star patterns in the night sky, I could never remotely fathom. "What Plough?"

Until I caught Janet and John taking an early lunch just before my scheduled finish I didn't see a single soul, Janet and Keith having presumably pushed well ahead from their advanced overnight location. With the derelict cottage near Cowling devoid of any Bronte-esque claim to fame there was clearly no need for anyone to explore this patch of beautiful open moorland. That seemed to suit the curlews, in evidence, irritated by my intrusive presence, almost every step of the way. They continually circled around me, sometimes landing on the footpath ahead, their shrill alarm calls a persistent notice for me to quit their nesting patch, and to entice me away. If they'd had half a brain they'd have kept quiet and left me in peace and I'd have never known they were there. Must be related to pheasants. Still, they've nothing on that vicious little bastard otherwise known as the Arctic Tern.

I discovered that creature's endearing way of discouraging visitors whilst strolling on a deserted seaside promontory a few miles south of Parnu, Estonia. A noise that I can best describe as a cross between machine gun fire and an old fashioned football rattle suddenly exploded in my right ear. It came from nowhere, and my immediate fear, as my ear still rung, was that I must have trodden on a military device. It was immediately dismissed as the rest of me was still intact, but before I'd had time to explore other theories a missile, accompanied by another ear shattering burst, flashed across my face, veered up into the sky then dived back down, forcing me to duck.

I retreated quickly as it repeatedly wheeled and dived, and despite wearing glasses (me, not the bird) my immediate fear was for my eyes. Once I'd reached its "safe" distance the attacks ceased, although it continued to circle, clattering away until I posed no further threat. A slim, elegant, small bird with a delicate forked tail, the Arctic Tern, as I learnt from a subsequent visit to the Farne Islands, off the Northumbrian Coast, is one of the bird kingdom's most aggressive members in defence of its nesting territory. The information sign on the main island informed visitors that their annual monitoring and ringing is a dreaded task. No volunteering for me, then, I'll settle for the curlews.

I'd found Janet and John propped up against the walls of an old ruin only a mile or so short of my destination. Unlike the curlews, they greeted me like a long lost friend. There was an increased camaraderie between the five of us as our daily fortunes and itineraries ebbed and flowed, and they asked of any news concerning

Janet and Keith, just as I'd been asked the same question of them yesterday. We walked on together until I bade them farewell as they headed several miles further north for their accommodation whilst I sat in a grassy field just above the busy A6068 Colne – Keighley road, trapped by the constraint of my ridiculously short day, Winterhouse Barn less than 200 yards up the road to my right.

It had been Hobson's Choice when I booked, the limited accommodation further on being fully occupied, including several unlisted recommendations, but I decided, signal permitting, to try the numbers again in the hope of late availability (and an equally late cancellation of my existing arrangement, plus loss of deposit) and the lengthening of today's wimpish seven miles for a corresponding reduction in tomorrow's sixteen. The phone worked, but four calls later I'd failed again. Five minutes on, after some confusion whilst I found the right door, thanks to instructions shouted across the road between the roar of the lorries by a man rounding some sheep into a trailer, I was introducing myself with the words "I'm Richard, sorry I'm a bit early". It was all of one o'clock and I wasn't even gasping for an orange and lemonade.

Mrs West, despite her surprise at seeing me, kindly showed me to my modern, cosy room with its choice of adjacent (unboarded!) single beds, sloping ceiling with opening skylights and, something I always valued, especially when I was shattered and wanted to retire early, a TV. She announced that they were about to go out – I'd have had to hang around until approaching teatime if I'd been a few minutes later – and left me an outside door key. I know it usually goes with the B & B territory, but it's still refreshing that a stranger can be trusted with the run of the house within a few minutes of introducing himself.

Showered and relaxed, and in returning shirt-sleeve sunshine, I ambled gently down the road to explore Cowling, unlike the thundering heavy goods vehicles that rumbled past the 30 mph sign, only to be brought to a halt in the middle of the village by roadworks and a temporary traffic light. It was a mixed blessing for me. Mr West had responded, in answer to my comment that the road was surprisingly busy, that it had got much worse over recent years and it used to be fairly quiet, but at least the contra-flow made crossing easier, although I could have done without the all pervading stench of diesel fumes.

Busy road excepted, I liked Cowling, a mill settlement – I think there may have been four at one time, but apologies if I'm mistaken – with its rows of terraced houses running at 90 degrees either side of the "A" road. The cobbled streets to the right climbed uphill into open countryside, and a well signed footpath onto the moors, with its miniature version of Stoodley Pike on the ridge, but I wasn't tempted, enjoying my afternoon potter and taking voyeuristic photographs of washing strung out across back alleyways, just as it would have been in its industrial heyday of archetypal flat caps and clogs. Only the wheelie bins spoilt the illusion.

I'm increasingly fascinated, as with Hebden Bridge, by these self contained purpose-built towns. Presumably, there'd have been a few cottages and some sheep, then wham!, in the space of a few short years up went the massive mills with their towering chimneys and pluthering smoke, densely packed workers' cottages, shops, school, Sunday school, chapel, pubs, the whole tightly wedged industrial machine simultaneously incongruous yet curiously aesthetic against an empty backdrop of rolling hills and moors. I wondered where all the workers had come from and what affect it must have had on the scattered rural population.

More to the point, what did they all do, now that the factories are long closed, the streams and rivers no longer drive the mill wheels, and the redundant chimneys, sadly, as they're an evocative and starkly beautiful symbol of this heritage, are, bar a handful of lonely reminders, demolished? The present citizens of Cowling, to my uninformed eye, seemed to be doing alright, the solid houses – better built, and more spacious, it seemed to me, than in many similar towns – re-glazed and well kept, and I got the impression that it's a thriving community where people want to live.

I certainly wouldn't mind, although that main road is both a curse and a lifeline. It once supported the industrial infrastructure of a booming mill town, exporting its products to the outside world, now it supports the commercial infrastructure of the modern world, exporting its labour as daily commuters to the likes of Keighley, Bradford and Leeds. I suppose that answers the question of what its current citizens do, paradoxically now attracted to this once grimy industrial enclave as a desirable residential base in the country, with "local" employment defined as anything up to twenty or thirty miles away. It used to mean a five minute walk to the factory gates.

Needing to recce somewhere for my evening meal I sought out the Harlequin bar/restaurant, which had been recommended at the B & B. More typically Parisienne than Northern Mill Town, there was an informal bistro type area and a separate restaurant and after checking with the friendly hosts that I didn't need a reservation for a "walking class" meal I decided to treat myself. That left the rest of the afternoon for a return stroll and a siesta, armed with a twin pack of Jaffa Cakes and a copy of the Independent, before my stomach reminded me, as early evening arrived, that man cannot live on Jaffa Cakes alone.

I felt slightly under-dressed and a tad self conscious in my hiking boots, but was made very welcome, enjoying an excellent meal and drink whilst eavesdropping on the foursome at the next table. Their conversation revolved around SATS, National Curriculum, Ofsted Inspections, Budgets, Fundraising, Discipline, Tests, Homework, Targets, New Initiatives, Form-filling, and how to cope with the sheer, bloody stupid, and bloody minded bureaucracy of it all, and how to have any kind of social life or stay awake, doing reports and assessments in front of the computer, beyond 9 p.m., a common theme to every teacher I know.

I have a mental list longer than The Pennine Way of why I'd like to administer a size ten hiking boot, with all the force and experience of my footballing days, up the arse of Tony Blair and his Spoof Labour cronies, but their victimisation and patronising contempt for dedicated "coalface" Public Servants (as opposed to the top management echelons) ranks second, only below his criminal Iraq obscenity. I have friends who are fiercely proud and dedicated to their careers in Teaching and the Health Service and their despair and permanent exhaustion as they fight their daily battles in the face of the dogma-driven onslaught and arrogant, cringe-making incompetence sends my blood pressure soaring. Blair will doubtless be gone by the time these words see the light of day, struggling (and, in the literal sense, failing) to make an honest living on the public speaking and patronage circuit. Regrettably, I can't see a successor, of whatever party, undoing the damage, or having the will, for that matter

Fortunately my silent seething was placated – and in fact replaced entirely – by other thoughts, as a very attractive young lady in tight jeans positioned herself at the bar, directly, but not deliberately – my long days in the sun hadn't fried my brain to such levels of self-delusion – in my line of vision. It would have been rude not to notice, and she did more for my well-being in those few minutes than our God-fearing Presidential Poodle had managed in three terms of office.

Like all good Way-sters I was back in bed for nine, despite enjoying a chat with the landlords just as I was leaving the Harlequin, and I fell asleep with pleasant thoughts and images filling my head.

I'd thoroughly enjoyed my half-day trip to Cowling.

~

Day Six. Cowling to Kirkby Malham.

"I tramp these acres and I feel, once upon a time"

Sixteen miles ahead, to my next B & B, The Victoria Inn, Kirkby Malham. It should have been nearer to eighteen, and my preferred stopover at Malham, but "Full up" responses to every one of a long list of accommodation bore witness to its popularity as a tourist centre, especially on a July Saturday, albeit that it's only accessible for vehicles via a narrow, winding, country lane. My map, and again it was telling the truth, showed my route to be easy walking through rolling hills and valleys.

On a pleasantly warm and quiet day, with welcome cloud cover screening the sun, I left Cowling and the open moorlands behind me, into a gentler pastoral landscape, with only Elslack Moor and its trig point at Pinhaw Beacon ahead as a lingering reminder. The path from the village was easy to follow, leading me to a short stretch of empty metalled road before climbing through fields to another road at the top of Cowling Hill, from where I looked back for a few minutes to take in the panorama of Cowling, my B & B and the silent toytown vehicles visible on the road to its right, and Ickornshaw Moor, which I'd crossed yesterday, on the horizon beyond.

One of the great pleasures of the walk, which never diminished, was that within minutes, sometimes seconds, of leaving my overnight accommodation I was in a different world, stepping out into open countryside, with no interminable urban sprawl, traffic noise, retail parks or "greenbelt" housing developments with their mocking "lifestyle" faux-rural obituaries to "The Oaks", "Chestnuts" or "The Woodlands". I'd passed one property that, in Estate Agents' parlance, was "in need of improvement", but "enjoys commanding views over open countryside", a forlorn, abandoned farmhouse halfway up Cowling Hill. Unlike most of the others it was substantially intact, including roof, and was the largest in the long line of these lonely relics. It would have made – with substantial investment – a wonderful family mansion.

The sun was playing hide and seek with the clouds, and with the temperature in the low 20s it was now a lovely summer morning. I strode on briskly, confident in my improving fitness – niggling tendon excepted – and stamina, admiring the distinctive black and white cows grazing the fields near Woodhead Farm, on the approach to Lothersdale. There's a cracking view from The Pennine Way over this hamlet, which is shoe-horned into the valley like a miniature Cowling, in this case, as far as the evidence revealed, a one-mill town, served by a small cluster of cottages, its chimney still standing defiant. It may still be operational for all I know, but there was no sign on that bright Saturday morning.

The whitewashed pub, which almost certainly would be, stood out against the predominant "industrial grey" and from my lofty vantage point it looked as though I could throw a blanket over the whole, tightly compressed, community. Even so, I couldn't find the Pennine Way path down. Whether through complacency – the route seemed so obvious and the view was so compelling that I wasn't concentrating fully – or a missing sign, I never discovered, but it was a simple task, only costing me a couple of hundred yards, to turn right where I met the minor road and follow its sweep round and steeply down into the valley, eyes fully peeled this time for directions left, out of Lothersdale and back up the opposing hillside.

No mistake this time, although I had to do a double take to navigate successfully up the hill and over the fields to the road and along the short track before – and again after a careful reconnoitre in the absence of a sign or obvious direction – finding the well defined path up and on to Pinhaw Beacon. From there I had my first distant view, over the valley, north towards the limestone escarpments of the Yorkshire Dales, and an instant surge of excited anticipation. Once I'd passed Malham, The Pennine Way would thread its path through the increasingly remote uplands of the central spine of Northern England and on to the Cheviots, and for the first time I felt that I was really on my way, both geographically and psychologically. I could almost taste the first, faint, tang of Scottish heather in the breeze.

Not before I'd negotiated Thornton-in-Craven, though. The approach was obvious, dropping off the moor to cross a minor road just to the right of the world's noisiest cattle grid, audible half a mile away as the occasional vehicle clattered over it, and straight on down another metalled road, before a flagstone path cut away "down to Thornton-in-Craven" as my map/guide comprehensively explained, although it didn't add "and the best of luck". I didn't recall my surroundings, but clearly remember that we'd got hopelessly lost and confused in this gentle patchwork of fields in 1970, cursing ourselves for our obvious incompetence in what is just about the easiest terrain in the entire Pennine Way.

Whether our self judgement was harsh, or whether I've learnt nothing since then I don't know, but 36 years later it happened again, despite my determination that it wouldn't. Descending somewhere above Brown House Farm I (correctly) dropped down a steep field to (again, correctly) an obvious but unsigned sharp left where the path met a track at right angles. It immediately struck me that a southbound Way-ster would almost certainly have misguidedly continued along the track as opposed to taking the unsigned sharp right up the open grassy hillside from where I'd descended, which had barely a trace of a defined path, bar a few re-assuring boot impressions.

I continued down, via a stile, into another large enclosed field, as the defined footway took a sharp right, in the wrong direction. I could see Thornton, and traffic streaming along the busy A56, so I wasn't "lost" in any directional sense, but couldn't work out a route over the fields, with their protective fences, ditches, hedges and high stone walls. According to my map I should be hard up against the stream to my left, so I dropped down, parting cattle, thistles and other scrubby vegetation, and ploughed on over rutted pasture before finding a gate, but no path or sign, and followed my nose to the farm, another gate, a sign at last (well, whoopee, that was useful, now that I couldn't possibly go astray) and the tarmac lane into the village. Perhaps I was being a bit thick, but a couple of relevant signposts or way-markers wouldn't go amiss, and looking at my map retrospectively I'm convinced that I didn't stray far, if at all, from the supposed route.

My abiding, possibly unfair, impression, reinforced by identical problems coming out of the village, and a similar dislike in 1970, is that it's the least "walker friendly" place on the whole Pennine Way, but if anyone on behalf of Thornton wishes to contradict me and explain the error of my navigational ways I'll be more than happy to listen. My one positive memory is of a deer – disappointingly, my only sighting on the whole walk – suddenly leaping out of the undergrowth shortly after I'd claimed the little lane, then disappearing "just like that" back into the thickets, never to be seen – at least by me – again. Now that's what I call magic.

With my mood somewhat darkened, unlike the weather, by my impromptu tour of the local fields I climbed up the grassy bank, following the clear "Pennine Way" sign, to cross, or at least try to cross, the A56 in the centre of Thornton. It must have been summer Saturday holiday syndrome. The traffic was relentless, and no sooner did a gap appear to my left than an unbroken stream roared past from the right. I can truthfully state that I've never – even in manic free-for-alls in India or rush hour Paris – taken longer to cross a road. After an eternity, a statistically favourable gap appeared and I marched indignantly across, thankful that I wasn't elderly, disabled, a child or a hedgehog. When I'd successfully negotiated the opposing kerb I let out, in a combination of childish anger and relief, a full blooded and unashamed cry, at full volume, of "Hooray!" to the amusement of two workmen who were cutting back an overgrown hedge.

There was a pretty cottage just up the quiet lane that led me away through the village and onto Sheet 4 of 8 on my "Pennine Way – Part 1 – South" guide and I paused to take its photo, but was otherwise glad to see the back of the place. I passed some welcoming "Keep out" signs (or words of similar tone) before more uncertainty and irritation in the fields above the Leeds and Liverpool Canal, with no clear path and no helpful sign or marker leading to the hidden stile at the bottom corner. Echoes of 1970 again, and I learnt afterwards that I wasn't the only one to get confused. There's nothing more infuriating on a walk than knowing the exact direction ahead, especially on a wimpishly easy stretch, but not being able to negotiate a zig-zag obstacle course due to lack of adequate signing. I added to my "Hooray" a "Good riddance, Thornton", as I finally traced my way to the canal.

It's difficult to get lost on a towpath, but The Pennine Way only allows that navigational luxury for a short distance before taking a right – path, track, path, track, in short sequence – and leading into open countryside again at the footpath signed "Gargrave". The field ahead had, for no likely reason that I could identify, been turned into a construction site, with huge mounds of excavated earth and levelled groundworks, and the path diverted around the unsightly mess, regaining its original course some distance ahead, or so I thought, until, and for the first time since leaving Cowling, fellow walkers appeared, and to my surprise, from the opposite direction.

The group comprised two lads with full packs and an unencumbered lass who, I was to discover, was their motorised support system. Like me, they were heading for Gargrave, but had turned back as they'd not picked up any signs since the diversion. I'd been similarly unsure, but my compass and map, plus guidance note to "navigate by following the stream in a north-easterly direction and climb up between two low hills to reach the post" had been followed, with the exception that the post was still worryingly invisible. After a discussion, and much cartographic consultation, I decided to press on, whilst they opted for a sandwich break and a further conference.

Half a mile of "surely this must be the right way" on, the marker post appeared on the distant horizon, like the pin – minus flag – on a golf green, (except much bigger of course) and I signalled back by waving my stick in the air like a demented idiot. I don't know if they saw it, but they'd certainly realise that I hadn't retraced my steps, and I noticed them later entering Gargrave whilst I was having lunch. The Pennine Way turned me into a dab hand at spotting distant marker posts, stiles, cairns, streams and other aids to way-finding, which is, trite as it may sound, an acquired and vital skill that I consciously developed as the days progressed, and which increasingly stood me in good stead.

I didn't need any further help once I'd spotted the post and browed the hill, Gargrave visible ahead along an easy path thanks to its church tower, and I was soon crossing another busy road, the A65 Settle – Skipton, thankfully with less trauma. I decided to stop at the corner café (a reminder of a poignant Bruce Hornsby song) for a spot of lunch, strangely fancying another cholesterol intake, in this case two fried eggs and chips, guilt assuaged by the knowledge that my levels, for some reason, had been confirmed during my various tests as much lower than average.

My outside table was next to the signpost – I can't recall whether it was there in 1970 – telling me that I'd "already" covered 70 miles since Edale, with another 186 ahead to Kirk Yetholm. That combined distance of 256 has now been updated to 268, excluding diversions such as the Bowes Loop and accommodation searches, hence my revised estimate for my effort of 280. Gargrave, despite its dissection by the main road, is an attractive, bustling centre, well recommended as a base for exploration of the surrounding area. It was also my second skirmish with the Leeds and Liverpool Canal as I crossed the bridge on the Malham road at the picturesque locks, thronged with narrow boats, nautical folk, canal-side strollers, children, dogs, ducks, all making for an idyllic weekend scene.

Within a few hundred yards I was alone again as "Malham" took a right and I continued along the "No through road" in the shade of Great Wood, until the Pennine Way footpath led me steeply up open, sheep-cropped, grassland and over the top of Eshton Moor. Mysterious sightings suddenly appeared in the distance as I dropped down. First, a lone walker, purposefully striding out towards me despite the bulk of a substantial back-pack, and almost certainly a fellow Way-ster. I anticipated our cheery exchange of greetings, possibly a short chat whilst I jokingly advised him that when he arrived in Gargrave he'd be almost home and dry, with only 70 miles ahead. It wasn't to be.

I dislike the current obsession with body language, which in my opinion generally serves only to make people more self conscious and awkward – at least in my case it does – but his body was sending out unmistakeable signals and as we closed he acted as if I didn't exist. He was fairly young, maybe borderline thirty, and when I tried to catch his eye he stared fixedly ahead, intent on blanking me out as our paths crossed barely a foot apart. "Afternoon", I ventured, which was reciprocated with a grudging mono-syllabic grunt as he sped past, still fiercely avoiding eye contact. "Have a good day!" I exclaimed, peevishly, and before I could stop myself, but after a few seconds reflection I was quite pleased with my knee-jerk sarcasm.

"Ignorant bastard" I mumbled to myself before, as I walked on, wondering if I was being over-sensitive, or maybe that the chap was having a really shitty time, but after further reflection I settled for "ignorant bastard". There's an unwritten code of friendly etiquette for walkers, especially so on lonely long distance trails, and I'm pleased to say that I only experienced one similar occurrence, a few days on, this time involving an older man, proving that it's not a "generational thing" exclusive to today's young whipper-snappers.

The surly walker consigned rapidly to history, an older couple with a small dog, travelling light – I think she had a handbag, the dog was wearing a collar – rapidly came into "Afternoon" range, after which cordial exchange they asked me how far it was to Gargrave and whether it was easily "do-able". Given that they'd already walked a mile from their accommodation, and our current location, opposite Newfield Hall, was three miles out, that meant a total round trip of eight miles which, in due deference to their age and the dog's short legs didn't, on balance, seem particularly "do-able", although I wasn't so indiscreet as to put it in those words, merely remarking that "You've done about a mile and it's another seven there and back".

Thanking me for my help, they decided to press on "for a bit" and I did likewise, and at quite a decent lick, alongside the River Aire past Airton, before a left would take me off The Pennine Way for a half mile detour into Kirkby Malham for the night. No sign all day of Janet and Keith, but about a mile short of my exit I spotted two walkers in the distance, subsequently identifiable, as I closed, as

Janet and John, and by lifting my pace even further to an exhilarating quick-step I just caught them. For the second day running we re-united like long lost friends, which, in a sense, we now were, and for the second day running our walk in tandem was short-lived, in this case a modest fifty yards.

We exchanged Pennine Way gossip and other pleasantries for a good ten minutes, followed by the usual parting "Good luck, see you again soon!" and I spun off left towards the village whilst they headed on towards the Youth Hostel near Malham. The rush to catch them, followed by our break for a chat, then the tarmac to the Victoria Inn, hadn't done my tendon any good and I was struggling to hide a limp as I completed the remaining yards into the pub, past the handful of customers still seated outside in gathering gloom. The afternoon had become increasingly overcast and humid after its sunny start, and with rain in the air I was glad to find shelter before it set in.

Kirkby Malham is a delightful little village and the stone built Victoria Inn, festooned with vibrant hanging baskets and tubs, looked the part, nestling seductively at its centre, the ancient church its nearest neighbour. I received an adequate welcome, and enjoyed a nourishing and substantial evening meal, taken in the bar as the restaurant was full, of fish, chips (second time today!) and mushy peas, plus a Guinness for extra calories and iron, but as for my room, the least said the better. At least my very basic en-suite had a telly, if not a bar of soap or shampoo, or much else for that matter, and a nice view as it backed directly over the churchyard, where I went for a stroll, my brolly coming into its own in the steady evening rain.

I just caught the vicar as he was locking up and he allowed me a quick tour of the church. After a couple of minutes, following another display of body language – he was stood by the door, jangling the keys – I took my cue and poddled off into the damp. I like churches – Southwell Minster in Nottinghamshire is arguably my county's finest building (excluding the architecturally stimulating Victoria and Broad Marsh shopping centres of course) and I find myself on three or four occasions every year doing the full external circuit followed by a meander inside, looking for the 26 - or 28 on

Sundays, when extra furniture is brought out - tiny mice that are mischievously carved at random locations in the wood, but as a committed 100% born-again Atheist I do have serious problems with religion – which brings me back to Messrs Bush and Blair, so I'd better stop there.

There's not a lot to do on a rainy night in Kirkby Malham, charming as it is, so after making a call from the Public telephone box, rustically enhanced by virtue of it having a wild geranium, in full flower, pushing up through the concrete base, I returned to my gloomy room and watched the second half of World Cup Diving, or more specifically Portugal (no further comment necessary) v. Germany in the Third Place Play-off. Thankfully, Germany won.

Needing an early start for a heavy day tomorrow I was chuffed to find that an eight o'clock breakfast wasn't feasible, not even an offer of a cold buffet or some cornflakes and orange juice, so I suggested a packed lunch which, of sorts, I received, and was truly grateful, as I was for my last view of my digs, the only one that left me acutely disappointed.

It wouldn't even begin to describe how I was to feel about tomorrow's weather.

~

Day Seven. Kirkby Malham to Horton-in-Ribblesdale.

"There's a south by sou' westerly force eight coming in strong"

Only fifteen miles today, one less than my brisk sixteen of yesterday, and even if I could limp through the nagging early soreness at the back of my right ankle into a tolerable "comfort zone", I couldn't dismiss the weather, which decided that if I didn't like clear, still, skies and hot sunshine with unbroken visibility it would show me what I'd been missing – and with a vengeance.

It started quietly, dull and humid with heavy clouds shrouding the hills, but only a light drizzle, and with my brolly now in action for the first time on "operational duties", necessitating stick plus carrier in one hand, I came to the conclusion that either the carrier or the umbrella would have to go. The brolly went back into its rucsac strappings and I decided to rely on my – allegedly – waterproof and windproof hooded cag, plus my unfounded optimism, based absurdly on the weather forecast, that conditions would improve.

The early getaway was prompted by a couple of stiff ascents ahead, Fountains Fell and Pen-y-Ghent, but first I retraced my steps along the empty lane back to the Pennine Way where I'd bid goodbye to Janet and John. It follows the River Aire upstream and past Malham to its effective source at the foot of Malham Cove where it emerges into daylight as a proper river after spending most of its infant life finding its way underground through the porous limestone from Malham Tarn. Just before reaching an eerily deserted, albeit fully booked, Malham – a combination of my early, Sunday, arrival and the miserable weather – I realised another unusual, at least for me, wildlife sighting, which I recognised as a creature from the stoat family (the first of two such occurrences).

Small, low-slung and mid brown in colour it emerged, startled, from the grass almost beneath my feet, settled for a few seconds at the base of the nearest tree, then disappeared into an overgrown gully that led into the river. Despite being armed with encyclopaedic knowledge of the natural world, including how to tell the difference between a weasel and a stoat – one's weaselly recognisable, the other's stoatally different – I still couldn't decide, and the waters were further muddied when it cropped up in conversation at my B & B that night and Keith suggested that it might have been a pine martin or polecat. Anyway, it was small and furry and scuttled about secretively.

I scuttled through Malham like the early milkman, a solitary figure after overtaking a small group of young women, evidently off for a day's hike, substantial packs at the ready as they discussed their route. I met them again a few minutes later as I returned, red faced, to recover my stick, which I'd left propped against the wall near the gate where The Pennine Way leaves the road and heads across for Malham Cove. For anyone on O2 network, I can advise that it's the first place where a signal re-appears after Kirkby Malham and Malham, and I'd digested and rattled off a few texts before, in the excitement of re-connecting with the outside world, dashing off up the easy path, stick-less.

My stick was certainly needed, invaluable in fact, after I'd climbed the steps cut into the rocky ground to the left of Malham Cove, in persistent rain and lowering cloud, onto the amazing slabs of exposed – and slippery – limestone paving at the top. The sheer face of the Cove is pretty special too, its scale only fully appreciated close up, where it's easy to believe, and wonder, in awe, at the mind blowing changes to our planet effected by the ravages of time. Following glaciation, and subsequent warming, (can't blame mankind for that one!) a waterfall to rival Niagara is said to have plunged in thunderous ferocity over that ridge. Today there's just the feeble trickle of the emerging River Aire at its base and a well stocked Outdoor shop on the right of the tarmac road coming into Malham. Makes you think – or it did me, anyway.

So did the weather, and I was relieved to stumble - almost literally, over the difficult, uneven, pavement – on two walkers with day packs, out on an excursion, plus, to my surprise, a family group determined to ignore the deteriorating weather and achieve their destination of Malham Tarn. We walked together through the mini Wild West canyon from the top of the Cove until the climb up a narrowing rocky path led, via a stile, to an expanse of bleak open moorland, then across a minor road towards the water. We separated as I pushed on around the Tarn, head down against a rising wind and sheets of rain sweeping in misty swirls across the choppy waters.

That was my moment to make a sensible, considered decision to put on my waterproof over-trousers, proven veterans of my Mongolian trek, before my jeans became saturated, but anticipating the forecast improvement in conditions (or "bastard incompetent weather men" as I venomously spat out as the day progressed) and not wanting to stop in the relentless squalls and excavate down to the very bottom of my rucsac I foolishly continued, inadequately protected against the elements, naively awaiting the predicted clearing skies and drying wind that would soon restore normal service. My top half, at least initially, was OK, thanks to hood pulled tight over my bush hat, but even that was found to be wanting on what became a dreadful, even foolhardy, trek to Horton.

One of my few clear memories of 1970 is of that tarn. It rained then, persuading us, in brightening afternoon skies but a rising gale, to abort Fountains Fell and Pen-y-Ghent, taking a low level route before dropping down, and saving a couple of miles into the bargain, directly into Horton. On July 9th 2006 Fountains Fell remained invisible as the squalls became more intense, heavy cloud descending ever lower down its shoulders, and for the first time on my journey I needed to keep moving to stay warm. Nevertheless, my fleece remained securely protected in my rucsac, which paradoxically proved to be a good move as it would have otherwise become, like my jeans, a heavy, saturated, liability clinging to my shivering body.

The thickening blanket had descended to only a few hundred feet, and from feeling apprehensive as I approached Malham Tarn I now felt afraid and vulnerable, acutely conscious of walking alone with no mutual support system, both moral, and in an emergency, physical. Furthermore, my narrow banded Pennine Way maps didn't extend to any contingency options, for which I was to blame, unlike Keith who had detailed Ordnance Survey extracts plus a Sat. Nav. system. What to do? My guide advised me, with regard to Fountains Fell, that "In mist the upper part of the path can appear faint and confusing. Care should be taken to stay on route". It then mentioned a groove down to the left that "if lost, this is a good feature to aim for". Hardly a ringing endorsement for crossing in appalling weather, given additionally that the fell is dotted with abandoned mine shafts.

Nevertheless it was Hobson's Choice again to carry on and hope for improved weather, but by the time I'd skirted Malham Moor, descended to cross the bleak, traffic-less, minor road leading to Arncliffe and climbed the track up to Tennant Gill Farm it was obvious that it was "in for t' day" as they probably say in those parts. One consolation, I'd hardly touched my water, proof, were it needed, that in terms of actual "degree of difficulty" debilitating, dehydrating, heat is the real crippler, as I was again to re-discover after today's aberration.

I'd made decent progress, and stopped to eat my hostelry-prepared soggy sandwiches, disappointed to note that large quantities of grated cheese had already escaped into every crevice of my rucsac from their sparse, and now split, foil wrapping. As for the rest of my balanced provisions, comprising my Bramley Apple sized tomato, it looked a bit tough, so I abandoned it to nature. (Incidentally, the world famous cooking apple was originally propagated from a seedling in Southwell, and the original tree, or evidence of it, is to be found behind the Bramley Apple pub, near the Minster.)

I "sheltered" – a euphemism if ever there was – under a dripping tree, creaking and swaying in the wind – both of us – and contemplated Fountains Fell, hidden directly ahead up the disappearing path. I'd decided I had no real choice but to go on, and if at any stage I couldn't find my way I'd simply turn round and come back, when two distant figures suddenly emerged across the road at the bottom of the track. On a wretched day when I'd not expected to see a soul I'd now encountered eight, not counting the young women in Malham, and I waited for this latest duo to catch me. After the usual brief introductions I walked with the back marker, who revealed that this was his second attempt at The Pennine Way and that he'd walked from Staffordshire and across the Peak District to reach Edale.

It was only then, as his presumed companion stretched away into the clouds, that I realised that they weren't together. "No, he's just passed me back at the road". Realising that I'd soon be losing the confidently striding front marker for good and, to my surprise, that I was considerably faster, uphill at least, than my new found colleague, I bade farewell and good luck and pushed on breathlessly to close, with difficulty, on the bloke who clearly knew where he was going.

"Leader" was emblazoned appropriately across the back of his jacket and as he was travelling light I idiotically, from his motif, assumed he was in charge of an outdoor group, feeling stupid when he advised me that it was just a logo. Obvious, of course, but he was polite enough not to say so. Stranger number one had already disappeared without trace somewhere in the cloud, wind and horizontal rain below us, but my concern was for my own welfare. The straggler was, like me, carrying a full pack, had made it this far and was clearly competent and equipped to look after himself at his own steady pace.

We climbed on into the murk, but the path was, despite the warnings, easy to follow, with regular marker cairns, and I'd have felt no misgivings if I'd remained alone. Despite my heavier pack, and maybe ten years seniority, I managed to keep up, learning that my co-walker was Ivan, a plasterer from Redcar who was walking The Pennine Way in weekend stages. Today was Malham to Horton, some two miles shorter than my total distance, where he'd left his car first thing before taxi-ing back to the start.

He was due to meet his mate in Redcar that night for their usual Sunday evening drink, and after asking him whether there was much to do there he predictably responded that there wasn't, to the extent that they'd come up with a novel way of spicing up their nights out. Instead of sticking to regular haunts they'd decided to rotate alphabetically through all the hostelries in the area, and were already on their second time around, having started at The Aardvark and progressed to The Zulu Warrior. (Actually, I've fabricated the names.) There were to be no exceptions, and he admitted to having spent wasted hours in some pretty awful dives.

In a variety on the theme, an old school friend (who shall remain nameless) and his mates used to indulge in The Carlton Hill Run, calling, in a sequence of pint, half, half, pint, half, half, etc, in every pub from the Nottingham end to their resident Carlton section of the A612, before falling over somewhere near Cricket Field. As someone who now has severe misgivings about the excesses and culture of alcohol I can at least say that there was never any violence or vandalism, other than an incident with a soda siphon in The Old Volunteer that invoked a ban by the un-amused landlord.

We stopped, in what was now a full blown gale, to inspect a mine shaft barely a few yards off the path and encircled by a wooden boarded fence, easily negotiated if you were stupid enough to do so, or had a death wish, and peered – very briefly, in my case – over the top. There was no sign of the bottom, and I mused that you could disappear forever down there. Doubtless the odd unfortunate wild creature already has. We disappeared on through the all-enveloping clouds, glad that the path was well defined, and the regularly spaced cairns within visible distance, before coming onto a sudden descent, much steeper and shorter than our approach, just after passing the summit cairns.

I daresay there would be smashing views on a clear day, but our surroundings vanished into the gloom and driving rain a mere hundred feet or so below us. Out of this strange twilight world, with the wind buffeting my body and trying – and succeeding, all too frequently – to tear my hood away from my face, two figures suddenly appeared, Southbound Way-sters, and we crossed with cheery grins and resigned comments about the conditions. "Thank goodness for Global Warming!" I shouted above the howling wind, words that would come back to haunt me when the sun put his hat on again. I was chuffed and relieved that Fountains Fell was over, as we dropped down towards the minor road to Stainforth, which we had to follow for just over half a mile before taking the track to Horton, with Pen-y-Ghent optional, and in my mind a non-starter.

The genial Ivan, who'd been both re-assurance and good company over the fell, had other ideas. By the time we'd reached the right fork, past Dale Head and on to Churn Milk Hole, with Pen-y-Ghent invisible but for its bottom couple of hundred feet – which was where we were – Ivan had confirmed that he was definitely taking the loop, via the summit, and I was equally emphatic in my confirmation that I'd be taking the left down the path just under a mile ahead. I was absolutely drenched, and my "waterproof" cag had given up the ghost, final proof that I should have replaced it, which I nearly had, when I was spending my vouchers.

Bush hat, shirt, underpants, jeans and socks were all ringing wet, and my feet were now literally sloshing in my boots, despite my half inch application of Dubbin, due to rivers running down inside from my clinging jeans and through my socks. I was suddenly struggling, after the water finally breached my defences, tired and cold – always a danger – and was shivering after we'd stopped very briefly at the roadside for remaining rations, sheltering in the shallow overhang of a farm doorway. It took a few minutes of steady walking before I warmed up again, anxious for my B & B, hot (for a change!) shower and evening meal, intent on the shortest route, especially if it meant avoiding the climb to the summit of Pen-y-Ghent which, again quoting from my guide, "may not be too clear in poor visibility".

We slogged up to where a path disappeared left into the clouds, but safely and directly back downhill to Horton, and The Pennine Way disappeared straight ahead into the clouds, but steeply uphill, visibility bugger all. Ivan clearly wanted me to accompany him, but for my benefit, not his, and had reminded me – without success – that if I was otherwise to complete the entire walk, missing this section would be a permanent regret, and all for the sake of a bit of extra climbing and a couple of derisory miles – or words to that effect. As I prepared to say cheerio, he reminded me that "It's only two miles extra out of the entire distance and you won't be able to wind back and do it again." "Sod it, go on then."

I surprised myself, as I'd no idea, up to that foolish, spontaneous, split second change of heart, that I'd be trudging, tired, hungry, perished, and quite literally soaked to the skin, up a mountain in the worst walking weather I've ever experienced, in any season, when I had the option of an easy and safe short cut. "Bastard weathermen" I muttered to myself as we ground our way upwards, ever upwards, but with no view, in the atrocious conditions, of a tangible goal. I'd long since dropped my steamed up, rain spattered, glasses into my bag, grateful that my eyesight without them – they're essentially for sharpening my distance vision – is still fairly good.

Ivan's superior stamina was telling, plus, I reminded myself, lesser years, much lighter pack, and two miles fewer walked, and he waited whilst I caught him, but unlike Day One with Mike, it was the ferocious wind that threatened to tear me from my scrambled footholds, arm aching as I continually thrust my stick down for extra support, pack threatening to unbalance me on the near vertical scrambles towards the top. Then, somehow, and trembling from my exertions and the fear of being blown off as that final zig-zag climbed over slippery boulders and rocks, we were on the shallow final ascent to the summit marker. I think it's a trig point, but I wasn't paying much attention, spotting it with relief as it suddenly appeared through the gloom from about twenty yards away before disappearing back into the mists some twenty yards after we'd passed it.

The descent was less severe, and easy to follow, on a good path, but we were still three miles from Horton, and even Ivan, with whom I was now evenly matched again after my nightmare on that final, and for me, genuinely frightening summit scramble, ventured that he'd had enough and would be glad to get back. I'd have been less than a mile away if I'd taken that undemanding short cut. The gale was relentless, not gusting, but an incessant, ferocious, storm that now chose to drive not rain, but sheets of horizontal hail stinging into our faces, the grey mass of cloud obliterating everything above, below, behind or ahead of us beyond a couple of hundred feet from the ghostly path, still fading out of sight ahead with every advancing step, like something from an Edgar Allan Poe horror story.

We squelched on towards the track and visibility gradually improved as we dropped below the heaviest of the cloud, although it was still chucking it down and blowing a gale. "Bastard weathermen!" Now here's an idea, and I admit that's it's an eccentric one. Why not have a daily nominated weather person who has to dress the following day as per their prediction, with a conspicuous logo on the lines of "Met Office – dressed as forecast"? That might sharpen up their act.

In fairness, the good weather on my Pen-y-Ghent day, after rain supposedly clearing overnight, was assumed from what they'd said on TV a couple of days previously and the Met Office may have changed their minds in the intervening period (which told me that they were pretty clue-less a massive 48 hours in advance, but that's another story), but that wasn't to be the case when I crossed Great Shunner Fell in thick cloud and freezing winds, that very morning's Radio and Television forecasts both guaranteeing – and they displayed the symbols on TV to confirm it – unbroken blue skies and warm sunshine.

Oh to have met the "Dressed as forecast" nominee, attired in tee-shirt and shorts, blue from Hypothermia. Just a thought, and a fairly stupid and unfair one on reflection, but it made me smile to myself as we plodded that endless final three miles, in the teeth of a "nice day after overnight rain".

My B & B, The Golden Lion Hotel, was at the far end of the village, directly across from the church (again!), and I left Ivan with a warm handshake – or at least as warm as conditions would allow – and best wishes as he headed off for his car and his alphabet pint. His company and companionship had taken the fear out of my assault through the dark clouds over Fountains Fell and I could look back, as he'd predicted, with satisfaction that however ill-advised – and it was, even more so with hindsight as I shuddered at my foolishness at the end of a long day, tired, cold, soaked to the skin, in the worst conditions I've experienced as a walker – I'd conquered Pen-y-Ghent, albeit with only three wheels on my wagon, but, as far, as the Pennine Way was concerned "still rolling along".

I got a warm welcome and a cosy, modern, room, with all facilities and two beds at The Golden Lion, and immediately made for my en-suite, where I stripped off, dropping each item of saturated clothing onto the tiled floor whilst I worked out what to do with it. My cag would dry on a hanger. I rinsed out my lightweight top under the hot tap and it too would be dry, on its hanger, by morning. Underpants were wrung out as dry as possible then draped over the shower rail, from where I'd stuff them tomorrow, still damp, into my plastic bag of dirty laundry for washing on my rest day in Hawes, my next stop.

As for my socks, I squeezed out as much of the gritty brown residue as strength would allow, wrapped them in a small carrier and dropped them into the rubbish bin – I'd plenty more, and due to the ease of effecting en-route laundry I was tending to re-cycle the same stuff. I finished my journey, despite wearing clean clothes every day, with several unworn pairs of socks and pants, a significant advantage of B & B over camping. My bush hat hung at a rakish angle on the door handle, but my boots would have to be worn tomorrow still wet, to dry out, weather permitting, as I walked. (It had been a daily feature of my trek through the marshy valleys of Mongolia's Khenti Mountains, so the prospect didn't unduly worry me, although with hindsight I'd have stuffed some absorbent newspaper into them overnight.)

That left my heavy duty black jeans, now so heavy that I could barely lift them, when, joy of joys, I spotted the heated towel rail, providence having allocated my sole such luxury to the one night when I needed it. Maybe there is a God! (although it would be arrogant lunacy to expect him – or her – to smile on me when children are dying of cruelty, starvation and cluster bombs.) I switched it on and painstakingly manipulated the legs and crotch so that they'd get maximum benefit, intending to turn them over later, after my evening meal. "Shit, money!"

I'd suddenly remembered that in addition to my supply in my plastic card wallet, snug and dry in its blue drawstring bag, I'd got about £200 in my trouser pocket. It came out, reluctantly, in one congealed, semi-welded, soggy mess and I spent the next few minutes gently peeling and separating the individual notes, laying each bedraggled fiver, tenner or twenty carefully on the adjacent single bed, where they spent the night. Jeans back on towel rail, relaxed and warm – but hungry – after my shower, I ferreted out a change of clothing, including my lightweight "evening wear" jeans from my rucsac, pleased that apart from a few wet patches at the bottom it had successfully repelled the elements.

If there's one useful lesson to be learnt from that atrocious day it can be summarised in one word – "bags". Put everything in easily identifiable and relevant sized self-contained bags, waterproof where possible, and bring along a few spare ones, then even if it throws it down for days on end, or you fall in a river (shades of Mongolia again) the bulk of your stuff will remain dry, even if you and your rucsac aren't. One other tip would be to bring plenty of cash – but keep it somewhere dry! – as cash dispensers are few and far between and most B & B's, especially farms, don't take plastic. I'm not sure what the going hourly rate for sheep shearing is, to pay for one night's accommodation.

I descended to the pub lounge where the sole occupants, to my surprise, were Janet and Keith. Another "long lost" reunion followed by an exchange of gossip, but only after careful selection from the menu. They were amazed that I'd climbed Pen-y-Ghent, having dropped directly into Horton via the track as, I subsequently discovered, had Janet and John, all showing a damn site more common sense than me, although I was quietly chuffed with my somewhat foolhardy achievement. Three excellent meals were followed, in Keith's case, and as he had done at the first night's pub in Padfield, and every subsequent opportunity, by an order for Sticky Toffee Pudding.

He'd designated himself as unofficial World and Pennine Way taster for this particular delicacy, a personal favourite, the definitive serving of which he'd experienced on holiday in Drumnadrochit (which, in case you didn't know, is in Haggis country not far from Inverness). I suspected that nothing would ever match his sublime Drumnadrochit experience, if only because it would bring the thrill of the chase to an end, but The Golden Lion got an "excellent", which he asked the waitress to convey to the chef. The whole place got an "excellent" in my scale of B & B ratings.

We moved across to the bar after dinner to join the locals and watch the World Cup final. Italy beat France, which was a shame, and Zinedine Zidane - surely the most exotically named player in the history of Football, or any sport for that matter - disgraced himself with his infamous head butt, which was an even greater shame. I suppose his notoriety does at least give him the claim that supporters the world over can instantly recall his final contribution to his International career. Who can remember the parting shots of other greats, such as Pele, George Best, Bobby Charlton, Eusebio et al?

The view from my window when I returned after the footie took my breath. The rain had cleared and a dramatic late appearance of Pen-y-Ghent revealed itself, stark and beautiful against the darkening sky. The final fling of the setting sun, saving its one brief appearance for the day's last knockings, threw a horizontal golden glow in a narrow band across the foreground. Pure theatre.

I could scarcely believe that a few hours earlier I'd struggled, drenched and shivering, to remain upright on its invisible storm-lashed summit.

Day Eight. Horton-in-Ribblesdale to Hawes.

"The years disappear like a ghost"

Janet and Keith had signed the famous – in Pennine Way circles – book in the Pen-y-Ghent café just up the road and had insisted at dinner that I remember to do likewise, reminding me in the morning at breakfast. I hadn't bothered yesterday when I dripped by as I was desperate for shelter and warmth. They were off ahead of me and I was content to enjoy what promised to be a leisurely walk to Hawes, where I'd booked two night's B & B, with a full rest day scheduled for tomorrow.

Fourteen miles today, and I'd already ceased to notice my soggy boots by the time I made my first stop, on a bright and pleasantly warm summer morning, a couple of hundred yards back up the road. The cheerful young man at the café proffered the large Pennine Way book for signature, then, in confirmation that this would indeed have been the place where I'd recorded my passing 36 years earlier, brought out volume one. I flicked eagerly through the pages from late July onwards, only to reach the end of August without success.

Backwards, then, but almost certain that we'd set off after the end of the school summer term, and of course Horton being several days into our walk, it shouldn't have pre-dated the middle of July. Nothing. Acute disappointment. Maybe it was another book. I turned a few more pages, the café man sharing my disappointment as I reduced my close scrutiny to cursory glances. Back a bit further. "Found it!" We celebrated, as I showed him the sequential signatures, Darrell Pulk (my brother), Richard Pulk and Steve Beer, plus respective addresses, 83 Ernest Road, Carlton, Nottingham and 324 Westdale Lane West, (amazingly, Keith's temporary stamping ground) Mapperley, Nottingham.

And the date. 10th July 1970. 36 years – to the day. You could have knocked me down with the proverbial feather – both of us in fact, the proprietor sharing my amazement and delight. He suggested that I take a photo of the page, but unfortunately my otherwise excellent Yashica "Point and Shoot" forgot to warn me that it was too close to

103

focus and the resultant images are blurred, rather like my memories. I signed the 2006 entry along the lines that I was back again, after exactly 36 years, and left the café walking on adrenalin fuelled air, the best wishes of the engaging proprietor following me, wondering just exactly what had happened to those intervening years.

It really was a nostalgia trip now, but apart from a view of the distant Ribblehead Viaduct – "I remember this bit" – and a particular rocky ledge that doubled as a seat on the approach to Hawes, with familiar views of the sweeping Yorkshire Dales - "I reckon we sat here" I said to no-one, as I parked my bum - my recollections remained shrouded in a Pennine fog. Not so the glorious open spaces of the Dales, now revealed, after yesterday's squally blast, in all their summer splendour, as I climbed the track out of the village towards Jackdaw Hole, although I didn't notice a hole, or any Jackdaws.

I passed another ruined farmhouse, where my phone suddenly burst into life with a flurry of text messages and I realised, by the time I'd responded, that thanks also to my café stop I'd only covered just over a mile since The Golden Lion, an hour earlier. Keith had insisted on lending me his mobile there as I asked the bar staff if they had a pay-phone, and it illustrated the hit-and-miss nature, in rural locations especially (although I had the same problem in St Ives, Cornwall) of being with the "wrong" provider, at least until fuller coverage is developed. Imagine a winter's night in Horton. You're dependant on your mobile for an important message or call, so, armed with sweater, sou'wester, boots, torch and emergency rations you leave the house with a parting "Just off to Jackdaw Hole, see you later".

I pushed on, chirpy and confident on what would surely be an excellent day. "Ouch, you bugger." An involuntary shout as my Achilles Heel (doubling as my eponymous metaphorical weakness) checked my first stride, after my texting, with a fierce stab, reducing me to a geriatric hobble until I managed to walk it into a controlled, stick-assisted, limp, a painful handicap that was to be my unwelcome hallmark, to a greater or lesser extent, for every remaining step of the way. Nevertheless I upped my pace significantly as I descended towards Old Ing Farm, from Rough Hill, when further adversity

104

struck, this time my first collective attack of the locally named "clegs", vicious horseflies that sting, draw blood and leave a nasty, itching, weal that can lead to infection – although Janet and Keith never sustained a single bite.

Where horseflies are concerned I seem to be a prime target. A sharp sting on my left hand betrayed the first successful attack, but it flew off before I could swat it – damage already done anyway – leaving a red spot oozing blood and guaranteed to swell and itch like mad later. Its mates joined in and I was soon waving my arms and bush hat like a hysterical kid protecting their candy floss from a wasp, but I still got bitten several times before, thankfully, they petered out again. At least my insect repellent top seemed to work, as it was to prove again under an even more sustained assault near Hadrians Wall, but exposed flesh – hands, wrists, neck and ears – was a permanent target, not just by the two marauding armies, but niggling lone snipers that persisted throughout from Horton onwards.

I became super sensitive to their alighting "tickle" on my skin and developed a lightning fast reflex swat that sent a good few of them spiralling to the ground before they'd drawn blood. I applied "Plix" morning and night and found it had an equally soothing effect on British horsefly bites as it had on Estonian mosquitoes. As for my wasp analogy, I have to say in fairness that they don't bother me, and I go to great lengths at home or work to evict them safely.

I've never been stung by a wasp, or a bee for that matter, and don't intend or expect to be. Demonised by Jasper Carrot in his nevertheless funny "What useful purpose do wasps serve?" sketch, he's got the wrong target (and they're good for the garden). Forget brightly coloured fast-moving stripey things that buzz, and won't attack unless severely provoked, it's the silent, dull coloured, sneaky, slow, hovering things like midges, mozzies and horseflies that warrant both his attentions and merciless extermination, the more so, as the saying has it, that if you kill one, thousands come to its funeral.

My flight from the scary clegs – and they genuinely are, when they attack in numbers – hadn't helped my tendon, but despite limping quite heavily I caught a group of four female walkers on the broad track of Cam High Road – A Roman road, in fact – over Cam Fell. The group transpired to be American citizens, somewhat eccentrically, and admirably, celebrating the 60th birthday of one of their number by walking from Arnside, near Morecambe, cross country to the Yorkshire coast. They'd flown over specially on an inclusive package, with pre-booked accommodation and emergency radios "just in case", and these junior Golden Girls were a credit, and deserved to be proud as punch. I stopped further on for lunch, just as the clouds thickened and a few light showers passed overhead, they overtook me, and I caught them for the second time near Dod Fell on West Cam Road.

We chatted again, admired the stunning view across Snaizeholme Valley – just one more in a litany of evocative place names – and concluded with a photo-shoot. They suggested a rendezvous that evening in our mutual destination, but I wasn't sure if I'd prefer an early night nursing my ankle, the back of which, above my heel, was swollen and tight, so I left it open. We parted with handshakes all round and I pushed on towards the final descent.

It was, ankle and clegs excepted, an easy day's walking on clear paths and tracks, with gentle ascents, a long stretch on flat ridges, and the steepest section an enjoyable drop, with fine views and returning sunshine, into Hawes, pre-empted by a surreal interlude when The Pennine Way cut across a council-type estate in Gayle. Through a final field, taking time out to stroke a horse with her nervously inquisitive foal – it finally risked an exploratory nibble of my hand – then a narrow cut-through between stone cottages and I was on the bustling high street, with its shops, banks, hotels, pubs, cafes and restaurants, fish and chip shop, traditional rope-making and Wensleydale Cheese attractions, museum, street market, and people, locals and tourists alike, all compressed into one attractive North Yorkshire village, from where the surrounding countryside can be reached not by travelling miles out through suburbia but the simple expedient of passing through a gate or over a stile.

The Bullshead Hotel, which wasn't, to my surprise, a licensed premises, although it must have been once, was slap bang in the centre, enclosed by market stalls, and I was given a choice of rooms. I chose the large one on the ground floor, with a huge bed, on which was sat an enormous teddy bear, propped amongst some carefully scattered cushions against pristine pillows on top of a chic duvet cover. The room was full of feminine touches – pot pourri, miniature soaps, perfumey things in bottles and pretty furnishings – and I thought it was smashing, glad that I'd booked in for two nights.

I had a shower and removed Ted, who was about five feet tall at his full height, to a suitable spot on the floor, where he fixed me with an unblinking, slightly spooky, stare, reminiscent of those sheep at Top Withins. The cushions had to go too, and I shuffled them into a heap at one side of the bed, and sprawled out on the remaining half an acre, musing that I could sleep sideways if I had a fancy. After a relaxing doze my stomach dictated that I seek an urgent appointment with food, and fish and chips called out loud and clear.

They were delicious too, enjoyed on a bench in the main street, happily watching the world go by. Then a gentle stroll, flexing my aching ankle, perusing the displays in the tourist shops, wincing at the house prices in the Estate Agents, and finding four familiar ladies waiting for their evening meal to be served. They waved me inside from their window seats and we spent the next couple of hours fostering Anglo-American relations, or in the case of one lady, Irish-Estonian.

Her Irish background, and family secrets, that she'd only reconciled with the understanding and enhanced self-confidence of her later years, following a first visit to her family in Ireland, bore remarkable similarities to my Estonian voyage of discovery (literally – the car ferry from Stockholm to Tallinn) to meet my half-sisters, nieces, nephew, aunt and cousin, in a whirlwind tour that left me physically and emotionally reeling. We learnt, through the candid exchange of repressed secrets that are so much easier to release between empathetic passing strangers, powerfully so if there's common ground, that we shared the same traumas of guilt, secretive "dark" family history and of being somehow "different" as a child, and, in my case at least, an enduring stigma after I finally became an adult.

Following our fond and poignant farewells I retired to my giant bed with the comforting thought that tomorrow was my "day off" and I didn't have to re-pack my rucsac in the morning.

~

Day Nine. Hawes. Rest Day.

"There's a sadness, there's a joy, there's a place, there's a song that will never die"

I opened my door en route to breakfast to find my clean laundry, neatly folded, waiting outside in a carrier bag, and when I returned to my room thirty minutes later Ted had somehow climbed back onto the very same spot on the bed where I'd found him when I first checked in, the pillows and cushions had re-assembled themselves, I reckon to within an inch of where they were, the pillows supporting Ted had fluffed themselves back to their pristine crispness, and the duvet was turned down to its immaculate spirit level precision. Amazing – and unnecessary. In fact a waste of labour, but it made me smile, and persuaded me to languish on the chair for a while lest I disturb the symmetry. I'd re-arrange (or "mess up") the bed and put Ted back on the floor when I came in later for an afternoon relax.

Ann, my landlady, was off to Harrogate with her husband for The Yorkshire Show, and I was off for a gentle tour of Hawes and its environs, including Hardraw Force, claimed to be the highest waterfall in England, but not before a knock came at my door. Ann handed me a postcard. "An American lady asked me to give this to Richard." It was from Kathleen and friends, wishing me a safe journey and leaving an E-mail contact. Unfortunately, they'd already left on the next leg of their walk, so I was unable to thank them in person, and being in E-mail "limbo" with no contact postal address I have, to my shame, not responded as I type these words. However, the situation is about to be re-dressed, and hopefully we'll exchange a warm correspondence.

My day in Hawes, in a mixture of pleasant sunshine and cooler, cloudy, interludes – ideal walking conditions – was very special and one that I hope to repeat one day. I returned to The Bullshead later in the afternoon to be greeted by the sole occupier, Tilly, the black Flat Coated Retriever. She'd got her own area and food and drink at the back of the servants quarters, "off limits" to guests, where she'd disappear by barging through the swing door, but with time to fill and an acute feeling of melancholy welling up I decided to do us both a favour and take her for a walk.

The problem was that I couldn't find her lead, despite looking in all the "obvious" visible places. I was averse to checking, however superficially, inside private cupboards and drawers, apart from a quick gleg in the likeliest ones near the main door, but unfortunately my situation had been somewhat compromised by then, with Tilly following me around expectantly ever since my cheery "C'mon then, let's go for a walk". I resorted to "Where's your lead, Tilly, where's your lead?" Whether by chance, or the doggy equivalent of Sat Nav, I'm not sure, but we found ourselves in the "off limits" corridor, next to a tall cupboard, in which hung a dog lead, and off we went – or rather, off went Tilly.

She took me for a circular walk that must have been her daily constitutional – across the road, turn left, then right up the entry between the houses and past the Pennine Way sign, through the fields towards Gayle, then a right somewhere round the back of the Wallace and Gromit cheese centre and across another field, before dropping back down suspiciously close to the fish and chip shop, where I had to tug her smartly away as she was about to snaffle an involuntary free sample from a little lad's takeaway. She paused (or should that be pawsed?) again as we reached a particular market stall just before home. "Hello Tilly, come for your toast?" As she eagerly devoured the crunchy offerings I explained why she hadn't called round earlier, and my impromptu role as substitute dog walker.

Just like most of my 1970 Pennine Way adventure, I'd also forgotten what it was like to take a stroll with a canine companion, but as I hung her lead back in the cupboard everything was coming back into sharp focus, not least the "Dog is for life" commitment. I wasn't sure whether I could ever take on that responsibility again, especially given the surprising demands and involvement of our one hour excursion, but I did feel honoured when I was informed later that Tilly would usually refuse to go out with anyone else.

Would that I had that affect on all the women!

Day Ten. Hawes to Muker.

"Through the silent miles, the empty spaces"

I caught two "hot off the press" weather forecasts first thing, one live from the weather presenter on the telly in my room, and a local one off the radio at breakfast, so I knew it would be a smashing day for walking – sun and blue skies throughout, and a perfect 22C – and that the cold, grey, blustery conditions in Hawes would soon improve, despite Ann's "Not very nice out there, they said it was going to be lovely and sunny today".

Only eleven miles to my B & B at Muker, roughly a mile off The Pennine Way down the track from Kisdon Farm, one mile on from Thwaite. The walk was essentially a traverse of Great Shunner Fell, which, my guide informed me, was the highest point so far, at 2,340 feet, with a slog of five miles continual but "easily accomplished" ascent to its summit and a steeper, three miles, descent into Thwaite. Given my improved fitness, and promised conditions that were ideal for making good progress, it should have been a doddle, especially after my rest day, and I anticipated a gentle easy stroll and sweeping views across the fells and valleys. Wrong on both counts.

My right tendon was now giving me serious concern, continually swollen directly above my heel, even aching and throbbing in bed, both before and after sleep, and the slightest direct pressure as I made an exploratory examination was excruciating. No choice but to reluctantly raid the First Aid kit, and on went the crossover elasticated support bandage, although despite wearing it for every single step from then on, later to be complemented by my tubi-grip as things got a bit desperate, I'm not convinced that it did me other than psychological good. My stick, however, was invaluable, and I would have been unable to continue without it.

I limped heavily out of Hawes, feeling a bit of a prat and hoping that I could walk through the pain until it subsided – it never disappeared again, after that day – to a tolerable level where I could manage a reasonably relaxed and steady pace. The biggest problem, once I'd got that first "loosening" mile under my belt, was that if I

111

stopped for a decent rest – and a proper lunch break was essential on the longer days – it was agony to get going again.

The sun never got going either, leaving his hat stubbornly on the peg, and the grey clouds rolled ever lower across Great Shunner Fell, which was hidden somewhere up the track ahead of me as I started my five mile trudge from Hardraw. The wind continued to strengthen, and whipped fiercely across my path as I drew the hood of my cag tightly over my bush hat, still at that early stage naively anticipating (despite my Pen-y-Ghent experience) a dramatic turnaround as the sun inevitably burnt off the cloud cover and the temperature rose by ten degrees, confident in the guarantee, in front of my very eyes, by some incompetent soothsayer who would have been better advised to scrap the multi million pounds computer technology and base the forecast on the simple expedient of looking out of the window.

They're fine predicting successive days of heat under a bloody great High Pressure system, but throw in a bit of "changeable" and I reckon a piece of seaweed sometimes does the job better. I know I'm whingeing on, but hikers, fishermen, sailors, and other outdoor folk are reliant, often in critical terms of safety, on the latest bulletins. A day-walker may well have ventured out less than adequately prepared. The good news was that it stayed dry, but it was freezing, and as I climbed towards the thickening blanket of cloud, and it lowered ever more menacingly to meet me, the penny dropped that I was stuck with it. "Bastard Weathermen!" I exclaimed, not, of course, for the first time on my walk, as the swirling grey murk enveloped me.

My "sweeping views" for the next three hours were of the path, thankfully of flagstones or closely spaced cairns, disappearing thirty yards ahead - even less, at the top - into the ghostly shroud, and equally eerily, when I paused to look back, ceasing to exist beyond my last few seconds' progress. Unlike that awful Sunday after Malham, I'd had no reason to feel apprehensive when I left Hawes, and the route is straightforward anyway, with no abandoned mine shafts, but the thick fog stole any perception of progress and nothing existed beyond my claustrophobic horizon. The relentless chill wind driving across the featureless, shelter-less, expanse dictated against stopping, even if I'd wanted to.

But what if I had to? For the first and only time on the Pennine Way I suddenly felt a mild sense of panic, acutely aware of my isolation and vulnerability, and quickened my step, in the same anxious way, I suppose, that a frightened woman might react when she suddenly finds herself alone on a dark, empty, threatening street. I stumbled on an uneven flagstone, triggering that niggling injury into a fierce protest and me into an appropriate self-recriminatory exclamation – "That was fucking stupid, Richard, slow down you prat!"

I don't know what would have happened if I'd come to grief, even whether I'd have got a phone signal (I didn't in Muker), but I did know that following my rest day John, Keith and their respective Janets were well ahead, and that no casual rambler would stray up here, on a weekday, in such horrible conditions. As it happened, I didn't see one person, in either direction, from joining the track after Hardraw to entering the little café in Thwaite, in something like four hours walking, and not one fellow walker all day.

It doesn't have to be a twisted or broken ankle, it could be illness, diarrhoea or a migraine, heaven forbid even a weak heart, and to be stricken up there, invisible, in bad weather and with no-one to hear a whistle blast was the contemplation that led to my temporary panic, and which might paradoxically have caused that very nightmare scenario. I trod carefully for the rest of the crossing, using my watch as the only measure of distance – "That's an hour, must be another two miles or more, nearly at the top soon" – and so I was, after a couple of fake summits where the path disappointingly clawed its way upwards again towards another invisible ridge.

Then, at last, it was dropping away, a sudden gap in the clouds allowing a tantalising glimpse down the valley before closing again, and eventually, buffeted by what was now a full-blown gale, my right shoulder frozen on the wind blasted descent, I met the track down to Thwaite. The skies finally brightened and the clouds lifted, affording my first view, looking back up the path, to the large marker cairn some two miles distant, invisible from twenty yards when I was there, but the summit of Great Shunner Fell was stubbornly cloaked in a lingering grey blanket.

The wind dropped too, from slamming the door petulantly behind me as I entered the very welcome café at the hotel in Thwaite, to a good tempered breeze by the time I limped out, re-fuelled on Ginger Ale for a change - not to be confused under any circumstances with the abrasive Ginger Beer - and steak and kidney pie and chips, with only two miles ahead of me. It stayed bright during those closing stages, as I ascended a steep new-mown field, strewn with grass cuttings obliterating the path, to claim the stile in the top-right corner, then followed the narrow way up and along the ridge with expansive views over the valley, and Muker and its church tower, to my right, before dropping down again at the farm track to my destination. The brighter interlude didn't last, and it was one of those evenings when it was cold, dreary, and dark from about six o'clock. I kept an eye open for an embarrassed and shivering weather forecaster dressed for a summer barbecue, but no such luck.

Bridge House was another excellent (and Hobson's, after exhausting other hopefuls) choice, a tall, attractive Georgian house situated, strangely enough, next to the bridge, at one end of the village. I received a warm welcome, depositing my boots and stick in the porch-way, and climbed two flights to my beautifully appointed room, adding it to my list of possibles for a future short break. In another Pennine Way coincidence, Alan, a fellow escapee from Insurance Broking, mentioned Swaledale as an attractive walking area whilst we were on an autumn six miler around Nottinghamshire's best kept secret, above Epperstone, the first gentle test for my ankle in the three months since The Pennine Way (verdict – "could be better"). It transpired that they'd recently stayed at, and been equally impressed by, that very same place.

As ever, the better class Tourist (as opposed to Way-ster orientated) accommodation seemed a bit incongruous – but nevertheless more than welcome – given my scruffy arrival straight off the moors, and absence of "appropriate" smart/casual change of wear, even a pair of shoes, but there was never a hint of disdain, notwithstanding that the other guests may have stepped out of their executive saloons in their Sunday best. I had my meal at the village pub and made a call from the phone box opposite, followed by a very short, and painful, wander, down past the Swaledale Woollen Shop, with the large black sheep perched on its rooftop, then back, via a mini detour to the church, to my digs.

My vague recollection of Muker, which I had expected to rejuvenate into familiar memories, was of an isolated rural community of scattered cottages, sheep farms, and not much else, so either I was mistaken or it has changed, as it's now a popular and very attractive tourist village, albeit a tad sanitised. It's easily accessible of course, in the way that just about anywhere is by car, and perfect for a few days holiday. My parents and those of most of my working class friends never owned a car, and the ubiquitous short break hadn't been invented, unless you count a day trip to Skegness or Mablethorpe. It's easy to forget not just what Muker may or may not have been like in 1970, but how the world has changed.

I had an early night, pre-empted by delicately massaging Ibuprofen gel into the swelling at the back of my ankle, step two of an assault that would eventually exhaust every available medical resource.

~

Day Eleven. Muker to Bowes.

"Now somewhere out on that ocean, lies our fear should we grow old"

The Ancient Unicorn in Bowes, some seventeen miles on, was today's destination, but not before another Ibuprofen rub, which was to be repeated daily - morning, evening on arrival, and before bed - and a painful hobble downstairs to breakfast, a new and daily struggle that had me descending like an old man, leading on every stair with my left leg so that the stretch on my right tendon didn't send me through the roof. I can understand why such injuries drive athletes and other sports people demented with frustration and anguish, especially when they're otherwise fit, often after months, even years, of preparation.

At least in my case I only had to continue at my own pace, and provided I could overcome the daily distance, and the pain, I'd limp on, but I had serious doubts that morning when even that scenario looked in the balance. I'd reached the anticipated stage where I'd walked myself into a decent level of fitness and stamina, even on the uphill sections, but if I was struggling to make the breakfast table due to a gammy ankle I was in real trouble. I limped self-consciously off after my meal, now reduced to cereals, two boiled eggs and toast, hoping that my landlord Alan Nichols hadn't witnessed my embarrassing departure and was shaking his head as to whether I'd make the first hundred yards, let alone Bowes.

It was a shitty first hundred yards too, but I gathered a momentum of sorts as I headed, in glorious early morning sunshine, towards Keld, three miles on, up the magnificent limestone valley of the River Swale. No wonder my friend Alan stayed here. A pleasant cooling breeze took the edge off the temperature as I followed the gentle ascent past Keld and up to the right into my next valley, parallel to Stonesdale Beck and the minor road below and on my left, devoid of activity save a battered Land Rover that lurched down the track off the moors, to splutter on and disappear down the tarmac, trailing clouds of black diesel in its wake.

Another climb, onto Stonesdale Moor, where I rested for a dive into my rations, having already covered nearly seven miles – almost half distance, perfect weather, lovely views, easy-peasy walking and still not midday. But for my injury, it would have been Pennine Way perfection, and I confess to feeling, as I did on many such days, somewhat robbed of my full and anticipated enjoyment by that debilitating, and not least, embarrassing, painful limp. As I reflected, reclining in my purpose grown clump of comfy heather and watching the bees single-mindedly going about their business around me, a couple of walkers overtook me, the advance guard of maybe a dozen men and women straggling behind in twos and threes, shouting out their greetings as they passed by.

They looked like a mixture of early and normal age retirees, and judging from their modest day-sacs I reckoned they were heading for refreshments at the Tan Hill Inn. It suddenly struck me uneasily that, health permitting, I was heading for that age group, before rationalising that it was a pretty good destination to aim for if it included the easy friendships of a mixed group of fellow ramblers out stretching their legs and enjoying life-affirming scenery. It was a busy day for fellow walkers, probably my busiest of the entire Pennine Way, and a total contrast to yesterday's foggy solitude. A couple of younger hikers, also lightly encumbered, breezed cheerily by, and as I approached the pub three or four others were resting outside.

At last, 1970 re-visited. The Tan Hill stands in total isolation at the junction of two very minor roads amidst miles of bleak, rolling, moorland and lays claim, at 1,785 feet, to being Britain's highest public house. Although it's apparently been modernised – sanitised, some say, out of its original, unique, character – I didn't go in, and it looked exactly as I'd remembered. A little mine wagon stands outside on its bit of railway, a reminder, as is Coal Gill Sike, the nearby stream that becomes the Frumming Beck before completing its journey to the River Greta as Sleighthome Beck, of earlier widespread mining activity. I believe the pub used to have its own shaft, and the notes in my guide stress the importance of keeping to

117

the tracks as the area "abounds in tunnels and shafts – not all are fenced or sealed off".

The Pennine Way cuts directly across the bleak expanse of wilderness falling gently away beyond Tan Hill, and the view was another familiar one, if not the path itself, my previous recollection being of a muddy tramp across undefined, cloying, peat. I have a photo somewhere, taken shortly after we'd left the pub, and it shows a distant rear view of my brother, and behind him, in single file, the diminutive, slightly built Steve Beer, bent double and almost dwarfed by his huge rucsac. Apart from these two figures there's nothing but emptiness – sky above, moorland below. It makes me wonder how we got as far as we did.

I plotted my course from the marker posts along the narrow, winding, and largely unpaved path, awkward on the ankles as it snaked through the clumpy tufts and mounds, including a few surprisingly soggy patches, of peaty heather and grasses, reminiscent of what most of the 1970 moorland sections were like, the Way following the triple named stream for a full six miles to Trough Heads Farm. I overtook another solo walker with heavy pack as he rested, affording me a cursory nod in response to my cordial "Afternoon!" and he was to be my other example of "Pennine Way reticence", irritating both myself and two others a few days later.

A cluster of people was stationary up ahead, and as I closed I was delighted to recognise Janet and John, although surprised that I'd caught them so soon after my rest day – they too had lingered over a couple of shorter days. They were chatting to a small, well equipped, group – I think it was a threesome – who I took as that rare phenomenon, southbound Way-sters. Janet, as I came within earshot, immediately called out "Knew it was you from the carrier bag!" having just asked the strangers whether they'd seen a tall, solo walker with a stick in one hand and a carrier in the other.

The added amusement was that a lady in the other group was similarly "accessorised", for exactly the same reason, and had also been subject to gentle banter. She was equally convinced that it was the logical alternative to unloading your pack every time a good photo opportunity appeared – and, consequently, not usually bothering – or in pursuit of a map reference, compass bearing, Mars Bar, whatever, and we congratulated each other on our common sense in the face of accepted Street Cred – or Way Cred – before we separated, to a chorus of "Good lucks", in our respective directions.

It was taken for granted that I'd continue in the welcome company of Janet and John, and it certainly broke the monotony of the long, stony, track that shadowed the stream for the final two miles to Trough Heads Farm. Thirteen gone, only four to go! This was the point where The Alternative Pennine Way split from the official route, on what is termed The Bowes Loop. It's reckoned to add an extra four miles if, like me, your itinerary dictates accommodation in Bowes. There's nothing else locally unless you're pushing on along The Pennine Way proper to the youth hostel in Baldersdale, as were Janet and John, but I'd decided from the outset that I wanted B & B's with private facilities where possible, thus narrowing my options and ultimately adding five miles, not the quoted four, owing to confusion the next day after leaving my accommodation.

My guide summarised the diversion as "a pathless and somewhat awkward alternative route down to Bowes" – which in part it was – and "a somewhat laborious (in route finding terms) alternative" – which was an accurate summary of the following morning's frustrations. In a return of worryingly hot sunshine and disappearing breeze, necessitating a corresponding increase in water intake, we rested at Trough Heads Farm, in my case briefly, before I bid a fond "See you again soon" to my companions and took the path designated "Alternative Pennine Way". That, as my guide predicted, was about it for signs for a while, ensuring that I got confused, through no fault of my own, as I followed the stream through the pretty, sheep cropped, valley. It was also, sadly, the last that I saw of Janet and John.

The map showed the path, some way to the left of the stream, taking the higher ground, but the logical route looked to be alongside the water, although they appeared to converge anyway, albeit vaguely, a mile or so ahead. I stuck with the map, ending up in an enclosed field - with the path having simply faded away - falling steeply into the valley bottom and full of chest high purple-flowering thistles. I was surrounded, for the second time today, by numerous bees foraging all around me in pursuit of nectar, but a nuisance now as I pushed my way carefully through with my stick. "Now where?"

After an anxious few minutes picking my way around the clinging, prickly, stems and buzzing insects, and wandering to and fro searching for an obvious exit, I spotted a gate at the very top, invisible on the initial approach. As I was about to take, with some relief and not a little irritation, the Pennine Way signed path I noticed, a few hundred yards behind me, the "talkative" chap, looking puzzled, studying his map, taking a few paces down the hillside, stopping again, then back up, then veering in my direction. He'd presumably spotted me, so I left him to it and continued on my way, well aware that to wait and empathise with his similar navigational difficulties would probably elicit little more than a grunt.

At least most of the remainder of the route was well marked, leading me down through farm fields, then a right, parallel to the unwelcome and relentless traffic roaring, a few hundred yards on my left, along the dual carriageway of the A66, the trans-Pennine link from Scotch Corner on the A1 to the M6 near Penrith, although I had another chance to go the wrong way as I closed in, tired, hot, ankle aching, on Bowes.

There was a noticeable difference in the standard and type of way-markers from district to district, often manifested not in their quantity, but in the common sense, or lack of, with regard to their siting – be it simple acorn logos, pointers or paint on boulders, walls, gates, fences or buildings, or stand-alone posts ranging from (my favourite) gnarled, rustic, wooden ones easily visible from a distance but with the ingrained "Pennine Way" or simply "P W" discernible only on close inspection, to varieties of modern ones, including metal. Bowes was one such example.

Someone, or more likely a committee, had laudably approved and commissioned a total overhaul of the "Alternative Pennine Way" route-marking, perhaps in part prompted by observations from mine and similar guides. The excellent and amply distributed aesthetic wooden posts were pristine fresh and easily spotted, leading me confidently on to a high quality purpose built pedestrian bridge that took me safely across to follow the River Greta. Then where? My map showed that I should fork left, away from the bank and onto a track for a short distance before cutting sharp right on a path across fields, to emerge at Bowes Castle and into the village, but surely, having been molly-coddled thus far, I'd be chaperoned by another helpful pointer. I wasn't. Must have run out of money.

I recce'd carefully up the grassy slope, found an access to an unsigned track, invisible from the riverbank - "This must be it" - and past a cluster of private houses before an elderly signpost thankfully pointed me across rolling fields to the square, towering, relic of the castle, perched atop the hillside. I wonder how many people have walked on for some distance along the Greta before having to re-trace their steps, and all because of a thoughtless lack of a sign. It was even more annoying, given that some of those on the approach were superfluous, as the way followed an obvious track. Strange.

Castles are splendid landmarks, evocative reminders of a bygone age, but I've never been impressed with their usually crumbling innards, preferring to use my imagination from outside the ramparts and save myself a pricey entrance fee into the bargain. Bowes was no exception. My Aussie room-mate on my volunteer month in India (Leicester based Salt of the Earth would be thrilled – and thoroughly deserving – to hear from prospective volunteers or donators) had an expression for it.

It followed a weekend trip to the undoubtedly magnificent and fully intact temples at Madurai and a previous visit to our local one in Tirunelveli, a huge, sprawling, mainly underground labyrinth where we'd stumbled, in oppressive heat, choking and compulsorily barefoot, through the dark, dusty, polluted filth of what looked to be something like a thousand year re-construction and renovation project at current labour and progress levels. As for Health and Safety, the least said the better – suffice it to say that Jeremy Clarkson would have been in his element. Nige and me had had enough of Madurai's, albeit totally contrasting, splendour, preferring to explore the vibrant streets. "ABC Syndrome", he exclaimed, which I discovered to be Oz tourist-speak for "Another Bloody Castle".

Bowes Castle was my first, and as far as I recall last, castle on The Pennine Way, Thirlwall excepted, but I remembered his words with amusement as I walked on. Whilst I'm being unkind to Bowes I might as well quote the brief summary jotted that evening in my note pad – "A one horse town, without the horse". I'd expected a bustling little centre, maybe a smaller version of Hawes, based purely, and unfairly, on my ignorant assumption that it was a familiar place-name next to a major road, and merited a similar sized block representation on my map, but I should have realised otherwise from the listing of one solitary B & B, The Ancient Unicorn. Hawes had seventeen.

Nevertheless it was very welcoming, and I was pleased with my bright accommodation in the separate single storey converted stables/barn type building, if not the dripping tap feeding the shower hose, which persisted all night despite my Herculean efforts to squeeze one final performance from the spent washer. After my shower and gel rub, twenty yards across the car park was followed by an enjoyable early evening meal served by the chirpy South African chef. If my tendon had been OK, and my heels weren't feeling sore and bruised – an indication of related "compression" damage, which I'd first noticed about two miles short of Bowes and had never previously experienced in all my years of football and hiking – I'd have gone for a stroll around the churchyard and castle grounds in what was now a perfect summer's evening.

Instead, I stretched out on the bed, drawing the curtain to screen the hot sunshine streaming in through the full height patio style window, cheesed off with my decrepit state and more than a little apprehensive of tomorrow's trek to the Langdon Beck Hotel, Forest-in-Teesdale. Anticipating my gradual build-up to "full match fitness", but not, of course, my injury, I'd assumed that I'd be well capable of longer stretches by this stage, and my accommodation, albeit in part also due to its availability, was staggered accordingly.

That meant, after today's seventeen miles, which had proved to be a good two more than reasonably "tendon tolerant", something like an intimidating twenty three or twenty four tomorrow, with the additional threat of deteriorating (as in, sweltering heat again) weather. I'd let out a thoughtful "Mmmm..." after I'd finalised the booking and re-examined the map, but with no realistic alternative, and needing to play "catch-up" to fit my intended later stages, I decided that it would be alright on the day. It was a day that should see me pass halfway, beyond Middleton-in-Teesdale, the high water mark of our 1970 effort.

I was only hoping that history wasn't about to repeat itself.

~

Day Twelve. Bowes to Langdon Beck.

"I've a will and I've a wanting, and miles to go before I sleep"

The day arrived. I had a 7.30 breakfast, thanks to the landlord suggesting that if I catch the catering lady first thing, when her vehicle pulled onto the car park, she'd happily sort me some snap so that I could be away for 8.00. She did, with a smile, and I was off, anxious to make early inroads into my journey from the very bottom to the very top of my map page number eight and tomorrow's ground breaking appointment with map page number one of "The Pennine Way – Part 2 – North".

To my relief, my ankle was already easing by the time I crossed the bridge on the minor road over the still quiet A66, and perversely it stood up well to my longest day of the walk, unlike my heels, which were already beginning to protest after yesterday's early warning. My further research following my Reactive Arthritis episode had stated that Achilles tendonitis and related heel pain are known consequences, although it didn't advise whether walking The Pennine Way with a heavy pack on sun-baked moorlands, stony tracks and melting tarmac would be a help or a hindrance. I got a combination of all three that day, and would settle, on balance, for "hindrance".

The sun was already blazing down from a still, cloudless, early morning sky, as I followed the tarmac away from Bowes and its dual-carriageway by-pass, across a moorland plateau, reassuringly highlighted in red lettering on my map "MOD. Poison Gas. Keep out" to the left of the road, and further on, to the right "MOD Range. Keep out". That told me then, but just in case I hadn't got an instructive map there were regular and prominent signs on both sides of the road, also in red lettering, that "There are some nasty military bits and pieces on these moors and if you touch them they will explode and maim or kill you, and serve you right too", or equally unambiguous words to that effect.

The metalled road presumably existed only to service these sites, with additional tracks leading off to the sinister remnants of what

124

were presumably World War Two (One, even?) and later, Cold War, encampments and storage locations, but there were no clues as to whether the area is still actively used. The road petered out, shortly after the last military signs, into a blessedly short-lived rubbly track – I hated those unforgiving, heat reflecting, ankle turning, dusty surfaces more than any other – before passing behind a couple of farm buildings displayed on my map as "Levy Pool", where a narrow unflagged way snaked up to a horizon over empty peat, grasses and heather.

That was where the money for relevant (as opposed to superfluous) Pennine Way signing ran out again, just where it was most needed, although in fairness I was now some three miles out of Bowes and it may have been beyond their perceived or actual jurisdiction. Nevertheless, I'd have liked the courtesy of a few wooden marker posts, after the first few ran out, at the cost of a few quid and half a day's labour, to help me navigate across a pathless, featureless, scrubby moor, with my map again showing "MOD Range. Keep out" to my immediate right.

Even the village idiot would have been odds on to navigate safely out of Bowes, given the choice of "Pennine Way, straight ahead along well-signed paved road, Death or Mutilation climb barbed-wire fencing and cross unpaved moor beyond enormous red warning signs", but this initially faint, and seemingly little used, "Alternative Pennine Way" path now petered out completely, as had the wooden markers that I'd followed confidently onto that first ridge of Cotherstone Moor, my map helpfully reminding me that "The way is undefined and hard to follow, although there are numerous sheep tracks through the bracken". Spot on. I knew exactly where I was, and using my compass as re-assurance, exactly the direct way ahead – except that there was no path, the terrain was overgrown, with hollows and ridges limiting forward vision, and the one defined path led in an infuriating U-turn (or Ewe-turn, to be precise) back down towards the gully of Hazelgill Beck, out of which I'd just clambered.

Taking an accurate bearing and striding on in a straight line on easy ground towards a chosen point is one thing, trying to stay on course whilst weaving through a confusing tangle of undergrowth, with no obvious horizon and a military range next door is another. After a flying start, I was confused and furious. "Why can't the prats put a few posts up? They've spent a bloody fortune where it's neither use nor ornament." Common sense. Or lack of. Or maybe, on what was probably a grouse shooting moor, malicious. Regardless, I was, to put it mildly, a bit pissed off, and still am in hindsight, as I type these words!

I reckoned on two miles to where the path was supposed to meet the minor road ahead, then another mile to re-joining the official Pennine Way at Baldersdale. I was certain to hit the minor road somewhere but not, even supposing there was one, the path that led to its access point, and for all I knew I might even end up trapped inside a boundary fence or ditch. It would be a sweaty, energy sapping slog, breaking in and out of waist high scrub, up and over uneven clumps of grass, into and out of hollows, and getting more and more disillusioned and cheesed off, so I decided to cut my losses and turn my supposed extra four miles on the loop to a guaranteed, hopefully safe, five.

I re-traced my steps to the point where I'd crossed a track traversing east-west. According to the map it then became a footpath, heading west, meeting the Pennine Way a couple of miles further south than I would otherwise have done, but apparently guaranteeing safe access. It looked well defined, so muttering a couple of well chosen expletives, and not even daring to dwell on the fact that my early start had gone for a burton, I went on my way. Angrily. Incandescent, in fact, such that I had to remind myself that there was nothing more I could have done and there was no point in getting hot and bothered over a few absent posts – especially as the sun had long since added to that equation by removing his trilby off the peg. I intended to write after my return, but couldn't be bothered, so these words are my irritable testimony.

Two miles of easy walking later, on a thankfully obvious path (they should make this the officially signed diversion), memorable only for the rabbits scattering for most of its length, I clanked a large gate firmly behind me and took a sharp right to re-join the Pennine Way.

A gentle, peaty, descent off Cotherstone Moor, overlooking Balderhead Reservoir, its vivid sparkling blue contrasting with the backdrop of the sombre Mickleton Moor, led to a tarmac lane winding down past Baldersdale Youth Hostel, and the realisation that Janet and John had started the day seven miles ahead of me.

The road swept around the western edge of Blackton Reservoir, where a handful of fishermen – I'd still to meet a fellow walker – were sheltering from the heat under giant umbrellas. It seemed like a good idea, but I had to press on, taking refuge under my bush hat, although it subsequently occurs to me that I should have used my brolly as a parasol, especially on tarmac stretches where the heat was at its most intense. It never once crossed my mind until now, but would definitely have warranted a try.

Then along a track, up a path, another short stretch of track, across a minor road, then up past Hazelgarth Rigg and down the moor, to cross farmland at Grassholme Reservoir. A few more anglers, a few more parasols, a few parked cars. A few hundred yards along the minor road, then back to me and the sheep, and the rabbits, and the curlews, and the lapwings, and the gulls and the oyster catchers, the latter, with their distinctive reddish/pink beaks, a novelty for me as they grazed a nearby field. And my other stoat sighting – or was it a weasel? Once again, I nearly trod on it, as it was taken unawares, slap bang in the middle of The Pennine Way, by the unlikely appearance of a Way-ster, before it scuttled away sharpish.

It was somewhere round here, a few miles short of Middleton, that I'd dropped my wallet clambering over a wall and into a grassy field, followed by that successful crack of dawn search and retrieve exercise, but nothing remotely resembled that vivid memory of a high stone wall and a large field of lush, long, grass. The weather couldn't have been more of a contrast, but this gentle pastoral approach on a well signed path up and across the B6276 Middleton-Brough road, and on to Harter Fell, had little in common with my recollection of a bleak, austere, scene, looking down towards a desolate reservoir, as we scaled that unplanned obstacle. I was disappointed, and despite pausing and taking stock every few minutes nothing came into focus.

My guide warned me that "The section over Harter Fell and down to Middleton-in-Teesdale is particularly difficult to follow, a mixture of farmland and rough grazing with many walls and fences". It was now well signed and easy, with obvious gates and stiles, but maybe that description held the key to what had happened to us, and my wallet, back in the rainy mists of 1970. My unsuccessful, albeit incidental, quest put me in mind of an amusing tale by Alexei Sayle recounting a mission, many years after the event, to try to find the place where he'd dropped – and in this case failed to rescue – his sandwich box down a ravine, somewhere in Spain if I remember correctly. Fired by a similar nostalgic eccentricity, his voyage of re-discovery did at least bear fruit, with his accidentally discarded container still visible, and inaccessible, in the scrub a couple of hundred feet below the site of his aborted picnic.

I dropped down the moor, slowly closing in on the scattered settlement that was our 1970 swansong and which, from above, gives little hint of its attractive centre. The Pennine Way takes a left up the track a couple of hundred yards after it re-joins the B6276 on its approach to Middleton, immediately before the bridge over the Tees, but I continued over the river and into Middleton, a pre-conceived decision to break my long day with a cooked lunch.

I opted for the little café on the left, just before the T-junction, and sat out on the pavement – so much easier than lugging my clobber inside – in a patch of shade where, following an enquiry from the proprietor, I was brought their Pennine Way book to sign and address. Her husband appeared a few minutes later, to shake hands with a fellow Nottinghamian and briefly reminisce about his old stamping ground, which coincided with mine. Once again, I was left to reflect that it's a small world.

My rest and re-fuel rejuvenated my batteries, but once I'd stopped walking the intensity of the midday heat hit me, and I was glad to be moving again, if somewhat stiffly at first. The right turn onto the track, as I re-claimed The Pennine Way, took me into uncharted territory, a small – infinitesimally so – step for mankind, but a significant one for me, taking me beyond our achievement of thirty six years ago. The track was soon replaced by a narrow, but well defined, path following the Tees upstream towards the magnificent Cauldron Snout, an eagerly anticipated landmark on tomorrow's section. No navigational problems, although the plethora of stiles was a nuisance, breaking my stride and forcing me into various unwelcome contortions as I tried to lever my body plus rucsac, stick and carrier through, over, across, round and beyond any number of ingeniously designed metal, wood or stone impediments to sheep and sundry other farm animals.

Despite being a real pain at times, stiles are nevertheless a definitive and timeless symbol of rural life, and warrant – if not already done – an authoritative photographic history. My thoughts were less philosophical at the time as I stretched my protesting thighs beyond the normal extent of their elasticity, over the high wooden cross-bars, taking care not to slip on the narrow planks that broke my descent. Their constant interruptions were both tiresome and surprisingly tiring.

Stiles are to walkers what kerbstones are to joggers – notice how joggers run ridiculously on the spot whilst waiting to traverse a busy road, desperate not to break their rhythm – the difference being that walking is an admirable form of exercise whereas jogging is one of the most pointless, stupid, activities known to mankind. Most of them seem hooked on traffic fumes, imprisoned in a strange, slouching, heavy footed shuffling gait that is actually slower than a brisk walk. Still, and despite that prejudicial tirade, each to their own, and who was I to criticise when I was slogging up the Tees Valley – and still, well into the afternoon, yet to see another walker – in debilitating heat?

The cool inviting waters, ever present just a few yards to my right, were even more tempting when I reached Low Force - the junior, gentler partner of the spectacular High Force just over a mile further upstream - where a woman and her dog were swimming in the lazy waters just below the rapids. This would have been the perfect spot, with a tent and an open-ended schedule, to finish for the day, go for an invigorating swim and stroll up this delightful stretch of river for an evening meal at High Force Hotel.

I'd passed a perfect location just a short distance back, an idyllic field containing tent, man, with can of beer in hand, tuning radio, and woman, lounging semi-horizontally in deck chair, drink at her side. "Is it far to the bridge?" she enquired, after we'd exchanged greetings. "About a mile" I responded, making a mental note that if and when I'd finished my mission I'd take a leaf out of their book. It was definitely a victory for the joys of camping, whether on a fixed stay or an impromptu Pennine Way halt, and it would have made for one of those glorious shining memories to illuminate the past.

Unfortunately I was too hot and tired to really appreciate Low Force. In fact I felt that its cheerfully sparkling waters and prostrate sun-bathers were mocking me, as I trudged past, lightweight top heavy with sweat, rucsac sticking to my back, but I was pleased with myself after I'd shouted out a friendly "Howdy, lads!" to a group of six or seven surly looking teenage youths, drinking from beer cans near the falls, when they all responded amicably, surprised, I think, that an adult had invited them, albeit temporarily, to share the same planet.

High Force was a revelation, and was also populated with sun worshippers littering the boulders and ledges on both banks, above and below the huge sheet of water smashing relentlessly down onto the rocks below. Unlike many famous locations, High and Low Force lived up to their billings, but I couldn't afford - would have felt out of place, to be truthful – to linger, with another five miles to go, and fatigue well and truly setting in. A few minutes later and I was alone again, apart from an industrial eyesore and its clouds of lorry induced dust scarring the opposite bank, a surreal feeling after the sudden tourist throng around the falls.

I was glad to be past this hideous blot and into the unspoilt, sparsely habited and wonderful world of the Upper Tees, arguably the most splendid of The Pennine Way's treasures. More rabbits, hopping about everywhere on the close-cropped flood plain, and then that rarest of sightings, a walker - the first in nearly twenty miles – approaching in the distance, with full pack. A southbound Way-ster, he was heading for his overnight at Middleton. "Best of luck!" was followed a few minutes later by a surprise, and disproportionately demanding as I really began to flag, climb up and over a protruding hillside, affording the consolation of a panorama back down the Tees, before I dropped down steeply, my stick digging in fiercely on the scramble at the bottom, to rejoin the river opposite Cronkley Farm.

I crossed the water on the paved roadway then turned left to follow the east bank for about half a mile before a temporary parting of the ways, the Tees forking left, my route following a minor tributary straight ahead for another mile, where it met a stony track on the other side of a footbridge. This was the point where the Pennine Way path took a left past Saur Hill Farm to re-join the river and I took a right down a dusty, heat-reflecting track to its T-junction with the B6277 from Middleton to Alston. The Langdon Beck Hotel address, from my booking confirmation, was "Forest-in-Teesdale", which was about a mile to the right in the Middleton direction. Langdon Beck was about a mile the other way, towards Alston.

When I'd originally telephoned I'd been told to take a left along the "B" road where the track met, but the niggling thought had entered my head that he might have meant the previous track off the Way at Cronkley Farm, in which case taking a left now would send me in the wrong direction. There were no clues. Langdon Beck and Forest-in-Teesdale are names on the map, but don't exist as self-contained villages, comprising just a few lonely buildings scattered over a distance of some three miles. I was fairly confident that I should go left, but there was no trace of anything up the road but open countryside and I couldn't face the prospect, knackered and desperate for my orange and lemonade, of trudging who knows how far until the desperate realisation that I'd got it wrong.

In the absence of a phone signal I sought re-assurance at the solitary farm cottage I'd passed on the track. They concurred with my assumption, but once I'd passed the well appointed – at least from the roadside – youth hostel, the likely overnight base for Janet and John and possibly Janet and Keith, the road just ground on and on, the sticky tarmac punishing my throbbing heels and swollen ankle. There was not one derisory building to give encouragement, just the occasional vehicle roaring past as I stepped aside onto the grassy verge, not in deference, but for personal safety.

As a motorist, I accept that mistakes are inevitable from time to time, but I do try to drive defensively. I'll never understand the bone idle, unthinking "buzzing" of pedestrians, cyclists or horse riders when all it takes is the tiniest of steering manoeuvres and about a millionth of a brain cell to give a responsible passing margin. Some of the worst offenders are the "Trilbies", who drive everywhere at 35mph regardless of speed limit or road conditions, hands gripping the wheel like a vice, tunnel vision ahead, selfishly oblivious to every other road user, and never, ever, under any circumstances, pulling in, as it suggests in The Highway Code, to let past the dozens of frustrated motorists streaming behind them.

The contrast between the approaching driver, sometimes with a respectful and always appreciated "seen you" flick of the indicator, moving in good time across to the "wrong" (i.e. correct, in the absence of opposing traffic) side of the road and the negligent brain dead zombies who give you about a foot clearance, with nothing coming from the opposite direction, could so easily be one of life or death. We need a concerted education campaign backed with strong TV and Newspaper advertising, and to hell with accusations of the "Nanny State". This, as evidenced by my uncomfortable Pennine Way skirmishes with public highways, and the carnage of a terrifying average of ten road deaths every day, is one area where there isn't enough "Government meddling".

If it hadn't been for the confirmation at the farm I would have had severe misgivings, as I wearily tramped the road to nowhere, but finally Langdon Beck came into view, nestling on a tight bend at the bottom of a hidden dip, or rather the attractively white-washed Langdon Beck Hotel did. There didn't seem to be much else. I'd expected, given its isolated location within an area of outstanding natural beauty, a "middle class" country hotel, but it was to my disappointment more of a tired village pub with restaurant and rooms, "Victoria Inn" rather than "Bridge House".

My single room was at least bright, and pleasantly cool, with a smashing view towards the Tees Valley and The Pennine Way where I'd re-join tomorrow. There was no en-suite, but I seemed to have exclusive use, in the apparent absence of any other overnight guests, of the basic bathroom tucked away down the corridor, which was a good thing as I managed to flood it. The shower was one of those "three-legged" rubber hoses, the two cups fitting over the respective hot and cold taps and the remaining one housing the shower nozzle. I'd found it lurking in the corner of the uninviting bath.

There was no shower curtain, nor did I even notice a fitting for one, so I took care, after forcing the attachments firmly over the elderly taps, to hold the nozzle in my left hand, pointing towards the plug hole, whilst adjusting the water flow and temperature from the respective taps with my right. "Bloody hell!" Water spurted from two puncture holes in the tubing, all over me and all over the floor. "Now what?" No way did I fancy "luxuriating" in that bath, and no way, as I stood there, stripped and stinking, was I going to forego my shower, essential pre-cursor at every B & B to a relax on the bed or a descent for food and drink.

There followed ten minutes of comic wrestling with the shower attachment, crouching down in the bath in a vain attempt to contain the water, whilst simultaneously twisting the tubing to direct the escaping fountains against the wall and away from the floor, dribbling what I could from the nozzle onto my lathered hair and body. It was farcical, and in the end I gave up the unequal struggle, decided "Sod the mess" and stood up fully under the triple-spurting attachment before stepping out, fully shampooed, rinsed, and smelling nice, into the expanding lake. I mopped most of it up with the towel – after I'd finished with it, of course – opened the window wide and left the rest to evaporation, grateful, for once, for the scorching weather. What a performance.

At least my laundry was trauma free. I simply gave the bag of washing to the landlord and collected it, contents duly washed and dried, after dinner. My meal was fine, and filling, and accompanied by a pleasant chat with my fellow diners, an older, non-residential, couple on the adjoining table, following which I retired for the traditional "Bed by nine", armed with a couple of walking magazines from the guest "library". With no mobile signal I'd used the payphone in the bar, but I did miss my late evening exchange of texts and the opportunity to re-assure well wishers that I was still alive, especially after 24 hour gaps in communication. I found incoming messages, from the simple "Keep going!" to "Notts thrashed Derbys in the 20-20" a great comfort and encouragement.

I was also encouraged by my ankle, still swollen and painful, but no worse than yesterday despite today's rigours – not far short of a full marathon, with a heavy pack and in blistering heat, over difficult terrain, up hill, down dale, lost and confused near artillery ranges and munitions sites, and no-one passing me nutritional drinks bottles and cooling sponges from roadside service stations – although I did have the café I suppose!

My heels, however, felt bruised and sore, to the extent that after arriving the pain had actually increased for an hour or so, even as I lay on the bed, and was to reach an excruciating, almost intolerable, level in the coming days. In conjunction with my damaged tendon, it came within a whisker of curtailing my adventure. So far, three daily gel rubs plus two support bandages and my ever faithful stick had nursed me along, but only a full scale medical assault would finally see me home.

Today was a scorcher, but I was to discover that the sun had been merely flexing its muscles.

~

Day Thirteen. Langdon Beck to Dufton.

"I feel a healing through this land"

Only thirteen miles today, to Brow Farm, Dufton, with the added bonus that my B & B was right on The Pennine Way. I was the sole participant at breakfast, confirming my assumption regarding bathroom exclusivity, and also generating a feeling of loneliness, accentuated by the large, empty, dining area, which I was anxious to vanquish by limping off on what promised to be a fairly easy day, with its inclusion of two spectacular natural wonders, Cauldron Snout and High Cup Nick.

The sun was already blazing down from a cloudless sky, and the early morning rabbits were doing their usual bunny-hopping and scurrying at my approach. There was not a breath of wind. Nor was there any sign of the Janets, plus respective John and Keith, either in the distance ahead, or behind, as The Pennine Way re-claimed the right bank of the Tees near Widdybank Farm, the stark outcrop of Cronkley Scar above the opposite bank closing in as the valley narrowed. The shallow waters cascading towards me over the rocks, stones and shingle reflected such a perfect azure that no painter could have captured the scene without accusation of indulgent artistic licence.

Looking back downstream, into the sun, the river was a dancing, sparkling, explosion of light, and I stood, entranced, for a full ten minutes before recording the images to photographic permanence. The Upper Tees valley is simply magnificent, and warranted every painstaking step as the path disappeared under haphazard piles of rocks and boulders that had tumbled down Falcon Clints, the rugged cliffs below Widdybank Fell. I had to scramble, meticulously placing every step and every stick propelled counter-balance in a zig-zag over the debris, the river at times lapping my boots, steep scree hemming me in to the right. Days of rain, or a torrential summer downpour, would surely have rendered this section impassable.

As it was, my progress was pitifully slow, until the crags retreated to allow a short stretch of defined pathway, some of it flagged,

135

presumably to keep feet dry from the river's potentially soggy flood plain – all a bit superfluous in the context that only the most determined of walkers would have overcome the previous stretch – but also no doubt to prevent erosion on that broad loop. Glad to be safely through, I took another few minutes to simply stand and admire – not rest, I'd scarcely covered three miles – that wild and dramatic valley, pleased, on reflection, that the fallen chunks of mountain, in tandem with the nearest vehicular access necessitating a hike down Widdybank Fell from the remote access lane to Cow Green Reservoir, should keep it that way.

It's home to species of Alpine plant that are found nowhere else in Europe, but even if they're protected and hopefully fairly safe from the disturbance of tourists and would-be gatherers our milder winters, with snow a rarity and prolonged frosts now exceptional, might seal their fate. Sadly, and whether or not man-made Global Warming is the culprit, I suspect that there's little that mankind can, or will, do, except to let nature take its course. You never know, another Ice Age might be lurking around the corner to take us all by surprise.

I continually kept an eye open for flora, as evidenced by my photographs of totally commonplace but always inspiring stalwarts such as pale blue campanulas, purple heathers and thistles, rose-bay willow herb, bright yellow dandelions or buttercups, white cotton grass, all posing as nature intended, sometimes aloof, sometimes in drifts of complementary colours. Alpine pinks burst defiantly out of impossibly narrow crevices, beyond the focusing abilities of my point-and-shoot, and tiny, brilliant white, star flowers illuminated ground hugging mossy clumps, but whether I spotted any unique specimens, as the path turned to the right, and I heard the muffled thunder of Cauldron Snout, I don't know. They were all beautiful.

In Mongolia I'd been impressed – to everyone else's indifference! – with the thousands of yellow flowering potentillas growing wild, some with their feet in the marshy valley floors, others clinging to drier mountain slopes, and all coping with a temperature range from plus thirty to minus forty, even fifty. They're also on sale for a few quid at my local garden centre, and when I checked the variety in a gardening encyclopaedia it stated "Mongolia. Hardy". Fair comment.

Cauldron Snout. What a name. The Zinedine Zidane of geographical locations. Just reading it on the map evokes images of nature at its rawest. A few hundred yards on and one of the defining places of The Pennine Way came into view, a spectacular, roaring, mass of water battering its way furiously through the steep narrow gap in the hillside and crashing down over ledges and boulders in a short-lived frenzy. A few hundred feet of wild descent in a manic unapproachable rage then, tantrum over, an invitation to dangle your feet into its welcoming embrace as it meandered gently in a calm, lazy, loop before tumbling on down the valley.

I'd not expected it to be so impressive, especially given the dry weather, and it may have been that the sluices at Cow Green Reservoir had been opened, but it didn't diminish the drama. I stood in awe for several minutes, thankful that pressures of time and distance weren't forcing me anxiously on, as they had yesterday at Low and High Force. It's quite a scramble up the moor to meet the track at the reservoir where the metalled access road finishes, and I took extra care not to over-balance, mindful of my heavy pack and the deafening torrent to my left, instantly accessible by one careless slip.

Once I'd reached the top I was surprised that the roar was already muffled, Cauldron Snout now invisible below the brow of the broad, steeply falling, hillside, but never fading from memory. The Tees threaded its way, in a shimmering narrow ribbon, way below me on its journey towards Middleton, and eventually Middlesbrough, another world away, and I pushed on in mine, amazed at the height I'd gained in that last half mile, from enclosed valley floor to elevated, open, moorland.

Two men with binoculars and shoulder slung haversacks, looking somewhat furtive to my possibly over-active imagination, were wandering the moor "off-piste" as it were, before passing me in the opposite direction, only one of them offering me a very cursory and reluctant acknowledgement, and having taken them initially as

137

"twitchers" my cynical side wondered if they were out looking for eggs, nestlings or similar illicit targets. Whether they were or not, such activities are despicable, and convictions should lead to severe redress, including confiscation of assets to support wildlife rehabilitation.

It's a sewer level act of selfishness, to deprive future generations a chance to enjoy our heritage, and if you are so sad and pathetic that you get off from collecting eggs – and potentially pursuing species to extinction – get yourself down to the free range at Sainsburys and paint a few spots on them when you get home. These odious creeps are practically beneath contempt, and on a level with the scum that will soon see the last wild tiger exterminated from our planet.

I followed the easy track towards Birkdale Farm, holding a gate open for a small group of approaching mountain bikers – the only ones, to my surprise, that I saw on the entire walk – acknowledged by a shout of "Good timing, mate!" and continued, as the track became a narrow path beyond the farm, across the moor towards Rasp Hill, where I was confronted by two farmers (one on a quad bike), one black and white collie on "active service" and a few dozen sheep, one of them also on a quad bike (sharing it, actually, with the farmer, who was either teaching it to drive or, more likely, giving it a lift because it was lame. Either way, it seemed quite content, insofar as I could judge from its blank expression).

Unsure of the etiquette or right of way in such matters, I decided to continue along the footpath – pausing only to take their photograph – and await instructions. "Can you just stand aside, please, up across the moor a bit?" I duly obliged, nearly sprawling all my length as I stumbled into a shallow gully where I waited, knee deep in clumps of wiry heather, ears assailed by the plaintiff monotone bleats from the gormless white tide as it slowly enveloped me, pausing at every opportunity to tear a chunk out of the undergrowth, then slowly disappeared, still munching and bleating, harassed by the workaholic canine on its single minded and dogged (sorry!) mission. The pedestrian farmer called out a "Thank you" and his colleague buzzed by with a wave of the hand.

I reckon most hill farmers would rate the quad bike as the greatest invention of recent times. They must save hours of trekking and hard sweat, although judging from the way some of them charge across the countryside they might be a mixed blessing. One young farmer defied gravity near Thornton as he threw his machine in a death-defying slalom across a steep bank in pursuit of his miscreant flock, and there are high profile examples of celebrities coming to grief, including, with near fatal consequences, Ric Mayall.

The path shadowed the Maize Beck across the moor, passing Meldon Hill to my right and Muirton Heads on the left, another military range which, according to my map, "should not be entered when the red flags are flying". There were no red flags, nor were there any green ones with banners proclaiming a warm welcome to ramblers, so I decided to stick to The Pennine Way, and its next natural wonder, High Cup Nick.

I'll quote verbatim. "High Cup (the Nick refers to the notch at the end of the valley) is a series of spectacular crags encircling a long straight valley with views to the Lake District." That doesn't begin to do it justice, any more than my attempt to fully capture the noise and drama of Cauldron Snout, but it's enough to whet the appetite, and in my case lift the pace, as I closed in on my eagerly anticipated lunch appointment, crossing the Maize Beck via the footbridge – the alternative, wet weather, path sticking to the right bank – and passing an oncoming group of young male walkers of Police or Military appearance, with heavy packs - possibly southbound Way-sters.

I tried to determine, as I tramped the last mile of open moorland before snap time, whether the compelling draw towards that "nick" on the horizon was accentuated by my prior knowledge or if it really would, to the uninformed, appear to be leading to the edge of the world. The last couple of hundred yards were unambiguous, the way dropping gently down to Britain's version of The Grand Canyon. Puny by comparison, but magnificent in the scale of its context, and sculpted by glaciation, not wind and water, High Cup, like Cauldron Snout, revealed itself at the last, shouting out "Here I am. Stand and be amazed!"

I did. And I was. What a view. And what a drop – to certain death. Unlike a few brave souls – day walkers who'd trekked up from Dufton – perched, soaking up the sun, at its edge, I kept a distance, content to enjoy its splendour – and take my compulsory photos – from the safety of a gentle grassy slope a good thirty yards back. Nowhere else on the walk was I more aware of being on the Pennine spine of Northern England, with the Lake District fells clearly visible to the west, and beyond that panorama, across the flat plain of the Vale of Eden, Carlisle, and the border. The smell of Scottish Heather was growing stronger.

I could also scent death if I strayed too close to that vertical drop and after savouring every moment of my thirty minute break, and every bite of my lunch, I took the higher, slightly longer, route up the side of the moor, leaving the direct skirting of the cliffs on my left to the adventurous, and the sheep. The paths soon merged, and I displayed my own devil-may-care streak by taking advantage of a bubbling stream in the infant stages of its journey from Backstone Edge to join High Cup Gill, a thousand feet below. I demolished my remaining half bottle of Langdon Beck tap water and filled both containers with freshly chilled natural reserves.

It was always a huge psychological boost, in the debilitating, dangerous, heat to find safe – or as safe as could prudently be assessed – watering holes and to know that I could drink "on demand" for the rest of the day, instead of having to eke out my rations – a particular problem ahead in the worryingly "dry" Cheviots – and struggle on with a raging thirst and potential heat exhaustion.

Just over three miles to go, all downhill, the first mile on a well defined path before a track took me below Peeping Hill (presumably, into High Cup?), dropping me right down into the valley at Dufton. I was to re-visit that unmade track just a few weeks later, which was good news for one of the few motorists who's ever driven a family saloon beyond the tractor (or maybe quad bike) line, and certainly the only one to attempt to turn round where the edge beyond the gravel and stones drops away down a slippery grassy slope towards an uncompromising dry stone wall.

The reason why I was there at all is purely due to the coincidence of my needing refreshment as I crawled, in an endless queue of traffic, along the A66 (as crossed by The Pennine Way at Bowes) towards Scotch Corner and The A1 (South), en route home from a short break, my "proper", post Pennine Way, holiday at North Ballachulish, near Fort William, and well recommended too. Hunger pangs demanded an imminent stop, and Pennine Way nostalgia directed me next left, and into Dufton, where pub grub would be available.

Afterwards, naturally, hiking boots on for an early afternoon stroll – or limp, but at least it was a relaxed one – to re-visit a tiny bit of my walk, which, amazingly, was this time just as I'd remembered it, apart from a 15C drop in temperature. And an elderly bloke trying to turn his car round. And failing. I think it was a Renault Clio, but whatever, it was sideways on and he'd managed to get the front end about three feet from said wall, halfway down the grassy slope, but every time he attempted to reverse, in a screaming, protesting, clutch-burning spin of the front wheels, it simply dug a bigger groove in the long grass and slid nearer to intimate knowledge of the local stone-masonry.

As I approached, he made another couple of desperate efforts, smoke pouring from the wheel arches, only to slide ever closer to his appointment with a tractor, not to mention the nearest Body Shop (probably Appleby, at a guess). He seemed surprisingly calm as he stepped out, explaining that he'd intended to leave his car as far up the track as possible, and was turning round to park on the verge before walking up towards High Cup. We reckoned he might have enough distance – about a foot now – and clutch left to have one more blast, but that would be it. Curtains, and the likelihood of the front end being buried under half a ton of wall.

Close inspection revealed that the front left wheel – which, because it was also on lower ground was responsible for most of the traction, or lack of it, as betrayed by its deep rut – was the problem, and I surprised myself by coming up with a possible last ditch (pun, with

141

apologies, inevitable!) solution. At my suggestion we piled handfuls of rubble and stones under and behind the wheel, tamping the first layers down into the mushy furrow, and chucking a load more on top. The car was sufficiently offset so as not to risk catapulting straight across and into trouble on the other side, and following my instruction not to worry about problems behind "just go for it, but slam on if it slides forwards again" he hit the gas, engaged the screaming clutch, and the car shot backwards and up onto the track in a scrabbling and rattling of stones and a cloud of dust, like a cork from a bottle.

He parked it at the side, facing Dufton, and I walked on, in the same direction, after a celebratory handshake, feeling pleased with myself, and last saw him disappearing up over the ridge. If I hadn't decided to walk The Pennine Way he might still be there! As it is, the tyre marks would have endured for a while, no doubt to the puzzlement of the local farmers, providing another – albeit temporary – fascinating landmark for passing walkers after the natural wonders of Cauldron Snout and High Cup.

Dufton is notorious for The Helm, a localised meteorological phenomenon of Storm Force winds blasting down across the valley, strong enough, some say, to hurl cattle hundreds of feet into the sky and strip the white lines off the roads. A slight exaggeration, maybe, but it was probably The Helm Wind that had forced the ultra hardy Scotsman, who I'd met near Crowden on his trek from Cape Wrath to Dover, to by-pass Cross Fell, one of my destinations tomorrow. He described the conditions as so stormy that any attempt over the fells would have been impossible (kilted or otherwise).

Scarcely credible to think that this would have been only some three weeks ago, but just to be on the safe side I flicked a feather, that was conveniently lying at the trackside, into the air, and was relieved to find that it floated gently back down to alight in exactly the same spot. It illustrated the lottery of planning a British holiday – a camping break would have been wrecked, literally blown away, and caravans overturned. This week, the local shops would have sold out of ice cream, battery powered fans and insect repellent.

The track becomes a metalled lane before meeting the road at a T-junction, where The Pennine Way follows it right, towards the village, but first, after about thirty yards, straight past the front door of my B & B, Brow Farm. The temperature had climbed relentlessly during the day, but as previously, the full affect only hit me after I stopped. I had an unexpected, and unwelcome, hour to kill, my landlady having gone temporarily AWOL.

Fortunately, her mother was "minding the shop", but couldn't immediately allocate my room, so I continued on to the village store where I invested in some "comfort" provisions – two bottles of orange flavoured Lucozade Energy drink, Jaffa Cakes (my dehydrating system seemed to crave orange, including my usual iced pint, so maybe that lady in India had something when she kept forcing them down me during my bout of diarrhoea) and a family sized bar of fruit and nut chocolate, all to enjoy immediately after my eagerly anticipated shower, and enough to keep me going until my evening nosh at the pub, if not exactly a balanced nutritional meal.

I strolled back slowly, exhausting both the remaining minutes of the suggested hour, and me. It was sweltering, and I couldn't wait to pick up my room key, enjoy my cooling shower and relax with my picnic on the bed, sore heels and aching ankle raised clear by placing supporting pillows under my calves. My heels and right tendon, no doubt accentuated by the heat, were threatening to become far more than just a persistent, but tolerable, niggle. Unfortunately, I was subjected to another of those ridiculous full boarded beds, and whilst I enjoyed my semi-upright late afternoon siesta I had misgivings concerning the prospects for a decent night's sleep, with the farm fully booked, and no space in my compact, but pleasantly cool en-suite single - looking out towards Great Dun Fell - to haul the mattress onto the floor. Nice view, shame about the bed.

First, there was the less challenging business of my evening meal. Dufton is the archetypal English village, its pub and attractive stone cottages bordering the spacious green, to a backdrop of open farmland and steep fells. It has a sleepy, timeless feel (albeit a turbulent history, prey in past centuries to advanced cross-border incursions) even on this scorching Saturday evening when every outdoor table at The Stag Inn, dating from 1703 and of similar vintage to my guest accommodation, was occupied, which suited me.

I sought sanctuary in the shady interior, shared with a few locals and a small dog, in which to savour both my steak and onion pie and the local accent, which seemed, to my uneducated ear, to be an amalgam of the harsher Cumbrian dialect, with a hint of North Yorkshire Dales, mixed in with the sing-song lilt of "Why-aye man", a reminder of how far north I'd walked. So were the unusual conical shaped hills that I'd photographed as I'd descended the track below High Cup. They looked almost man made, like long reclaimed spoil heaps, plonked incongruously outside the village, but are actually extinct volcanoes, putting me in mind of Edinburgh's rock, to which they are doubtless related. Scotland, here I come!

But not before I'd attempted to negotiate my second Pennine Way night in a bed with a maximum realistic height limit of five feet ten inches, and no room on the floor of the cramped single to lay the mattress. Hopeless. Having wedged myself diagonally in a familiar and predictably unsuccessful attempt at sleep, and finding that any movement or re-adjustment ended with me bashing my feet, head, or both, I finally gave up at 2 a.m. in a mixture of anger and despair. This simply wasn't fair, regardless of the fact that I especially needed a good night's sleep ahead of a demanding day tomorrow, one that I'd summarised to my cousin on a text, whilst sitting on a bench in the main street, as "make or break" as the prospect of Cross Fell loomed large, now rendered more intimidating by the intense heat and my potentially crippling injury.

So, with misgivings about tomorrow, and pissed off with the thought of tackling the day, through no fault of my own, bleary eyed and already knackered, I went in search of better accommodation. Or rather, sneaked down to the double room along the corridor, supposedly occupied, but with no sight or sound of fellow guests, it suddenly dawned on me that despite the "full house" notices it was empty, awaiting tomorrow's arrivals. I'd been allocated – quite reasonably, other than the "apart-height" problem – the single.

Next morning, after a four hour sleep (which was four hours more than I'd otherwise have had) I carefully re-arranged the double

144

bedding, flattened out any trace of my imprint in the mattress and sheet, fluffed the pillows, and gently stretched the duvet cover back, an exercise that to most blokes, me included, is not one that sits easily with the word "precision". Still, I reckon it was a pretty good effort and I wouldn't have known that anyone had slept there. Whilst I would have had no qualms about confessing to my pleasant landlady, she would presumably have been obliged to do the laundry for both beds, and I'd hardly slept in either.

So, least said ……..

~

Day Fourteen. Dufton to Garrigill.

"As I climb the mountainside, breaking Eden again"

Sixteen miles, over the fells to Garrigill, and directly north again after yesterday's east-west leg. The white "golf ball" radar installation atop Great Dun Fell appears, from the green at Dufton, to be no more than an hour's casual stroll away, but it's a full six mile climb from the valley to its 2,780 feet summit, then nearly three more across Little Dun Fell – inferior by just nineteen feet – to the trig point on Cross Fell, at 2,930 feet the highest point on The Pennine Way, and anywhere in England excepting a handful of Lake District peaks.

My "make or break" message wasn't melodramatic, I really was viewing this section with foreboding – if the heat and the ascent didn't get me, my tendon and heels might. I hobbled off along the road, taking The Pennine Way as it cut right from the village up a short track, then a path, left, to another track past Coatsike Farm, then more path, narrow, hemmed in by shady hedgerows and inconvenienced by stiles, then another track, with expansive views suddenly ahead towards Knock Fell, my first target, and one that, at 2,604 feet, would break the back of the day's climbing.

A path was signed right, to Dufton Pike, one of those distinctive conical volcanoes, with Knock Pike, its smaller sister, on my left. As the Pennine Way dissected them my thoughts strayed briefly to surreal images of primeval eruptions and flows of molten lava. Could it all have happened? Did a glacier really bludgeon the construction of High Cup as the ice advanced? Were there any fragmented human settlements to witness these momentous periods? Animal life? Dinosaurs? If not, how and when did they arrive? Wolves, bears, and hyenas (the remains of which have been found in a cave at Creswell Crags, North Notts, a stuffed – and very scary looking – example greeting visitors to the Information Centre) were followed by mankind's dominance and uncontrolled – and so far uncontrollable – onslaught. Until when?

Permanent settlements. The M6. The Pennine Way. Me. Here, now, millions of years on, just the immeasurably tiny flicker of one life flame. What would a time-lapse camera reveal, fixed, say, on the appropriately named Peeping Hill, re-playing the previous millennia, and more? We would scarcely believe it, and we'd recoil in terror at the prospect of a similar "fast forward". Where will that motorway be in a modest fifty years, a hundred, or a thousand? Will future generations excavate and wonder, as we do with Roman remains, or will there be no future inquisitive explorers? Only one thing is certain, that time will inevitably come, and it can drive you mad in frustrated curiosity and wonderment thinking about it, at least until, two miles out of Dufton, in July 2006, the expedient of an urgently needed drink re-focused my thoughts.

I climbed on, breathing and sweating heavily, but walking more easily than expected as the pain, and my limp, subsided. As the track traversed the left shoulder of Brownber Hill I caught two very heavily laden walkers, of late middle age, who I took for Northbound Way-sters, to find that they were in fact on a West-East traverse across the fells, camping en-route. A short distance ahead of them a solo male, also middle aged and with pack, was approaching the gate that introduces The Pennine Way to the footpath up and onto Knock Fell where the track deviates to the right before coming to an abrupt halt.

I recognised the chap as the "talkative" bloke who'd practically ignored me as I crossed the moor after Tan Hill, and with no more than five yards between us, as he swung the gate open from its locking bar, I was about to shout a cheery "Howdy!" before thanking him for the common courtesy of holding it for me to pass through. He caught my eye, allowed the gate to slam shut, turned his back and strode on, leaving me with a strangulated "How ....." and a disappearing smile. I was initially incredulous, then incandescent. I'd have been cross if it had happened in a busy shopping centre, but in this situation, and with the four of us just about the only people between Dufton and Cross Fell, in addition to our paths, as fellow

147

Way-sters, having crossed just a few days ago, it simply beggared belief. So much for any notion of Pennine Way camaraderie.

I was so appalled that I waited for the friendly couple to catch me. I just had to get it off my chest. "I've got to say something, you won't believe what's just happened." They did believe me, commenting that he'd more or less blanked them as they ventured an exchange when he'd overtaken them. Strange. And even stranger, when I caught and passed him a few hundred yards on, as he sat tucking into his rations, he called out a cheery "Hello, there!" to which I responded with a surprised "Hi!" as I continued, without pausing.

Maybe he'd got the message. Maybe he was so self-engrossed, or weighed down by his life problems (aren't most of us!) and pack, that he genuinely was indifferent to the normal etiquette of casual human contact on a lonely long distance trail. As they say, slightly south of those parts, "There's nowt so queer as folk". At least he wasn't potentially excused by being engrossed in one of those wretched I-pods, the concept of which I was possibly the last remaining person on the planet to understand, having seen the name in print as an "essential" accessory and having no idea what the bloody hell they were on about. Now I do, I still fail to see the point, and can report, with unconfined joy, that in twenty days of Pennine and Cheviot rambling I witnessed not one single wearer. That alone made my 280 mile journey worthwhile!

I battled on up the steepening moorland terrain on a winding, peaty, path, heavy on the breathing but soft on the feet, and generous to my water supplies, as it shadowed first Swindale Beck, then up the course of Knock Hush (I never tired of the myriad, sometimes evocative, sometimes eccentric, often mysterious place names en route – where did this one come from?) to the cairn at Knock Old Man, just short of Knock Fell summit.

My guide advised me that "In dry weather Swindale Beck is often dry, though water can usually be found further up in Knock Hush". I duly took full advantage, draining the remaining contents of one bottle, and making inroads into another, before filling them both from the stream – as always choosing a spot where it tumbled in a collectable, clear cascade over rocks, never the gravelly or muddy bits - not that it probably made much difference - and usually involving an unflattering position splayed out above the source, trying not to fall in whilst simultaneously holding my bottle in one hand under the fountain.

I rested for a few minutes when I reached the sub-summit at the cairn, basking not only in the strong sunshine but the massive psychological boost that I'd hauled myself up onto that fell much more easily – and enjoyably – than I'd anticipated, drunk as much as I needed, yet still had two full 0.75 litre bottles of chilled water and was, surprisingly – albeit still fairly early in the day – enjoying not a breeze, exactly, but slightly cooler air that made for a glorious summer's day, with sweeping views to boot. The Pennine Way dropped down the moor to briefly follow the traffic free lane leading towards the "Golf Ball" installations on Great Dun Fell before forking right to skirt them on a footpath up the hill. Then half a mile of descent, followed by half a mile of ascent, with a nett loss of that nineteen feet – though no excuse for an inferiority complex, the difference doesn't show – saw Little Dun Fell come and go.

Cross Fell's broad shoulders sprawled ahead, its rolling mass, with no defined edges, giving no impression of its lofty status, unlike Kinder Scout, which at a substantial 842 feet lower actually appears higher, and certainly more impressive when viewed from its Grindsbrook approach, and that's despite Edale's elevation, higher than Dufton's, making further inroads. Regardless, that great lump of exposed moorland, notorious for its banshee storms, its thick, clinging, cloud and mist, its lingering springtime drifts of winter snow, simply couldn't have offered a more benign welcome.

I dropped down to cross the little stream at Tees Head – presumably the infant beginnings of the eponymous river – walking as easily as I had for some days, before making an unbroken, steady, assault (one fell swoop, as Mike had done on day one approaching Kinder, whilst I paused and gasped for breath) on my final "proper" ascent of the day, and a well earned snap break on a half-collapsed stone wall in the shade of the summit shelter, where a very pleasant chap erecting a huge mast kindly offered to take my photograph. I learnt that he was an amateur radio enthusiast, pursuing his hobby from the highest available point, emphasised by my mobile instantly displaying its full set of signal bars.

Just as I had yesterday, I sat and gazed towards the Lakeland Fells, across the Vale of Eden and towards the Scottish border, glowing not just in the hot sunshine, but the satisfaction and relief that here, on this highest point, accomplished with relative ease, I was now well and truly able to envisage my Pennine Way adventure coming to glorious fruition. It was, literally, downhill from here, but I didn't suspect the extent to which that would also be the case metaphorically, although I knew that there were still a good few ups and downs, including the Cheviots, lying in wait.

I'd seen two or three other walkers on my final climb up to Cross Fell, but it was otherwise surprisingly quiet for a midsummer Sunday, with only the radio ham and one other at the top, and of my four co-Way-sters, no sign all day. As I was tucking into my cheese and pickle sandwich I was distracted by four young walkers, two men and two women, with packs, ascending from the Garrigill direction. I took them, rightly or wrongly, as University students, cheered that they'd made the effort, with heavy packs – possibly, Southbound Way-sters – to slog up here on a scorching day, and even more so when they elected to sprawl out in the sun rather than seek the cooling shade.

The two young ladies stretched out their tanned legs and exposed thighs, their skimpy – just about covering the bum – shorts complemented by hiking boots and woollen socks, the unlikely ensemble exuding, to this interested party, a sexiness on a par with any Paris catwalk. Just like the lady in The Harlequin, they'd alighted right in my pre-existing field of vision, and lest anyone think I'm a voyeuristic pervert (which I categorically am not!) I can honestly say that I record these moments merely as part of my overall Pennine Way experience, where such pleasures are every bit as noteworthy and enjoyable, albeit in a different way, as, say, an unexpected sighting of a stoat – coincidentally also occurring on just two occasions.

I doubt there have been many days where it's possible to sit, shirt-sleeved, at the highest point on Cross Fell, in the shade, and still have to wipe sweat off the brow – and not just because of the two sun-worshipping ladies – with not a breath of wind to stir the atmosphere. The early afternoon sun had seen off any trace of lingering relief but at least I was just over halfway and the remainder was, give or take a short climb here and there, one continual descent, the last four and a half miles, according to my guide, along "a clear farm track".

The plateau(ish) of Cross Fell had surprised me. Unlike Kinder in appearance or composition, and much flatter overall, with no peaty gullies or high ridges, it was nevertheless an irritatingly difficult crossing, riddled with thousands of small, shallow craters, indentations, humps and hollows. I presume they're an entirely natural inconvenience, but in view of the many local mine workings I couldn't be certain. Still, I'd had a cracking first half, just about the opposite of my pessimistic expectation, and with ankle and heels so far holding up well, as were my water supplies, and the rest of the route set fair, I was cheerful and confident.

I took a compass bearing from the shelter, just to check that my initial direction was correct, before dropping down quite steeply on a surprisingly poorly defined – and even more surprisingly, quite boggy – stretch of moorland, doubting whether I could have done it in those Pen-y-Ghent conditions. I picked up the "Pennine Way" pointer, plus its arrow, showing right, attractively imprinted on a large rock, below another arrow, left, indicating a cross Pennine route, and added it to my growing collection of signposts and markers photographic memorabilia.

The narrow path cut away across the slope of the huge expanse of desolate moorland towards that farm track, dropping down past Greg's Hut, a stone built bothy that had the appearance of an abandoned quarry premises, before it climbed back towards the horizon. I sat near the top of the ascent for a final break ahead of the five miles to my B & B in Garrigill, inaccurately named, given that I couldn't even buy a stamp there, "The Post Office", although presumably it must have been once. As I enjoyed the sweeping views

151

a woman appeared, with a small dog, surprising me by stopping for an unsolicited chat.

I was just about to move off again, before my ankle stiffened, but we were still exchanging Travellers' Tales a good twenty minutes later. I learnt that she was Liz, from Penrith, and given that she was heading up towards Cross Fell her round hike from the road at Garrigill must have been something like an admirable, and challenging, on a sweltering day, fifteen miles – no wonder the dog's legs were so short. I left each of them with the parting gift of a Werthers Original and creaked off in the opposite direction, trying desperately not to limp until I was out of sight over that ridge. Nice company, shame about my vanity!

The track appeared shortly after I'd passed Rake End and pursued its undulating progress past Cash Burn, Long Man Hill, Pikeman Hill, Rotherthorpe Fell and Black Band, before finally, just as it seemed it would grind on forever, turning right and dropping sharply down to meet the valley road. Having thoroughly enjoyed the expected "difficult" first half, to Cross Fell, and the next couple of miles beyond its trig point, I hated every step on that endless track. I jotted an unusually long resume in my notebook that evening:

"Cross Fell just over half of sixteen miles total. Did well. Very pleased with time and climb. Cross Fell to Garrigill anticipated easy and gentle descent, but awful endless track – semi industrial legacy (old mines in area) plus rubble, stones, rocks, aggregate infill – like a dusty quarry road and horrible underfoot. Hated every step of endless, boring, six miles. Over wild moors, but permanent concentration on track ruined views. Even Garrigill, unlike Dufton, refused to show itself until nearly there. B & B OK, basic but at least no boarded bed. No phone signal as usual in valley. Full one on Cross Fell – dead handy that!"

About two miles out I thought I heard a distant motor vehicle climbing up the narrow track, to find myself confronted, a few hundred yards on, by an oncoming Police car. He stopped as we drew level. "Man with carrier bag!" he exclaimed cheerily. "Don't you start as well", I replied, with an amused smile, "I've had that for the last 160 miles". He continued "Can you tell me where the dedicated open access starts, and it's no longer a designated Public roadway?" Resisting the temptation to say "How the bloody hell should I know, you're the local village Bobby", I advised him that I didn't, to which he asked if I'd seen some blokes on trail bikes illegally tearing across the moors, which I hadn't.

He'd been sent up the track to investigate reports that they'd been seen heading this way, and before disappearing in a wheel-scrabbling cloud of dust he asked me to keep an eye open, and if I saw them, to record it as evidence on my camera. Sound advice. Me, a solitary walker, in the middle of nowhere. "Excuse me, gents, could you just hang on a sec. whilst I take a photograph of your illegal scrambling, for passing to the Police. Thanks, lads, I appreciate that." No chance.

My view on those anti-social selfish morons who think they have the right to rampage noisily across every convenient scrap of countryside, whether on quad or trail bikes, or 4 x 4 off-roaders, destroying wild life and responsible citizens' legitimate enjoyment in the process, is unprintable, but the solution, were there any Political will, instead of Government hand wringing and crocodile tears, is blindingly simple, the prominent display of two word signs, backed by legislation and strong policing, stating "Crush Zone".

Any motorised vehicle illegally transgressing, be it a £1,000 second hand trail bike to a £60,000 top of the range 4 x 4 to be confiscated and scrapped, at owner's expense. No argument, no compensation. If it's a company or "borrowed" vehicle, user pays. Draconian, but a few early, high profile, convictions "pour encourager les autres", would soon have the problem solved. The ideal catch would be Jeremy Clarkson, the witty but environmentally challenged champion of "It's my thrill, so sod everything and everybody else". What about "rights with responsibilities, and respect for others"? Thankfully, progress is belatedly being made in some areas with regard to the urban menace of mini-bikes.

My heels were sore, ankle aching and swollen, as I plodded the final few hundred yards on sticky tarmac to the village centre, and my accommodation, a terraced cottage all of three doors away from

"The George and Dragon", evening meal conveniently sorted. After my warm welcome and cool shower I nursed my aches and pains with the usual gel rub and pillow support, but it was over an hour before the hot, pounding, pain in my heels and the aching tightness in my visibly swollen right tendon eased sufficiently to tempt me the few yards over the road to the Public telephone box.

It was like a furnace in there, and I made a hurried call, half outside, phone wire fully extended, door propped wide open with my foot, before taking a quick photo of the attractive village centre and retreating indoors for a pre-meal snooze – except that, having hauled myself wearily up the two narrow flights of stairs I couldn't find my keys (one for my room, one for the outside door in case I fancied a late night, which I didn't). Slight panic, hobble back down, wedge my hiking boots back on, and conduct a head down, meandering search, around the patch of grass – Garrigill's mini "village green" - where I'd strolled to take my photo.

"Twenty quid." I looked up, to see an elderly man sitting on a bench outside the pub. He held a key ring between his fingers, two keys hanging conspicuously below. "You can have them for twenty quid. Just picked them up off the grass." He didn't say "Why-aye, man", or "Wor Jackie" (or "Wor Bobby" – Stokoe, for that matter, assuming he might have had red and white affiliations), but he didn't have to. He was definitely a local. I bartered him down to a warm handshake and a "Thank you" and retreated, for the second time, for my snooze.

Having commented on my arrival that "This heat's ridiculous" my landlady told me that she'd allocated the coolest room, on the shaded side, but even with the window wide open it was still hot, and I dozed fitfully for an hour or so before taking the long trek to the pub where I indulged in Cumberland Sausage - I hadn't realised it came in one circular, forgive me for saying it, turd-like spiral - beans and chips, and ice cream for pudding, preceded by an orange and lemonade and followed, for added nutrition and calories, by a pint of Guinness.

All very nice too, as was the Sunday evening atmosphere, as I enjoyed the local accents and wondered at what major canine bust-up had resulted in the conspicuous sign at the entrance limiting dogs (although presumably written for the benefit of their owners) to a maximum of three. Coincidentally, full capacity had been reached, comprising two proper specimens quietly minding their own business, and a handbag-size excuse, hiding under its owner's legs and predictably yapping ferociously at the other two, who treated it with the contempt it deserved. I profess, certain "macho" breeds excepted, to be a dog lover on balance, but I wanted to squash it. Another dog – plus owner – arrived. Now what? More yapping, again ignored by the grown-up one, and no "full house" sanction by the landlord. He should have booted the hysterical diddy one out into the heat.

I'd observed the changing local accents as my trek progressed ever northwards, and it's a subject that intrigues me. My own flat East Midlands accent, our country's definitive way of speaking, (listen to Su Pollard for an unrefined example!) stretches in a huge triangle, give or take some local variations on the theme - for example, some villages on the Notts/Derbys borders have unique, and sadly disappearing, words, expressions and dialects – from Leicester, Loughborough, Derby and Nottingham, north-east to the mouth of the Humber at Grimsby and east to an area bordering The Wash, where, despite an absence of geographical impediments, it changes dramatically, around Spalding and Peterborough, to a rural Worzel Gummidge "tractor-speak".

Even stranger, the "ethnic" speech of the tiny Black Country enclave of Wolverhampton, Walsall, Dudley, West Bromwich, etc (and not to be confused with the more "sanitised" Brummie accent) is so strong, where still in undiluted evidence, essentially from older citizens, as to sound like a foreign language. It's a fascinating social representation of tribes, communities, immigrant influences, agricultural and industrial development and incoming labour requirements, and is thankfully now being increasingly recorded for posterity by such as local radio stations, libraries, study groups and sundry local historians, and also as part of a National archive.

I wonder if they'll record the contemporary and slovenly "Estuary English" of the disappearing consonant, spreading like a plague through general speech, and Student culture in particular - my local, like, Nottingham Trent University is, like, riddled with this, like, seemingly incurable, like, epidemic (sic) - of which one expression has stuck in my mind. It was spoken by a BBC expert co-commentating on an International Swimming final.

His actual words were "Commerweff meh-ughwwww", which I was able to translate, purely from the context of the TV pictures, as his pathetic, bone idle, mouth full of gobstoppers, attempt to say "Commonwealth medal". I suppose it could have been worse. He could have said, and probably soon will as his intonation evolves, as an intended statement of fact "Commerweff meh-ughwwww?", as if questioning my intelligence in understanding. "Yeah?" Give me strength.

I certainly needed it after that heat-reflecting track, which had aggravated my injuries by continually rocking and jarring my feet and ankles sideways on the uneven stones and rocks. My tendon had been continually wrenched this way and that, heels punished by the unforgiving, sharp edged rubble – all four miles of it, give or take a few welcome grassy verges eroded into a well defined path by other walkers escaping the debris-strewn, un-compacted, track.

The words of my landlady, when I'd confirmed the booking, regretting that I'd failed to get accommodation a few miles further on, came back to me. "Most people have had enough for the day by the time they get down here off Cross Fell." She was right!

~

You have been warned! (just after Bowes)

Approaching Blackton Reservoir, near Baldersdale Youth Hostel

As if there weren't enough real ones! (Near Low Force)

Looking down the Tees Valley,
shortly after Middleton

Low Force

Harebells, near Low Force

My B&B, Langdon Beck

The Tees sparkles, looking back downstream....

....and is a breathtaking azure, as I follow it North

A tricky scramble over fallen rocks....

....is rewarded by the magnificent Cauldron Snout, the Zinedine Zidane of evocative place names!

Looking back from above Cauldron Snout

High Cup - or at least half of it. The opposite side is equally dramatic

Golf balls at Dufton. Great Dun Fell's radar installation, six miles on, is visible top left

Descending from Cross Fell

Garrigill. The mini Green where I lost my keys. My B&B is just out of shot to the right of the white building

"Cnoc na Feille" (The hill at the Market Stance). Alston shares Buxton's claim as England's highest market town

Forget MOD warnings, this is really grim! (Approaching Slaggyford)

Hadrians Wall

My birthday, and an unforgettable one, for all the wrong reasons. A cow seeks shade at High House as temperatures top 30c again

More wall, crippling in the record breaking heat

Glad to see the back of that bloody wall, although I'm only minutes away from a mass attack by clegs

Cleg City (with sanctuary ahead in South Wark forest)

En route to Bellingham, the stiles are still an inconvenience....

....but the flowers are pretty

Bellingham (pronounced "Bellinjum")

Looking back next morning, cooler, drizzly weather returns for a few hours

Crossing the moors north of Bellingham

Approaching Byrness

Byrness, nestling below the
Cheviots ("Cheeviots")

Janet and Keith ascending Byrness Hill (Byrness below)

Byrness Hill

The lonely Cheviots - approaching Windy Gyle

Uswayford Farm, England's remotest B&B, hides away a few miles ahead. Even its correct pronunciation is a mystery

Then on towards the finishing post

Made it, saving my Forest top for the last 20 yards!

The Border Hotel, Kirk Yetholm (Roof sheeting to the far left, following fire damage)

Day fifteen. Garrigill to Knarsdale (and back to Slaggyford).

"Cnoc na Feille"

Another scorcher, but only twelve miles, on easy terrain, so even if Janet and John and Janet and Keith were ahead it was doubtful if I'd see anything of them. Trough Heads Farm would prove to be my last contact with the Wigan Two, but the others were to be my semi-permanent, and very welcome, companions over the closing stages. In the meantime, another solitary march lay ahead, fellow Way-sters – in fact walkers of any persuasion – a rare commodity.

After the usual palaver with the gel and the two strappings I popped into the local shop, a couple of doors the other side of The Post Office, where I was correctly, and to my surprise, advised that I'd get cash-back, an urgent requirement given that I'd used up my last cheque (never thought of checking before I set out, despite the warning of having already received a replacement book) and my "readies" were diminishing. There are few dispensers along The Pennine Way, not that I've ever used one, preferring to draw my supplies, and avoid queuing, whilst I'm paying for shopping, indoors, at the supermarket.

I was heading for Stone Croft at Knarsdale, a tiny hamlet a mile or so north of Slaggyford, the B & B that I'd booked following a recommendation, having exhausted the listed ones, but not to stay overnight. I'd picked up a message on Cross Fell that my room was unavailable due to an overstay by workmen completing a delayed renovation contract on the nearby "big house", presumably the local equivalent of the Wembley Stadium fiasco or, closer to home – at least, my home – the multi-million pound, very welcome and long overdue re-build of Nottingham's tired and embarrassing "Slab Square".

It's the largest market square in England, if not Britain, and as the programme approached its second year of a scheduled one, with the lengthy over-run long obvious even to the impatient pigeons, and predictably denied until the last by the arrogant council - who'd have us believe that mobile cranes, diggers, bloody great holes, trenches, piles of paving, plastic sheeting, portacabins, wooden pallets, skips, pipes, tons of clutter, vans, lorries, generators, temporary floodlights and yellow-clad workmen were part of the completed design - when we were finally offered a lame excuse (despite piles of unlaid paving lying around everywhere) about "problems sourcing foreign paving materials from China and Ireland".

I won't go into greater detail, especially as it's got little – nothing, in fact – to do with The Pennine Way, but the words "brewery" and "alcoholic celebration" spring to mind. Nevertheless, I can't wait for it to be finished, currently re-scheduled, as I write, for March 2007, some four months late, but I'm not holding my breath. Hopefully it will be worth it in the end, maintaining Nottingham's status, despite recent adverse publicity based on erroneous statistical data - which isn't to say that it doesn't, like most of Britain, have its depressingly high quota of yobs - as one of the Country's more attractive city centres (provided of course that you ignore the chewing gum and cigarette ends).

My overnight status was to be revealed on arrival at Stone Croft, where a lift was to take me to my contingency digs, dropping me back at Knarsdale the following morning. I'd been assured, with profuse apologies for any inconvenience, that it was a nice place and that I'd be well looked after, which proved to be a huge understatement. My first five miles towards my goal followed the River South Tyne through a pastoral landscape of farm fields along a narrow path, partially shaded by trees and hedgerows, punctuated by stiles, and involving the odd bit of ducking under the occasional branch.

It took the west bank for a couple of miles, then over a footbridge to continue on the other side to Alston, or at least its outskirts, where The Pennine Way re-crossed, sharing the bridge with the A689 to Brampton. I saw just one person in that first two hours, a bloke with a dog emerging through the trees alongside Alston's churchyard and, with embarrassing echoes of my surprise meeting with the epic long-distance Scotsman, the timing was inconvenient. "Those Cherokees are after me, they look mad, things look …."

"Morning." "Morning." And on he went, as did I, reminding myself that at least I'd never see him again.

The Pennine Way went left, temporarily following the Brampton road over the bridge, but I continued straight on into Alston, partly to get some en-route supplies, partly to secure my second £50 cash injection of the day, and also because it seemed a shame, on this short, easy, stretch with no taxing climbs, to miss England's highest altitude Market town – a claim, incidentally, shared by Buxton in Derbyshire, a place that never ceases to depress me on the rare occasions when misfortune dictates that I pass through it.

Not so, Alston. Much smaller, and prettier, its tiny market stance on the hill, where I sat in the shade, having augmented my provisions, and cash, at the adjacent Co-op, sits on a bend in the steeply climbing eastbound A689 leading out of town. Another place to add to the list for a possible future short break. Mine lasted about fifteen minutes before I reluctantly retraced my steps, back down the hill and left along the main road, swung right across the bridge, then a right onto the track from where The Pennine Way shadows the Brampton road as they both head north along the valley of The South Tyne.

So did a little steam train, chugging enthusiastically up the South Tynedale Railway. I caught a brief glimpse through the trees before it disappeared again, leaving a tell-tale streaming banner of blue-grey smoke and a fading staccato beat in its wake. This restored section of line runs for a modest three miles from Alston, but the Preservation Group have aspirations to extend it beyond Slaggyford, much to the consternation, as I was to find, of the owners of my re-scheduled B & B. According to my map, the disused section meets the Newcastle-Carlisle line at Haltwhistle, with an earlier spur near the little village of Lambley towards the site of an old colliery, which I would pass tomorrow.

Lambley village just outside Nottingham is the only other listed Lambley in Britain, and was one of my childhood haunts, through the local beauty spot of Lambley Dumbles. A redundant railway line, still, in this case, with track, pending possible (and highly unlikely) resurrection for passenger services to Nottingham, also passes nearby, to another disused colliery, what used to be Gedling Pit, and to complete the coincidence Gedling was served, along with other local mines, by an influx of North-Eastern miners following the closure of the Durham and Northumberland coalfields.

Whenever I find myself on a disused rural railway I have a desire to be transported back to its golden era, maybe the 1920s when the local stopping train delivered the post, papers, and milk, in huge metal pails, to isolated village stations intensively manned by a Station Master, Porter, Ticket Clerk and a lad to feed the cat and trim the flowers. The closest I'm ever likely to come was my journey across the Western Ghat Mountains from Kerala State to Tamil Nadu on the narrow gauge diesel-hauled rattler, but I suspect that India's railways – I believe they're the country's biggest employer – will eventually, albeit perhaps to a lesser extent, go the historic way of ours as the private car, road infrastructure, fragmentation, privatisation and economic demands all take a toll. There's no stopping progress, but its affect on India's high manpower economy and potentially fragile social structure will be an interesting challenge.

I turned from the disappearing train through the familiar company of scattering rabbits as the path took me on to cross the A689, and a climb across open fields, dropped down sharply to traverse the Gilderdale Burn on a little footbridge, then back uphill above and beyond Whitlow Farm, and the Roman fort of Whitley Castle, another morsel of Pennine Way history, where I paused to make out what little imaginary reconstruction I could from the sheep and rabbit razed grassy outline.

Then it was time to renew my acquaintance with the lightly used A689, re-crossing to follow a gentle route through attractive valley farmland backed by rolling moors, the road out of sight to my left, hidden river and (now disused) railway track down to the right, and only a minor "inconvenience" – the perfect collective noun - of stiles to check my steady progress – and a vital notice hammered on a post, drawing attention to walkers that the Kirkstyle Inn at Knarsdale is the last available pub before Greendale, where the Pennine Way meets Hadrians Wall. It also turned out to be only fifty yards along the lane before my pick-up point, which was to come in handy.

I'd not seen one other Way-ster since leaving Garrigill and, Alston excepted, not a soul apart from the involuntary public performance to the bloke and his dog, so it was a pleasant surprise to exchange greetings with a succession of oncoming groups of youngsters, led by young team leaders, one bunch marching briskly to a US military style chant. They were on picnic outings from a nearby centre – it may have been Barhough House, visible below the woods across the valley – and the cheery spectacle gladdened the heart. Leaving their songs and excited chatter fading behind me I ploughed my solitary furrow to re-visit and follow the A689 for half a mile into Slaggyford.

Thankfully, and despite its "A" road status, there was almost no traffic to squish by on the soft tarmac, or impede my crossing it yet again as The Pennine Way decided it was time to explore the other side for a while. I was disappointed with Slaggyford, which was my fault, not Slaggyford's. Like Bowes, I knew the name, it merited a grey blob on my map, and it was on a main road. Unlike Bowes, it was pub-less, and, as far as I noticed – although I may be mistaken – shop-less. It didn't have a castle, but its village station, slap bang alongside The Pennine Way, the abandoned railway having crossed my path on a blue-brick bridge, was preserved as a private house, with intact platforms and track bed – cue possible visit by that little steam train if The South Tynedale Railway get their way (and the finances) but not if the affected (or should that be "impacted on", in current cringe-making media-speak) locals get theirs.

I didn't realise it at the time, but I'd walked right past my re-allocated accommodation, which bordered the disused line just a few yards up from the station. I continued for about a mile and a half, past Merry Knowe Farm, and rejoined the road again at Burnstones, where workmen, including the ones who'd nicked my B & B, were in evidence renovating the imposing house just up a track on the left. The Pennine Way continued on ahead, but I crossed the A689 again, just for a change, and followed the narrow lane down past the church and the Kirkstyle Inn to Stone Croft, a beautiful bungalow in large grounds and a perfect rural setting.

A toddler was splashing in a plastic paddling pool and another littlie was romping on the lawn. The lady of the house, supervising from the comfort of her picnic blanket, shouted out a warm "Hello!" and bade me dump my rucsac, carrier and stick in the lobby whilst she telephoned to tell the lady at Slaggyford to expect me shortly. She'd thoughtfully left the original arrangement intact, knowing that I had a short day, rather than me stop one and a half miles earlier and have to add it to tomorrow's eighteen mile itinerary – and a good thing too, given the nightmare that lay in store.

Due to my early finish it seemed a good idea, especially as I was desperate for my orange and lemonade, plus ice, to pop next door, and I left my stuff accordingly, to return an hour later. Having established that the pub no longer served food, it was an easy decision to accept the offer of an evening meal courtesy of my stand-in landlady, made during the call to say that I was on my way. I was dropped off by the pleasant "Mr Stone Croft", leaving Mrs to entertain the children, and learnt, during the few minutes journey – it had taken me ages to slog the opposite way in blazing sunshine – that he was a farmer and that they had initially only accepted the bungalow on a mutually agreed short-let basis before getting the opportunity to buy. He reckoned they were just about getting it right, and it looked perfect to me.

So did the immaculate detached house occupied by Irene and George, an elderly couple who, at least in my case, provided a rescue service for travellers in distress, including a pristine double bedroom and exclusive use of a large luxury bathroom, my first port of call. I might not be attired for "smart casual" at dinner, but at least I wouldn't stink. Nor did my dirty clothes, after I'd taken Irene's offer of a laundry service, risking an outside airing on the whirly-gig as the early evening temperature hovered around 30C.

My heels were on fire, tendon puffed right up, but there was no point worrying, which in all honesty I never did, beyond the dread that the pain might prevent me from continuing as it intensified over those closing days. The unprecedented heatwave, with the next two days forecast to possibly register as the hottest on record, piled on the agony, and it became a toss-up between my injuries and a raging thirst as to which was the likeliest to finish me off. It hit almost 37C in the south, and given that there wasn't much relief further north, I felt confident in stuffing my fleece and cag, as I re-packed every morning, well and truly into the bottom of my ruc-sac.

Unsure of the "etiquette" following my welcome, more like a family friend than a paying guest, where I'd normally retire to my room or guests' lounge, I was left in no doubt when Irene, as she bravely shepherded my washing into the machine, suggested that George, who was relaxing in the garden, would love some company, particularly as he was just recovering from unrelated orthopaedic surgery following heart problems. I happily obliged, and we were joined by one of the neighbours who'd nipped round for the same purpose, accompanied by her friendly Spaniel, who'd come round for a tummy rub. Another neighbour, also with dog, chatted briefly as she passed by.

We sat on comfy chairs in the shade of the fence screening the house and garden from the railway, iced drinks in hand, smell of cooking wafting irresistibly from the kitchen. I felt guilty for a moment – this was supposed to be The Pennine Way, not a middle class garden party – but I soon got over it. Dinner was superb, a full "silver service" occasion, enhanced by it being presented in large serving dishes which, given the relatively light appetites of my elderly hosts and the generous portions, meant that I was "persuaded" to finish off all the spuds – new and roast – the vegetables, including tender asparagus tips, and Yorkshire puddings, on top of meat pie, followed by fruit crumble, all deliciously cooked, and served with beverage of choice (I had a lager).

George told me that he had been self-employed for most of his working life and that he'd had connections with Sunderland AFC. He was surprised and impressed that I was able to name all their opponents and results, including replays, from their famous 1973 FA Cup winning run, a sequence that started in circumstances that, as an analogy of life, is a bizarre illustration of the finely balanced, almost surreal and often absurd, wafer-thin borderline that can sometimes separate abject failure from unmitigated success.

I was there, in Sunderland's Third Round fixture at Meadow Lane against Notts County, who are, incidentally, the League's longest established team and hold the record in that throughout their disappointing and undistinguished history they have never once had the benefit of a questionable refereeing decision. County were one-nil up, with a minute to go. Sunderland, a poor side struggling to avoid relegation from the (then) Second Division were dead and buried, season over. As a Forest supporter who disliked Notts (still do, childishly!) I was amongst the hordes of Wearsiders, including exiled Nottinghamshire based Durham miners, behind the Spion Kop goal that Sunderland were attacking, more in desperation than any likelihood of scoring.

If I'd suggested at that moment, with the ref poised to blow the final whistle, that they would equalise, let alone, as Division Two relegation candidates, go on to win the Cup, at that time England's most prestigious trophy outside the League Championship, the men in white coats would have taken me away, and quite rightly. Yet that's exactly what happened. The ball came across from the right and Dave Watson (I think) headed it firmly into the net, to scenes of delirium from the Mackems at our end of the ground. The rest, as they say, is history. From the ridiculous to the sublime, sixty seconds from a first match cup exit at lowly Notts, and probable subsequent relegation as morale nose-dived, to a storming, passionate Cup winning fairytale allied to consolidation in the League.

Almost unbelievable, definitely so if written as Fiction. An extreme example, but taken as a microcosm of life it's a heartening analogy. The following week at work, before the Roker Park replay, I was so insistent that Sunderland would go on to win the Cup, based on that last minute drama and the extraordinary celebrations of their fans and players, that a friend checked the Bookies odds – a typically ungenerous 300 to 1 – and suggested I put my money where my mouth was. Never having placed a bet, I prevaricated, kept my quid in my pocket, and missed the chance to turn it into six months salary.

Nottingham Forest last won the Cup in 1959, in similar circumstances, coming from behind late on after facing an even more shameful exit, also in the Third Round, against non-League Tooting and Mitcham. To quote the famous Moody Blues song title, "Isn't Life Strange?" Having reminisced on the absurd vagaries of Football, and Life, until late – well past nine – we retired, in my case with the appalling thought, given that I still had a mental age of twelve, that tomorrow was my 55th birthday.

It turned out by a country mile – eighteen of them, in fact, plus an extra bit going round in circles – to be my worst.

~

Day Sixteen. Knarsdale to East Twice Brewed (Hadrians Wall).

"Travellers on an olden road, with all the baggage of our days and years"

I ignored my birthday. George was still in bed when I left, clearly exhausted by my stimulating conversation the previous night (on a serious note, continuing his recuperation) so I bade him a fond farewell by proxy, via Irene, who prepared a predictably special breakfast before running me back up the road to Knarsdale. It was already ferociously hot, with not a breath of wind or merest hint of a cloud, and by the time I'd crossed the A689 to strike the Pennine Way track, having been walking for all of ten minutes, I knew that it was going to be my toughest day so far.

I was subsequently told that it had been the hottest day on record in those parts. Whether or not that's true, I can't vouch, but the headline story on the local TV news that night was of the gritters being sent out, spraying the roads with a gravel compound in an attempt to hold the melting tarmac together. Road temperatures were reported at 50C – that's not a misprint, an egg-frying fifty degrees, on which my final, exhausting, end of day tramp was undertaken.

As I passed the big house at Burnstones, a workman pointing up a wall, and stripped to the waist, asked me where I was heading. He shook his head upon my response, in the universal language that implied I'd been eating funny mushrooms. "That's right up the Military Road by Hadrians Wall. Bloody hell, man, you'll do well to get there in this heat. Ha'way, best of luck!" "Mad dogs and Englishmen" I replied, with a faux air of cheery optimism, trying simultaneously to hide my limp, and acutely aware that there were still another three hours of rising temperatures to go before Noel Coward's midday sun, and another four or five after that before it peaked, and that even the mentally challenged dogs were sheltering indoors.

The track led up and onto the shoulder of a moor (unnamed on my map) with the main road below, to my right. My footpath was called Maiden Way, an old Roman Road, but had been abandoned at some time in favour of the A689. I wondered whether any treasure trove had also been abandoned here, but could see no more trace than I had in 2000 of Ghengis Khan's alleged fabulous legacy, buried somewhere in Outer Mongolia's uninhabited wilderness of the Khenti Mountains. It was the very area we were trekking, but despite keeping my eyes peeled, nothing – not even an old button.

I watched my local non-League team, Hucknall Town (1) play Blyth Spartans (2) this season – and pretty dire it was too, the Yellows typically throwing it away at the death – and most of the Blyth supporters were wearing Roman helmets with flamboyant plumes, plus, in some cases, shields and swords, but on closer inspection I sensed that they weren't authentic local finds (given also that Blyth is up on the coast, north of Newcastle and Wallsend!) but replicas, possibly of a modern plastic material.

The path dropped sharply down to negotiate, in quick succession, Small Cleugh (not "Clough") and Glendue Burn (which sounded encouragingly Scottish to me), before crossing open moorland and descending to cross, for the final time, the A689 and leave it behind for good. The path on the opposite side proved a bit tricky to find, and I had an irritating few minutes up and down the sticky tarmac – obviously reluctant to let me go after our recent association – before re-claiming The Pennine Way as it set off across scrubby, derelict industrial, cum moor, cum farmland, past the site of that old colliery, near Lambley. Still, the unattractive landscape suited the rabbits – but what didn't?

It had been good walking so far, some three or four miles, but the heat was beginning to get to me, and my heels, despite the yielding ground, were already sore. My right ankle was doing what it always did, swelling and tightening above my heel, but otherwise coping fairly well with my adapted, slightly limping, style. "Three wheels on my wagon, but I'm still rolling along." Onwards, ever onwards! I gritted my teeth, whilst the council were out gritting the roads, and pressed on as the next landmark came into view, described as "High House (ruin)", and they were right on both counts. It stood, roofless, on the top of a hill, occupied by a solitary cow that had taken sanctuary between the walls in what little shade it could find, its head and front quarters in shadow, the rest gently roasting.

I was disappointed to find – "Shit!" – that the crossing of Hartley Burn necessitated a disproportionate expenditure of time, effort, and, not least, sweat, steeply down, then steeply up, for about 0.1 of an inch on my map, before I crossed rolling fields and cut down between some farm buildings known as Ulpham. In the worrying absence of any clear stream water I'd been frugal with my supplies – already tepid, despite the supposed thermal insulation of my containers – and was thirsty, a dangerous sign, with most of the day, including the hottest part, still ahead, and no sign of natural replenishment. I hadn't seen another soul since the workman, and his words of encouragement, and nor would I, until my skirmish with the golf course at Greenhead.

I took a short detour, and tentatively, lest there be an insane dog on patrol (there wasn't, it was too hot) made my way through a gate and across a yard where I first knocked, then hammered, at the farm door, to politely ask for water. Silence. Nobody came. I searched in vain for an outside tap before beating a disconsolate, and very apprehensive, retreat. Six miles to Greenhead village centre and its pub, but that included a full one mile detour – although if all else failed I would have no choice. Then, disaster.

The Pennine Way crosses over a metalled lane to Greenriggs, immediately after Ulpham, before traversing the featureless moorland expanse of Round Hill and Black Hill, accurately summarised in my guide "The route from Greenriggs over Round Hill to Black Hill is very vague". It was reminiscent, in appearance, weather conditions and lack of signs, to that stretch after Bowes, except that there were no contingency "safe" tracks if you strayed, nor, to my eye, defined footpaths of any sort. It was appalling. I stood for several minutes, certain to within inches of my location, absolutely spot-on at that point, but could I make out the way ahead? Could I buggery. Just a vague moorland horizon.

I took a compass bearing. Didn't help – no way through the thick scrub. I made my way back to my inch-perfect location at the end of the short track adjacent to the buildings. I re-scrutinised my map, took unnecessary "belt and braces" compass bearings. Same result. I wandered around in various directions anticipating a path, or a cairn, or a post, and always ended up re-tracing my steps. I was tired, I was hot, I was thirsty, my heels hurt, and I was getting angry and flustered. "This is fucking pathetic!" I shouted out in frustrated fury, but totally ignored by the few desultory sheep. (I learnt later that Janet and Keith had been in a similar quandary but had found their way across thanks to Keith's sat. nav.)

No choice but to make an educated guess, or in my case, uneducated – pig ignorant, in fact. I followed a faint path for a while, initially in the correct direction, only to find, to my consternation, that it was dropping down to my left, not an encouraging prospect as I should be traversing higher ground. Mindful, however, that paths are re-routed from time to time, and given that it was the only such semblance – almost certainly, in hindsight, a sheep-track – I continued to follow it until I saw a gate some way below, providing access to an enclosed field. I dropped down to the bottom of the hillside, found the gate to be padlocked, and that it hadn't, it seemed, seen active service for some time, but in a petulant, totally pissed off and heat-induced tantrum, decided "Sod it, I'm carrying on now".

I should have traipsed back up the moor and at least maintained a course on the higher shoulder of Round Hill. Instead, I clambered over, deliberately, in a childish act of "just retribution", hauling my full weight and pack over the "wrong", opening, end (as every rambler knows, gates should always be climbed at the weight-supporting hinged end). I was seething. "If the bastards don't want us on their precious Grouse moor why can't they put a decent signed path round it?" And all this despite perfect visibility – I shudder to think where I might have ended up in fog and rain. I'm sure I was partly to blame, and no doubt someone will write, putting me straight, but a couple of conspicuous wooden marker posts, at 500 yard intervals, wouldn't have gone amiss.

Unlike me. I was totally off track, and as I ploughed stubbornly on the vegetation became more and more difficult, hummocks of tall grass throwing me off balance – I would have been semi-

169

permanently on my hands and knees without my stick – and disguising deep gullies and troughs, some only negotiable after exasperating "Now where?" diversions. I stumbled on, heading vaguely towards an indistinct horizon to the right, until the forest edge, conspicuously outlined on my map, appeared straight ahead. I should have cleared it on higher ground, passing above, with it lying a half mile below on my left, so presuming I headed sharp right uphill until I could, path or no path, find my way above and beyond the wall of thickly regimented conifer trees, and eventually spot the wooden hut landmark past the power cables, I should be back on course. Easy.

All I had to do was head directly through an almost un-walkable jungle of chest high grasses, ankle wrenching hollows, muddy sinks, dry stream beds and treacherous scrub, then climb up and across the moor until eventual salvation. It might sound exaggerated, but at my snail's rate of haphazard progress, with the temperature approaching 30C, wet through with sweat, and with no immediate prospect of escape I began to wonder if I'd ever get out of there. Even more so when my progress was stopped, as I approached the unrestricted moor, by a six foot dry stone wall topped with wire, and no gate in either direction.

Only one option. Find a section with a foothold, haul myself halfway up, and throw rucsac, carrier, and stick over before attempting likewise, terrified, as I leapt, of catching myself on the wire, or finishing off my ankle on landing. I aimed for a large, soft looking, grassy hummock and rolled, parachute-landing style (not that I've ever done a parachute jump, but I've seen them on the telly) on contact, to end up prostrate in the undergrowth, where I felt like staying. "What a way to spend a birthday."

At least I'd escaped the worst of the rough stuff, and after climbing up the hillside I was able to claim a path approaching Black Hill, before dropping down off the moor. Even then the way wasn't signed, but I was unquestionably back on route, as I passed the hut, ("A wooden hut in the corner of a field indicates the correct path") only to be taken by surprise, some way further on, by the first "Pennine Way" sign I'd seen since Ulpham, as it directed opposing walkers left, as opposed to straight on and past the hut from where I'd come. All very strange, and the anger returns as I type this account. It's no fun battling jungle in a heatwave, frightened and lost, and if I'd come to grief through injury, illness, heatstroke or other mishap there'd have been no passer-by, unlike on the Pennine Way proper, to potentially find me, or any clue as to my whereabouts.

It's a peril of walking alone, but I didn't countenance the possibility of such a nightmare, exacerbated, if not caused, by a negligent lack of signing, even more of an insult if the original path had been diverted. Looking at my map afterwards I reckon it cost me no more than half a mile, as in effect all I did was take a "dog-leg" to the left from the direct route (assuming there is one), but that modest distance and the frustrated route-searching pre-amble took me an hour of exhausting, morale sapping, thirst-inducing time and effort that I could ill afford on my designated eighteen mile day, and it caught up with me with a vengeance over the closing miles.

Buoyed by my extrication from the "Nightmare on Round Hill", and accepting again that I may have been partly responsible, certainly for pressing on in a temper when I first realised I must have gone the wrong way, I felt re-invigorated for a while, striding on purposefully, in an attempt to recover lost time, on an easy path, past a family of horses – three or four adults and a couple of foals – bunched together in the shade of a large tree, but the feeling sadly subsided as the heat, and my thirst, took centre stage. It's worth repeating that without my bush hat, dunked at every available opportunity – albeit few and far between on this dry stretch – I couldn't have continued, and would have been a likely candidate for heat stroke.

The path met a track leading from a spot marked "clay pits" on my map, to the busy A69 between Haltwhistle, four or five miles east, and Brampton, some ten to the west. I crossed quickly, well ahead of a thundering articulated lorry, and was glad to regain the tranquillity of open fields after climbing the path up the opposite embankment. The Pennine Way then cuts across a golf course, and I felt slightly ridiculous as I tramped, with boots and heavy pack, sweat stained and gasping for a cool drink, like a washed-up renegade from the Foreign Legion, past mocking sprinklers, vividly manicured greens and broad fairways dotted with tee shirted (appropriately), fully hydrated members pinging golf balls hither and thither and positively revelling in the hot, still, conditions.

To use that word again, which best expresses how I felt, it all seemed a little surreal, a tad like the native Gambian on the beach – his beach! - peering wistfully through the fence at the rich tourists from another planet on their sun loungers in the Five Star hotel compound. Well not exactly, as that contrast is shameful - although there is the counter-argument for the Tourist Dollar - and in any case I could afford to play golf if I wanted, but having tried, and failed, I didn't. Given my parched condition, I almost asked for directions to the club house, where at least they'd re-fill my containers, but then decided they might be a bit snotty about it, and pressed on, where fate was about to deal me a kindly turn – and about time, too!

The path led me steeply down from the golf course, past some attractive drifts of wild flowers – I took their photo, as proof – to cross the "B" road half a mile north of Greenhead. A man was pottering in his open garage next to the house across the road, and was more than happy to re-fill my water bottles and to advise me, when I asked how far it was to Hadrians Wall, that it was all of a hundred yards away. And so it was. I crossed a railway, and the remains of Thirlwall Castle suddenly towered above me. Built almost entirely of stones pilfered from the wall, it stands at the western end of its most dramatic stretch, a section followed for most of its length by The Pennine Way. First, the good news: "The route along the wall is easy to follow". Now for the bad: "This section is surprisingly tough due to the amount of up and down involved. Indeed, there is little level walking and some very steep climbs".

I faced seven miles of it, plus a mile and a half "off track" up the sticky Military Road (B6318) from Steel Rigg to my B & B, The Craw's Nest at East Twice Brewed (in fact it is East Twice Brewed!), not to be confused with Twice Brewed, next door, which comprises its eponymous pub and a couple of cottages, and Once Brewed, next door but one, consisting of the youth hostel, a small hotel/lodge, a modest camp site, and a couple of cottages. And not forgetting East Bogg, a farmhouse up a track off the "B" road. The fact that there's almost no development to spoil this bleak and atmospheric - although I wasn't in a condition to appreciate it at the time - legacy of our Roman history, and their greatest constructional achievement (on budget, and in half the time of Wembley Stadium) is cause for rejoicing, but it did give me problems in securing accommodation, and I'd thought at one time that I might be sleeping in a field.

The same thought crossed my mind as I slogged up the first vicious climb to cross the minor road at Walltown Quarry, surprised that I'd seen only a handful of explorers, presumably due to the particularly exposed aspect of the spectacular craggy ridge – from afar, like a giant wave, about to crash down onto the shore – in that searing heat. I had no choice. I'd stopped for a cold drink, thus conserving my supplies, in the shade at a tiny café just after Thirlwall, and stopped again at the first visitors centre for another long drink, and sandwiches.

I felt pretty awful, almost spent, struggling to make those excruciating inclines, fully exposed, as I had been all day, to the sun's relentless assault. It didn't help – although at least it was re-assurance that I wasn't over-reacting to the conditions – when a chap at the centre commented to his partner, after they'd walked all of thirty yards from their car, "I can't stand being out in this, it's unbearable". I felt like saying "Try walking eighteen miles in it over the moors with a heavy pack, dodgy heels and a gammy ankle", to which the correct response would have been "More fool you".

If it wasn't for the café breaks I couldn't have made those last miles, and I still had another seven to go. I'd only managed one and a half, including my two stops, since Thirlwall Castle, and that was over an hour ago. Seven miles. The prospect appalled me, but the two breaks in close succession, with food and drink, gave me renewed energy. I'd seriously contemplated dropping straight down onto the Military Road and waiting for the Hadrians Wall bus that would trundle right past the door of my B & B, but Ivan's valuable Pen-y-Ghent lesson persuaded me to plod on. The four remaining days would have been hollow, and my motivation massively eroded, with the knowledge that I'd skipped a section, the equivalent of claiming I'd done a marathon when I'd had a lift for a mile near the end.

The final clincher was a good mobile signal, so if I broke down on the ridge – a real possibility – I could phone ahead for emergency transport arrangements. The other sustaining thought was that if I made unbroken progress I might still be at my digs for tea time, so what was a miserable three hours ahead of me, out of everything I'd achieved so far, when I could look back soon, showered, flat out on cool, clean, sheets and anticipating dinner at The Twice Brewed pub. That simple philosophy got me through. Instead of gauging progress by distance covered, just use time. Usually, I hardly looked at my watch, other than an occasional glance, but on this day's desperate final leg I deliberately split my remaining distance into achievable time segments.

Seven miles to cover, say three hours. It sounds slow, especially compared with that twenty five mile "sprint" in five hours back in my youth, but at just over two miles per hour, fully loaded, on that terrain and in those conditions, it was a good, and just about manageable, average. My mental technique was to continually remind myself of that philosophy - it was nothing to do with distance, only time. Three hours was nothing, a mere blip, just a lazy afternoon watching Six Nations Rugby on TV, or a trip to town and back, and whether I gave up in despair or struggled on, it would inevitably pass, and, in hindsight, quickly – and I so desperately wanted to look back at the end of it with satisfaction. As with Pen-y-Ghent, I wouldn't be able to go back and do it again.

So on I tramped, "up and down", as my guide euphemistically summarised it, grinding out the ups, pausing for recovery and to take in the history, and the stunning views – insofar as I was still interested – at the top, and absorbing the knee-jarring, (fortunately my knees never offered so much as a twinge on the entire route) heel-pounding, downs. "Good, half-past two. Soon be three, and nothing I can do to stop it." Head up, stay relaxed, try to forget the now ferocious stabs of burning pain that greeted every step, every load-bearing downward pressure on my heels, whilst my boot was tightening around my swollen ankle.

I was no longer limping, but hobbling, but 3 p.m. still came and went, as I knew it would, as, equally inevitably, would my overnight oasis, if I just kept going. There was no Pennine Way romance here, alongside Britain's most evocative and famous Roman site, no distant skirl of bagpipes or whiff of Scottish heather, just an agonising sliver of time to endure. Somehow, I did, the last hour slogging up the B6318 Military Road, built with archetypal "straight line" Roman precision. "It's a long road ...." Endless. Dead straight, on my map, but an excruciating up and down over the contours. Hardly any traffic, but the unmistakeable diesel rattle of a bus came from behind shortly after my boots hit the sticky liquorice-streams dribbling down the camber into the verge.

It was the Hadrians Wall midi-bus, and I had time to cross over and flag it down. Now or never. If the driver had pulled in to ask – as has happened to me in rural Wales, and on the Isle of Lewis – I would definitely have given in, but I stayed on my side of the road, facing the traffic, and he merely slowed, before accelerating away, as I resumed my trudge. 4 p.m., and I was almost on my knees, but I'd resisted that final temptation, my "Pen-y-Ghent moment", when I could have taken that safe and easy track down to Horton. It's been said that I can be a bit stubborn when I make my mind up to something, and I must have drawn on every strand of that dubious characteristic.

Strangely, it occurs to me only now, as I type away furiously (by my pathetic standards), irritated by the red lines that Word keeps throwing up as I try to finish this chapter before tea, that I never had even the slightest hint of a headache, despite the extreme conditions, throughout the length of The Pennine Way, and apart from that crippling heel/tendonitis flare-up, legacy of my Reactive Arthritis, only one minor problem, a small blister on the outside of my right ankle, caused by my adjusted walking style – which, on reflection, is pretty damn good. My clear head was, I believe, due to my fixation with water intake, with en route supplements, including streams, at every opportunity, fully dunked and dripping bush hat, and literally pints of tap water on arrival at accommodation.

Unfortunately, the pain in my heels and tendon reached the point, as that final hour ticked by, where it was almost unbearable - "Half four, only thirty minutes left" - and if the Craw's Nest had been another mile on – maybe if I'd not seen the bloke in his garage, and had to add that extra mile diversion via the pub in Greenhead – I couldn't have made it. My landlady told me when I booked that it was 500 yards on, towards the brow of the hill, from the pub, and I counted the steps, so desperate was I to take my mind off that final ascent. I'd reached four hundred and ninety something as I turned right onto the gravel drive that led round the back of the sturdy stone buildings, set in isolation overlooking, from my room, farmland and moors, with that bloody wall, out of sight from my side, stark against the opposite horizon atop its craggy ridge across the Military Road.

It was, incredibly, exactly 5 p.m., my estimated time of arrival based on my calculations. Mrs Watson greeted me warmly, and showed me up to my very pleasant and refreshingly cool quarters – a welcome feature of most of my daily accommodation – then re-appeared, before I'd even made the shower, with a large jug of diluted and iced fruit drink, which I promptly demolished before consuming two pints of water from the tap. I stripped for my cooling shower, to find that, having come to a halt after that last three hours on baking hot surfaces, I was unable to stand, as I couldn't bear the ferocious waves of pounding pain throbbing and stabbing through my heel bones.

I sat for a few minutes, then hobbled, in agony, into the shower, where I managed to remain standing only by leaning against the cubicle and transferring my weight – effectively walking slowly on the spot, like a sad jogger waiting to cross the road – from one foot to the other. I lay on my back afterwards, pillows under my calves so that there was no pressure – not even the soft mattress – on my heels or tendon, but couldn't relax, as the waves of pain kept coming. I couldn't even bear the faintest pressure on my badly swollen ankle, so my gel rub would have to wait.

By 7 p.m., my pre-determined pub time, a) because I would be hungry and b) to see me in bed – thankfully, not boarded! – by nine, it still hurt so much that standing was a problem. There wasn't the remotest possibility of walking on tomorrow in my present condition, but I was banking on the restorative qualities of a good night's sleep, with only four days to go, whilst aware that I was ultimately fighting a losing battle as my injuries deteriorated under the relentless pummelling and heat. Lengthy rest would be the only possible treatment, if not - as I type, heels and ankle still far from rehabilitated - a guaranteed cure.

First, I had to negotiate that 500 yards back down to the Twice Brewed Inn, and not least the embarrassment of giving the appearance that it was my 95th, not 55th, birthday. I've long since ceased to "celebrate" birthdays anyway, but this had definitely been one to forget, and paradoxically one that I never will. The pub was pleasantly busy, but within seconds of approaching the bar I'd spotted, and been spotted by, Janet and Keith. Keith immediately sprung up and shepherded me to their table, then insisted on getting my drink whilst I perused the menu. They'd just ordered, and I quickly followed suit, before we caught up on the Pennine Way gossip, but no news of Janet and John.

It was a powerful personal morale booster, and I showed them my postcard from the American lady, Kathleen, forgetting that it contained reference to my birthday – the Golden Girls' July walk was a celebratory idea for one of their party's 60th – which I was most definitely not going to mention. Cue Keith, ordering and paying for my dessert, and another drink, as my birthday present. There was no arguing, and I accepted with good grace. Keith, surprisingly, had Sticky Toffee Pudding, which again he rated as excellent, "Can you tell the chef, please?" but not, of course, quite Drumnadrochit standard. Janet asked after my ankle, which I played down, scarcely mentioning my heels (nor at any time my Reactive Arthritis), although I was to be grateful for her medical expertise the following evening.

The Bury St Edmunds Two were staying at the hotel down the road and, like me, in Bellingham (pronounced "Bellinjum") tomorrow, but at different digs. Unlike me, their schedule had allowed for what was almost a rest day at Hadrians Wall – the equivalent of my seven miler to Cowling – and they'd had time to discover one of the recommended sites, only to remember, when they arrived, that they'd already been there during a holiday a few years earlier. They'd still had an excellent day, though, a slight contrast to mine.

The final entry in my brief notes, written up just before bed at The Craw's Nest, reads "Sod Hadrians Wall, it's murder!"

~

Day Seventeen. East Twice Brewed to Bellingham.

"Every river I try to cross, every hill I try to climb"

My morning fitness test was inconclusive. My ankle was quite swollen, unusually so, given that I'd had a good sleep and only walked a few paces to and from the bathroom. My heels still felt bruised, another first, before I'd even got my boots on again, but at least the waves of stabbing and throbbing had subsided. So, I could make a start, if not a promising one, and hope for the best. Only fifteen miles, three less than yesterday, and fingers crossed for no "off-piste" excursions.

There were no settlements, not even a tiny hamlet, on today's section – nor did I see another walker, Janet and Keith included – but my map showed a scattering of isolated farms, and if the walking became impossible I'd have to seek assistance accordingly. For all that, I felt a renewed tinge of excitement as I surveyed the succession of blue names on my route, water features with a hint of tartan:

Crag Lough, Greenlee Lough, Jenkin's Burn, Broomlee Lough, Gell Burn, Goften Burn, Fawlee Sike, Warks Burn, Blacka Burn (Rovers?), Kirk Burn, Houxty Burn (how evocative is that!), Slade Sike, and finally, at the very edge of Bellingham, to remind me that I was still in England, the River North Tyne. Just to check their origins and specific meanings I subsequently referred to the Collins New English Dictionary:

Burn – a small stream, a brook, a rivulet.
Lough – a lake or arm of the sea. The Irish form of loch.
Sike – a small brook, a rivulet.

No mention, to my surprise, of any Scottish connotations, but they sounded Scottish to me, and I was confident, despite my unintended rambles yesterday, that I wasn't about to stray within Irish territorial claims.

Negotiating the stairs down to breakfast, crab fashion, was difficult enough, before even starting my northbound inroads into the local water-scape. I hobbled, embarrassment and pain in equal measure,

179

the half mile or so up the Military Road and took the track on the left that was crossed a few hundred yards on by The Pennine Way, the path leading me steeply and breathlessly up the first, and only, severe incline of the day, and back onto that bloody wall at Hotbank Crags. The famous Housesteads Roman Fort, and museum, according to my guide "lie less than a mile beyond Ranishaw Gap. If time permits it is well worth walking the extra distance."

I followed the Pennine Way sign at the gap without a moment's hesitation. My progress was a little easier, as my ankle eased, and the soft moorland ground cushioned my heels. It was, naturally, hot again, but a pleasant cooling breeze took the edge off the temperature and I was already anticipating my first objective, the dense conifer plantation of the South Wark Forest, two miles ahead, and, as far as I could recall, the first meaningful foray through blessed tree cover in over two hundred miles of walking. The open, exposed, area I was traversing was described on my map as a marsh, and although only slightly soggy, it doubtless is in normal conditions, evidenced by the single most frightening experience of my entire journey.

I'd fended off two or three clegs late yesterday, but a couple had still got through, with a sharp sting, leaving their trademark bloodstain followed by furiously itching red lump (I've still got the remains of one on my wrist), followed by a soothing application of "Plix". I'd casually mentioned to my landlady at breakfast that the clegs were a bit of a nuisance in these parts, and she told me that the horses at the farm that shared her drive had had to be brought indoors as they were being driven mad, despite being sprayed with a repellent, and were on the verge of bolting. I'd never given it another thought as I headed for those trees, quietly optimistic that with my injuries holding up well I'd soon have over three miles safely under my belt.

"Ouch, you bugger." I tried to swat it off with the back of my hand, but even if I'd got it, the sting and tiny spurt of blood told me that the damage had already been done. Then another one, and another, both batted away as they went for my hands. Another sharp sting, just behind my ear, below the floppy rim of my bush hat. "Shit." They were suddenly everywhere, each and every one of the vicious little bastards with the express intention of attacking me. I've been chewed to pieces by midges in The Lake District and Scotland, and savaged by mozzies in India and Estonia, amongst other places, but this was much more sinister.

With horseflies you feel every stinging bite, every bite leaves a nasty legacy, and they circle, and attack again and again until they get you, or you get them. If anything vindicated my decision not to wear shorts, this did. They went for every exposed bit of flesh. I pulled my hat down as tightly as possible over my ears, waved my arms and stick around manically like a super-animated dervish, and marched at double time, head down, arms continually swishing, in a blind panic, adrenalin temporarily overriding my familiar walking pains. It seemed to go on forever, but was probably no more than five terrifying minutes, whilst I accumulated half a dozen more bites, keeping the bulk of them at bay with my panic-fuelled quick-step theatricals.

Just as suddenly, they'd gone, and I slowed, to realise that my ankle and heels hurt, and my sweat-soaked shirt was sticking to me, but had also, with echoes of that lesser attack near Horton, lived up to its billing that the insect repellent impregnation would deter just about anything – not one bite through the lightweight material, despite them landing on it in numbers. Another echo of that first experience was the stagnant water – this was a marsh, and there were also a few boggy bits around the site of that first assault. I've used the word "terrifying" as an objective description. They scared the shit out of me.

Imagine you're alone, in the middle of nowhere, attacked by hordes of silent, sneaky, circling insects after your blood, with no means of escape except to flee, in panic, not towards a safe place, because there aren't any, but because there's no other option. That's why horses and cattle go mad, and bolt. So did I. I recounted my experience later to Janet and Keith. Predictably, they responded, as they had following my previous account, that they'd yet to see a cleg, let alone be bitten. I've a friend who possesses similar immunity. When my brother and me were being eaten alive by midges on a

camp site near Keswick he was relaxing with smug impunity. Not
one single bite.

It's time the scientists isolated the magic ingredient – be it in the
blood, skin, sweat glands or whatever – and bottled it. I'm sure it's
not for lack of trying – it would be worth a fortune. And here's a
sobering thought – the mosquito is responsible for more human
deaths than anything else on the planet – and that really is scary. On
that considered reflection, maybe the horsefly has got less of a case
to answer, and at least you know the second you're being attacked.

I'd made better than expected progress thanks to the clegs, having
practically run across the marsh. Adrenalin is a good anaesthetic –
it's a pity it soon wears off. The man-made plantations may be
almost sterile, but at least that meant no clegs, plus the eagerly
anticipated bonus of welcome shade, the downside being that the
scenery is non-existent, everything closed in by tight, dark,
claustrophobic ranks of raw material for furniture, flooring, DIY
super-stores, toilet rolls or whatever's best produced from that
particular environment and crop.

My niece's husband in Estonia has a forestry management business
and took me on a sat. nav. aided boundary marking hike in February
2006, along with their daughter, who was thrilled that she'd got the
day off school due to the morning temperature having failed to reach
the stipulated minus 24C (It was minus thirty overnight). Apart from
the weather, and the bears (Toomas saw one near their house the
previous year), wolves, occasional lynx, and ever present elk – of
which their tracks through the deep, sparkling, snow were much in
evidence – the scene was similar to my current surroundings, and in
fact he's visited the nearby Kielder Forest (of which Wark Forest
may be a splinter) commercially.

As for the elk, or moose, (and in case you're wondering how to tell,
you can't rub elk into your hair) I've yet to see one, despite forest
excursions, both on foot and by road and track, in Estonia, and also
Sweden, yet there are warning signs to motorists everywhere, and
these peculiar animals are the size of small barns. It had become a
personal mission to see one in the wild, but having recently been

disavowed of my understanding that they are reclusive, shy and harmless (they are in fact merely reclusive and shy, but will attack, and often kill, if surprised) my quest is now somewhat lukewarm.

I'd naively laboured under the absurd misapprehension, as also conveyed in films like Jurassic Park where the stranded cast are seen, gooey-eyed, stroking gentle, harmlessly grazing dinosaurs, that vegetarian equates to friendly and tolerant, which is of course absolute bullshit – and there's an example. Not forgetting the hippo, Africa's top killer of man in the mammal stakes, and the rhino, elephant or buffalo (incidentally, what's the difference between a buffalo and a bison? – you can't wash your hands in a buffalo). Even domestic cattle can be a bit touchy, and best keep away from the deer in the rutting season. At least with the big cats and bears, if they've eaten you're reasonably safe. With the big vegetarians you can never be sure.

Musing on those irrelevant thoughts – at least in Pennine Way terms, but worth remembering if you encounter an elk in an Estonian forest – I emerged, a mile and a half on, out of the trees, back into eye-watering sunlight, and scenery, an open, easy, moorland traverse of Hawk Side, passing the site of a ruin, presumably another deserted farmhouse, with just a few crumbling remains as evidence above the overgrown foundations. More trees - a tunnel of similar length through a section of Wark Forest (Central) - a brief skirmish over a clearing, and down a lane, passing dwellings at Willowbeg and Ladyhill, then a half mile through Wark Forest (North) into an attractive landscape of rolling fields and low moors.

Just on halfway, and I should have been well pleased, but my tendon and heels were suddenly playing up with a vengeance and I was already back where I was yesterday. So was the heat - the breeze, like the tarmac on the lane, having melted away. There was no Military Road with a possible rescue bus, only the thought, positively cringe-inducing, of knocking at a farm door for help. The prospect was appalling. I'd hobble on somehow to Bellingham, take stock – almost certainly a devastating retirement – and try in the meantime to ignore the shocks of pain searing through my heel bones with every excruciating step. At least, water wasn't a problem. A lady at Leadgate Cottage, conveniently pottering in her garden, re-filled my containers from her outside tap, re-assuring me – not that I needed it – that her fresh, cold, springwater supply would do me no harm.

On I went, angry and upset that what should have been a gentle coast towards the Pennine Way finish line had been rendered almost impossible through injury. I grimly battled on, resigned but still determined, at least to make today's destination, mentally ticking off the names on the map – Lowstead, Linacres, Esp Mill, and the unfortunately named Shitlington Hall, near where a black and white collie went absolutely ballistic through the bars of a gate, snarling, snapping and foaming – and that Noel Coward song came vividly to mind as I scuttled past.

The transmission tower on the ridge above Shitlington Crags lay across the valley, but not before I'd forced my way through a herd of lively bullocks, parting them apprehensively with a brisk pseudo-confident wave of my stick, whilst keeping one eye firmly on potential escape over the fence to my right, as they scattered around me, except for one – there's always one – that stood defiantly in my path trying to stare me out, before reluctantly responding to my desperate cry of "Shoo!" just as I was running out of options. As always with fields containing cattle, progress was difficult and potentially ankle turning, through the now hard-baked ruts, holes and ridges gouged out by their hooves, but at least they didn't follow me.

The path meets the access track to the transmitter at Ealingham Rigg, after its sharp ascent back up the other side of the valley, and I refuelled and mopped my brow at the stile, climbing done for the day. Two and a half miles to The Cheviot Hotel, where I faced that agonising – but seemingly inevitable – decision. The B6320, unbeknown to the passing motorists, duals The Pennine Way for the final mile into Bellingham, or should that be duels, as I was criminally "buzzed", as I hugged the verge, by one moron who preferred the risk of knocking a struggling walker into the hedgerow ahead of the intellectual effort required to give prudent clearance. Never mind road rage, pedestrian rage would have seen my stick

184

thrust so far up where the sun doesn't shine that he could have used it for a tooth-pick. Just what is wrong with these people?

At least, it took my mind off the pounding, jarring, pain racking my heels, if only for a few seconds and thankfully the final approach was along a protective pavement, before diverting right down some steps to follow the North Tyne into Bellingham. I should have enjoyed a gentle closing stroll, possibly stopping for a few satisfying minutes on the pleasant riverbank, before savouring the remaining steps through the tiny market town of "Bellinjum". Instead, I hobbled self-consciously into my digs for the second evening running, where I presented myself at the bar, to demolish my pint of orange and lemonade before tackling the stairs to my room.

Two friendly locals, fellow walkers, engaged me in conversation, impressed by my efforts in the heat – "you should crack it now". I smiled, but otherwise gave nothing away, evoking sympathy on less sensitive ground by limiting myself to the clegs, where a common hatred was revealed. "Why aye, man, those little buggers can send you demented. Sometimes it's so bad they drive you off the moors." Precisely. Lifted by their chirpy accents, and conversation, the only one, Leadgate excepted, since breakfast, and my refreshing drink, I completed my mini rehabilitation with a cooling shower, albeit only by repeating yesterday's agonised tap-dance, before crashing horizontally on the bed, flat on my back, pillows under calves. My room was tiny, but it was cool, and the bed was unboarded.

As had happened yesterday, the heel pain actually intensified after I stopped walking, to the extent that I could hardly bear to stand again for a full two hours after I'd showered, and a rehabilitating doze was well nigh impossible. It felt as if a knife was being driven, and twisted, deep into the bones, in relentless red hot stabs, such that my swollen tendon, excruciating to touch, and consequently to apply the anti-inflammatory gel, was nevertheless now a secondary consideration. It was almost intolerable, a punishment for my continuing to hammer them onto the ground, with today's finish, like yesterday's, on tarmac so hot that it was the headline local news story.

End of Pennine Way adventure. A full three hours after my arrival at The Cheviot I could still barely hobble, in my cushioned, clean, change of socks, into the restaurant for my evening meal. I was the only one present, which hardly lifted my sprits. I ordered a commiserating Guinness ahead of my food, but had scarcely made inroads when a familiar voice called out "Thought we'd find you here". Janet and Keith were joined a few minutes later by Alan, an early retiree if I recall correctly, who was on his Land's End to John O'Groats epic, and who revealed, as the conversation evolved, that he was already contemplating an extension to take in The Orkneys. Although he was married, he seemed to anticipate no problem in extending his lengthy pass-out, despite the fact that he'd been away since May.

Alan had bumped into Janet and Keith in Bellingham – I think they may have been sharing the same digs – and they had polled up at The Cheviot knowing that I would be there, and that it was recommended for a decent evening meal – albeit that no-one else turned up, their restaurant trade that night entirely due to the enormous commercial value of The Pennine Way! I had to confess that it would be the last I'd be seeing of them, as I simply couldn't go on, so much had the pain in my heels intensified over the last few days, and I'd finished the last two, especially today, practically crippled.

Doctor Janet offered, and carried out, an examination whilst we were waiting for dessert (Keith had ordered Sticky Toffee Pudding), diagnosing my likely heel condition – I forget the medical terminology – and carefully inspecting my badly swollen ankle, nearly sending me through the roof when she applied modest pressure. Rest, as I knew, was the first recourse, but she ventured that it would be dreadful if I had to give in, with only three days remaining, but that I couldn't continue unless I could get the inflammation and pain reduced. My current medical assault now comprised: Stick, unfortunately coming into its own as a disabled person's accessory rather than a trekking aid, Ibuprofen gel (already well past recommended dosage and frequency), 2 x support bandages (1 crossover, 1 tubular), and animal wool, layered behind and below my heels.

I'd taken no painkillers, partly because I seldom use "over the counter" medication, partly because of my daily immune suppressant tablets (which, as I write, have been prescribed for a further three months, having reduced all my relevant blood readings to normal, to date with no adverse side effects) and partly because, in contradiction to my first statement, I was close to exhausting that large tube of gel, bought over the counter at Boots. Janet suggested that the only thing that might help, notwithstanding the gel, was Ibuprofen tablets, at maximum permitted dosage, and the sooner the better if I was to have a chance tomorrow.

Needless to say, I had everything but in my medical kit. And the other three, likewise, although Aspirin, Paracetemol and Anadin were available by the bucketful. The little chemist was long closed, although another suggestion was that they might have orthopaedic heel supports, so if I could get my tablets somewhere else, and some supports first thing tomorrow, there was a glimmer of hope. I heard a comment during a Formula One Grand Prix commentary after my walk, describing a remarkable comeback and arguing that you should never give up until the last possible moment, in life or sport, whatever you do. Shades of Sunderland's and Forest's barely credible F A Cup wins, and, corny as it sounds, a metaphor for my determination to continue.

The hotel staff directed me the hundred yards to the Co-op mini supermarket, open till ten. As in Alston, and Ballachulish, and, nearer to home, Lowdham, they're a lifeline in smaller towns and villages, and a welcome comeback niche for the Co-op, an echo, full circle, of the revolutionary Spar stores of my childhood. I bought "Extra-strength Ibuprofen", from the surprisingly large selection of remedies on offer, given the proximity of the chemist, (who doubtless have less appreciative thoughts about the late- night Co-op) and retired to my room to see if they worked.

One advantage of walking solo was that my handicap didn't impinge on my colleague(s) in the way that Steve's blister also put paid to the aspirations of my brother and me back in 1970, and I could adjust my pace and itinerary, or potentially drop out, without any external constraints. Paradoxically, I suspect that the empathy of a sympathetic companion might have seen us less likely to continue, and similarly I would have had difficulty with the moral dilemma of watching a friend hobbling as I had, unsure as to whether they were struggling on, and possibly causing themselves serious damage in the process, so as not to disappoint me. It was my decision, and affected no-one else, and in that respect those are life's least complicated, and rarest, of choices.

My scribbled diary for the day, jotted just before I hobbled off to dinner, and my medical consultation, related:

"Fifteen miles, hot again, refreshing breeze first thing. Desperate struggle with right ankle and very sore heels, basically hobbled it, almost dead stop at times. Ruined what should have been fairly easy day as little climbing after last bit of wall, and well signed, unlike yesterday! Clegs bloody nuisance, stinging, blood sucking horse flies, all the locals very aware, horses brought in despite being sprayed, can drive them mad, make them bolt. Had scary time where loads. Nearly killed by wanker on road in. B & B fine, though room tiny, but can I make tomorrow? Looks desperate."

I swallowed my tablets and turned the light out.

~

Day Eighteen. Bellingham to Byrness.

"I'm alive on a lifeline, come to the mountain and climb"

A barking dog, patrolling outdoors in its compound scarcely a stone's throw from my bedroom window and exploding furiously at every perceived presence or threat, had kept me awake until well past midnight, but I still felt rested when I roused from my belated slumber. The swelling behind my ankle had subsided and I made the bathroom, in comparison with yesterday morning, in a gait that was a passable imitation of walking. My heels were still sore, but the overall improvement was sensational. Last night, I couldn't have made half a mile. On these early impressions I began my pre-breakfast rucsac routine and filled my water containers from the bathroom tap. I also took two more Extra Strength Ibuprofen (to be followed by my usual three daily prescription medication with my breakfast), next instalment due four hours later, at eleven.

There were two of us in the dining room and we shared a common interest in walking, with my fellow guest on business in his capacity as a software programme writer for the Forestry Commission. He'd had a horrific insect experience once, whilst trekking on his own through Canadian wilderness, when a cloud of mosquitoes enveloped him and he had to run for his life, pursued by the swarm. When he finally shook them off he was in a terrible state and his back was one huge mass of bites. If escape and protection are impossible the ultimate consequence doesn't bear contemplation. Would you, I wonder, eventually die of the shock, and poison, or is a "saturation" point reached where there's no further benefit – or unbitten flesh – for them to attack. Gruesome.

A real-life horror film in the making. "Attack of the Killer Clegs!" maybe, followed by "Revenge of the Killer Clegs!" the first posse having been wiped out (bar one pregnant female) just as all seemed lost, by the risky, but desperate, release of toxic chemicals by our despairing group of young and scantily clad attractive hikers from a strange orange device embedded in the moor, underneath an MOD sign warning of inevitable death and destruction for anyone tampering with strange orange devices found embedded in the moor. It could lead to a whole new genre, following on from sharks, spiders and snakes. I didn't explore the theme with my fellow guest, preferring to leave him with at least a vaguely favourable impression.

Halfway through my second boiled egg we were joined by a non-resident. Janet had nipped round, hoping she'd find me sufficiently improved, thanks to the anti-inflammatories, to be stoking up ahead of today's sixteen mile challenge, and was as chuffed as me when I gave her the good news. They were off shortly, but my nine a.m. appointment at the chemist was still nearly an hour away, and in any case I wanted to test myself at my own pace and time. "See you in Byrness!" The Byrness Hotel, to be specific. Along with a small church, a fuel station, and a few cottages, it is Byrness, a tiny speck on the A68(T) between Otterburn and Jedburgh where it cuts through the impressive rolling expanse of Redesdale Forest.

At one minute past nine I was in the chemist shop, enquiring as to the cushioned heel supports, where I was introduced to the one remaining pair. Good news, for a change, and I snaffled them up. Bad news, as I broke open the pack in the street outside to discover that they were for size range four to eight. I wouldn't have bought them if I'd noticed, but it went full circle, and rather than pop back in for a refund the good news was reinstated when I doubled them up inside my size ten right boot, so at least my worst side would be cushioned, and balanced, after a fashion, by a thicker wedge of animal wool in my left. And off I went. Not exactly walking on air, but a damn site more comfortable than yesterday, and psychologically I was up in the clouds.

The tablets had performed a miracle in reducing the inflammation, the heel inserts were doing their bit, and, wonder of wonders, the weather was lending a helpful hand. With a relatively easy sixteen ahead, albeit even more sparsely settled than yesterday's should I need assistance, the blazing sun had stayed indoors, curtains firmly closed. My scribbles summarised the day as "Relatively easy walk, horrid bit excepted, grey and some light rain first half of day, but no visibility problems or low cloud. Bright later, warm and sunny again by tea time. Big change to have good walking conditions".

I followed the minor road in still, humid, and overcast weather, uphill out of Bellingham, where I was surprised to see Alan a mere hundred yards ahead of me, and even more surprised when I quickly caught up, his measured climbing even slower than my endeavours. We exchanged pleasantries, then I pushed slightly ahead at a pace that suited me. It was never a problem when walkers came together – there were no egos, no competitive jockeying for position, just a casual ebbing and flowing, and I bade him a "See you later", which I duly did.

My only contention, shortly after leaving the metalled road and exiting the subsequent track at Blakelaw Farm, was with the comment in my guide that "A much used and signed alternative leaves the official route. As the official route becomes boggy and indistinct, the alternative is to be recommended". Not by me, it isn't, at least with the benefit of hindsight. Following the advice, I took the alternative route, left at the moorland fork on the shoulder of Highstead Hill, but my option quickly faded into a narrow, almost indiscernible, path through peaty clumps of vegetation, weaving this way and that on the rough lower slopes of the moor, necessitating vigilance throughout to avoid turning an ankle or falling into a shallow ditch. It rejoined the official route a mile and a half on, near Hareshaw House, shortly after crossing a track, where I could see Alan, following the higher route, only a short distance behind. He told me later that the official section had been straightforward and easy to follow, unlike mine.

Both routes ran parallel to Hareshaw Burn, a quarter mile or so below, and on the left, which, according to my map, had its source on the hillside at Sandysike Rigg, laid claim to a waterfall, Hareshaw Linn, and completed its four mile journey by flowing into the River North Tyne at Bellingham. I also discovered, to my surprise and delight, whilst watching an excellent Channel Five programme about Northumbrian folk music only a few weeks after my return, that "Hareshaw Burn" is the title of a song, performed on TV, by the highly accomplished and respected fiddler and traditional music teacher Kathryn Tickell.

Light drizzle had turned into steady rain, and I used my umbrella for only the second, and last, time en route – I consigned it to the bin in my room at Byrness – as I followed the track around the foot of Abbey Rigg, where it met the B6320 again, my old friend from yesterday's agonising final slog. What a contrast, not just in the weather, but also in my condition, plus the bonus of having to negotiate only thirty feet of tarmac this time as The Pennine Way cut directly across the road. Through a gate on the other side, and onto a large expanse of featureless moorland, entirely covered, on my map, with blue marshland symbols, and the ominous comment "The route is very wet and, in mist, difficult to follow", with a further reassuring text "In poor weather, circumnavigating this section by walking along the motor road to the west should be considered, particularly for those unfamiliar with the use of a compass".

Nevertheless, the peaty path seemed obvious enough, and despite the steady rain, and the inconvenience of my compensating brolly, having also resorted to my cag (my bulky fleece never saw active service) I pushed on in high spirits. The underfoot conditions were soft and yielding, ideal for my heels and tendon, which were becoming troublesome again, but still within tolerance level, with a painkiller boost due in an hour. In the absence of clinging low cloud or mist – or clegs for that matter, too mardy to venture out in the cooler weather – the marker post at Deer Play (didn't see any!) was visible on the horizon.

Up past Lough Shaw, then the marker, then Lord's Shaw and Whitley Pike and the final ascent on an obvious path which had been recently re-cut, since the last update of my guide, in sharp, sunken, relief into the soft peat. Then a descent to cross a minor road, and back up to a summit at Padon Hill. I waited for Alan and we descended in tandem towards the corner of Redesdale Forest, my umbrella back in its rucsac fastenings as the rain petered out – never to return – and the skies brightened. The next quarter mile was undoubtedly, by unanimous agreement of Janet, Keith, Alan and me, by a country mile the worst bit of the entire Pennine Way.

The map showed the path ascending back up the hillside, tight against the boundary of the forest on its left, wall and fence to the right, to a modest brow at 1,191 feet at Brownrigg Head, described simply: "Throughout this section the route runs alongside a fence, greatly simplifying navigation in mist". It didn't mention that The Pennine Way had been totally abandoned and no longer existed as a footpath, all the more mystifying and infuriating after the sterling maintenance efforts back on the moor. Typically, there'd not been one single southbound Way-ster (or anyone, for that matter) in the four hours since leaving Bellingham, but we were gratified to find faint signs of trampled grass and bracken, witness to Janet and Keith's recent endeavours.

The designated route ahead was absolutely unmistakeable, wedged in as it was (and as described) tightly between the impenetrable forest and the unscaleable barrier, but access looked impossible. It was a steep, scrambling at times, assault through a saturated, head high, jungle of grasses, tree branches, and bracken, up a treacherous stream bed – if it had been a couple of degrees steeper and in full flow it would have qualified as a waterfall – wet and slimy in parts, rocky in others, with cloying, heavy, mud at the edges, and thick vegetation clinging to boots and clothing and attacking face and head at every exhausting upward step.

The thought had already crossed my mind, but Alan cheerfully voiced it - "Watch out, this is perfect for ticks". Not for the first time, I was grateful that my shorts remained in my pack, keeping my fleece company, and that my cag, hood pulled up over my hat, should prevent opportunists attaching from above. Heavy jeans, socks and boots should protect my lower half. They lie in wait and drop from the edges of disturbed bracken – hence the expression, "With fronds like these, who needs enemies?"

Returning from the rain-drenched Lakes many moons ago I was giving Sal her daily grooming, when I noticed a small lump on the back of her neck. When I investigated, it wriggled. I pulled the revolting parasite out with disinfected tweezers, but the still moving head remained embedded, and I had to dig it out, dousing the remaining excavation with Savlon. I'm not sure what a vet would have made of my DIY efforts, but it healed perfectly. That horrible experience flitted across my mind as we battled on, but I chose not to dwell on it.

Scramble. Sweat. Stop. Nowhere to go. Pine branch up my left nostril, right foot hard against the wall. Near vertical slippery rocks and mud, topped by malicious, eye-poking, thickets. Straight ahead. It has to be, there's nowhere else. Solid, dark, wall of trees intruding from the left. Ducking and weaving under branches, sometimes on hands and knees. Hemmed in on the right. Massive relief spotting a northbound bootprint in the gunge just above my eye level. Haul myself up and on. Alan has dropped back, his head and the top of his pack just visible down below as he forces his way through. Keep going, no choice. No escape route, but must run out of contours soon – the map can't lie. It doesn't.

Finally, after battling through The Pennine Way's only designated (not counting my previous "off-piste" rambles) section of jungle I emerged onto open ground, and lo and behold, the defined path re-appeared to bisect the tree-line to the left, moorland plateau to the right, on an easy, level, course. I called down to Alan that he'd be out of it soon, before we expressed shared incredulity that, especially after re-building so much of the path over the moors, they'd left this bit as almost a "no-go" area, more suited to machetes and ropes than hiking boots and trekking poles.

A slight exaggeration maybe, and I would never wish to underplay the daily horrors experienced, for example, by World War Two veterans in the Burmese jungle, but in the context of The Pennine Way it's an aberration that makes a mockery of the Forestry Commission's sign that "welcomes Pennine Way walkers" into Redesdale Forest. I'm not sure who takes responsibility for that short climb, but a little maintenance is long overdue, and a few willing hands, maybe from a volunteer Conservation weekend or similar, would soon clear a defined path.

I adjourned for a break, and to take stock, whilst Alan walked on. Despite this setback we were making excellent progress, already over half way, with most of the rest along forest tracks, boring but relatively undemanding, although my guide warned that it was "easy to follow, but hard on the feet", an accurate summary. Unlike yesterday's section on narrow, enclosed, paths, the broad track and undulating landscape afforded some expansive views, to my right over the moors towards Blackwool Law, and ahead and left over the swathes of dark green conifers carpeting the hillsides across to Raw Hill and beyond. I caught Alan again and we walked together for a while before he dropped behind, and our next contact would be around the dining table at The Byrness Hotel. His pace was slightly slower than mine, but in another contrast to Mike, who waited for me on that first day every time his superior fitness took him ahead, he seemed happier in his own company, which I respected.

My heels were hurting, but the painkillers were holding the worst of it at bay, and there was never a doubt now that I'd reach Byrness or, it seemed, with a rising feeling of elation and regret, that two days from here I'd experience the mixed emotions of passing the finishing line. I was already slightly sad that my adventure, and the experiences and scenery on the way – good, bad, or indifferent – would soon be consigned to memory, and a couple of photograph albums. Such challenges are intensely personal, but the feelings, whether it's upon completion of your first half-marathon or a trek to The North Pole, must be similar.

I saw a sad, deluded, macho type in town once, wearing a tee-shirt with the highly offensive slogan (on a par with that infantile and vacuous anagram of "fuck") "Second place is for losers". That's 99.99% of the world's population dismissed, then. My Pennine Way achievements, in the face of the hottest July ever recorded, advancing middle age, and debilitating injury were a personal victory, and even if, heaven forbid, I didn't ultimately make it over those final stages I'd given it my best shot, and in that sense I'd still be a winner.

As it was, any remaining self-doubt was evaporating, along with the puddles, as warm sunshine returned, and I closed in, with less than three miles to go, on the tiny settlement – just three buildings, I think

– with the splendid and absurdly disproportionate name of Blakehopeburnhaugh, where The Pennine Way met another track, imaginatively titled "Forest Drive", before crossing the River Rede on a metalled road. I'd dropped down into the valley, which the route shared with the empty lane and the re-visited A68(T) to my right, the little river sparkling away on my left. The narrow path hugged its bank past Tod Law, re-crossing via another small bridge, and along a track through the trees, the church at Byrness beckoning me on from across the valley.

My guide advised me that "The signposting is poor and it is easy to become lost. Study the map carefully", but perversely I'd had no problems, safely negotiating the couple of premises that comprise the hamlet of Raw, then a final crossing of the river and around the back of the churchyard to meet the A68(T) full on – but not before I'd taken evasive action, insofar as humanly possible, to avoid the hundreds of tiny frogs that were crawling across the way. Keith mentioned them later. Janet had been oblivious, and was less than impressed when I ventured that she must have squashed dozens, but we refrained from inspecting the soles of her boots for evidence.

I crossed the main road, then up the short, steep, incline to find my way, with more navigational difficulty than any part of the previous sixteen miles, to the door of my accommodation, more of a tradesman's back entrance than a hotel foyer. The welcome, however, was warm, including two Dobermans and a smaller breed – it might have been a Jack Russell, or something similar, to which I'd taken a childhood dislike that has endured ever since, after two of them broke into our Guinea Pigs' compound on our fenced and private back lawn and ripped them to pieces.

The Bury St Edmunds Two were already in situ, Janet calling out a greeting as I made my way to my room at the end of the offset corridor linking theirs, and the fact that they were both delighted that I'd made it reinforced my quiet satisfaction. As I lay on the bed after my shower, half dozing and for once enjoying the rising temperatures as unbroken sunshine returned, a movement distracted me. I'd left the door ajar, as I often did at my B & B's, both to help with ventilation, and also because it often felt claustrophobic and solitary, although these were pleasantly bright and fairly spacious quarters.

A pair of doggy – Doberman, in fact – eyes were staring at me from about three feet away, and when I reciprocated the animal launched into a furious tirade of high decibel barking, standing its ground, but making no advance in response to my friendly "Hello, come here then". I was slightly reluctant, "dressed" as I was in just my underpants, to introduce myself more intimately, especially as it continued its excited cacophony, propelling unappealing eruptions of saliva onto the bed and, more disturbingly, me. The stand-off was resolved when the landlady rushed up the stairs to fetch him back. "Sorry, he does that sometimes, but he only barks", which is a good thing if you're running a guest house.

I'd always been wary of Dobermans, archetypal "villains of the piece" in many an American TV programme, where they generally end up ripping the baddie to shreds or chasing the hero over a wall (two were portrayed as murder weapons on a recent repeat of Columbo, attacking and killing the hapless victim who'd repeated the murderers "trigger" word unknowingly back to him over the phone in front of the primed canines), but experience of a near neighbour's softened my view (and Columbo got his man).

They lived a few doors away, but chats about our newly planted gardens – it was a brand new estate – led to plant swaps and visits, and my close acquaintance with their Doberman, a "rescue dog" that had been subject to mistreatment before Pam and Clem adopted it. It took a shine to me, and would gently nuzzle against my waist, demanding my arm around its neck, where it would, given the chance, happily remain forever, protesting by shoving its head back whenever I moved away. I used to enjoy our little sessions, having "conversations" for minutes on end in quiet soothing tones that were therapy for us both.

Not so this feisty one, it would have been a shouting and screaming affair. As usual for the breed, it had only a stump for a tail. I'd love to be a judge at Crufts – "Sorry, there's a bit missing. Mutilation means disqualification". That would be all the Spaniels and Boxers gone, for a start, although I saw a Spaniel with a full tail the other day – what a nice change, and a credit to its owner. Having enjoyed that imaginary rebuff to Crufts, I wiped the dog spit away and resumed my relaxing countdown to dinner.

The hotel had just three listed bedrooms and a cosy dining room with one central table, which made for a perfect guest environment. Dinner was scheduled for seven-thirty, and as usual I was punctual, joined a couple of minutes later by Janet and Keith, and shortly afterwards Alan, and a convivial evening, accompanied by alcoholic beverages, was enjoyed by all. Alan was off at the crack of dawn tomorrow, straying from the Way to Jedburgh (if I remember correctly) as he continued his mammoth trek, if it was to include the Orkneys, for something like five months – I know blokes who aren't allowed out for more than five hours! As for the Way-sters, we just had the twenty nine mile crossing of the Cheviots (incidentally, pronounced "Cheeviots" – I was put straight on that one back in 1970 by my uncle Harry!) and we were home and dry.

It can be done in one day, but it's not recommended. Apart from the distance, it's the remotest stretch of the entire walk, and there are almost no streams, so it would involve, especially in hot weather, carrying copious amounts of water. There's just one viable B & B, roughly half distance, although it involves dropping down nearly two miles off route – and of course back next morning – so Mr Hobson, as on many occasions, had the last word. "I presume you're staying at Uswayford ("Ooozyfud") Farm?" ventured Keith, followed by the presumption that we'd set off together in the morning.

I was chuffed when Janet added "and we'll all arrive at Kirk Yetholm together"

~

198

Day Nineteen. Byrness to Uswayford Farm.

"There hangs an open landscape, a wild and huge frontier"

My "Pennine Way – Part 2 – North" guide, map section 15 (out of 16 in total!) saw fit to highlight, in red lettering, helpful information for those of a nervous disposition, firstly: "Note – Danger Area. From Byrness Hill to Chew Green the Pennine Way follows the edge of the MOD property to the east. Do not stray off the path, and pay particular attention when red flags are being flown". It didn't state, but could have added, "Notes 2 and 3 can be disregarded, along with the remaining map section, if this advice is not followed".

Then came: "Byrness to Kirk Yetholm – a note to walkers. Apart from two emergency refuge huts there are no facilities and there is no accommodation along the route ...... it should be noted that most of this walk is high and exposed ...... the going underfoot is tough. Walkers should make sure they are adequately equipped with extra food, emergency survival bags and torches and should seriously consider postponing the crossing in bad weather", to which I've added, in neat biro on my map, as the heat returned after its one day interlude "including a 30C heatwave".

Just in case the message wasn't getting through, a third section followed: "Crossing the Cheviots, a note to walkers. If forced to leave the Pennine Way in an emergency, walkers should drop down into the valleys indicated on the map by broad black arrows. The mileages shown indicate the distances to the nearest public roads and habitation. It should be noted that no public services are available at these places and that all the farms named are isolated from major centres of population".

Not recommended on a Pen-y-Ghent day, then, but the sun had got his hat on again, right from kick-off, and my combination of external support system (stick, bandages, animal wool and heel inserts) plus localised gel and painkillers had me cautiously optimistic that Janet and Keith wouldn't be regularly sat down in the distance ahead, looking at their watches. It was a perfect summer's day, maybe low twenties when we set off from the valley, and little higher, the altitude and a cooling breeze for once compensating for the sun's increasing strength, as we hauled ourselves up onto Byrness Hill after a steep, breathless, climb through thick forest and over rocky crags.

The Cheviots are a series of rolling, usually steep, hills separating deep valleys with little in the way of habitation, and I was struck by the dramatic emptiness of the landscape, a glorious expanse of bare undulations meeting a huge sky. And the obligatory MOD signs of course, the first bold red warning coming almost immediately over that first ridge and recorded on Keith's camera. The military are a mixed blessing, their presence at least preserving the open spaces, and so far on our walk unobtrusive, although that was shortly to change.

I was reminded of the Khenti Mountains, where I was continually expecting to see, whenever we browed another hill, a road, farm settlement, maybe even a village or small town, in the next valley, only to find it empty again. The Cheviots, unlike that Mongolian wilderness where you could travel northwards for days, into Siberia, and not see one sign of civilisation, are surrounded by human infrastructure, and the Romans have been there in strength, but in contrast to the equally inhospitable Pennines further south, industry and settlement has not pushed its way through the valleys, although there is evidence of early mine workings.

Centuries of cross border conflict mitigated against stable communities, and presumably there's never been the economically viable equivalent of "gold in them thar hills", nor suitable water sources for mills, to render large scale exploitation feasible as Industrial Britain developed. The legacy is that without roads its glorious scenery is not accessible for modern day settlers, be they commuters, artisans, second homers or retirees. There's almost nowhere you can drive a car. Shank's Pony has endured as the best means of access, farmers' quad bikes excepted, and sheep, of which the hardy Cheviot breed is an obvious example, the predominant source of income and sculptors of the hillsides.

We walked on in high spirits, over Houx Hill and Windy Crag (not that there was much today) with commanding views over the exposed hillsides to the right and Redesdale Forest below on the left, always skirting "Danger Area", with their ever present warning signs. On, over Ravens Knowe and the ominously named Ogre Hill, dropping down into a shallow valley between Coquet Head to the left and Harden Edge on the right. The three mile stretch from Ravens Knowe to the Roman camps at Chew Green was accompanied by the continual rumble of muffled artillery fire ("Fuaim A' Bhlair") from the range to our right, but not the slightest sign of human activity, explosions, or smoke.

They were presumably somewhere beyond the ridge, invisible and "sanitised", but the blood chilling thought came to me that the sole purpose of the activities was ultimately dedicated to the destruction of property and mutilation of human flesh, maybe in support, at a collective cost to the British taxpayer of billions of pounds, of Blair's squalid and illegal Spoof Labour macho adventure in Iraq. Doesn't one of the Ten Commandments, with which Blair apparently professes a keen belief, say "Thou shall not kill"?

It's also strange that we never picked on any of the myriad other dubious regimes, conspicuously those where we actually knew that they did possess "weapons of mass destruction". That expression is a damning indictment, lest we ever forget, "move on", and "learn from our mistakes", as Blair and cronies aggressively and self-righteously lecture us, that was indoctrinated and regurgitated, parrot fashion, for months on end into every response to every question – even just asking for the time of day – by every Spoof Labour representative, nauseatingly echoing the jingoistic days of Empire by tacitly questioning the loyalty and patriotism of anyone denigrating "our brave boys" out there. I think it was Wilfred Owen who said "The same old lie".

Despite those temporary musings the gunfire didn't detract from my appreciation of the stunningly bleak surroundings. There wasn't much remaining of the Roman camps, where The Pennine Way took an uphill to the left along Dere Street Roman Road, although fresh archaeological excavations were evidenced by appropriate warning notices, in this case to protect the delicate works from the tramp of heavy boots rather than the unfortunate hiker from the likelihood of being decapitated by a half-buried Roman mortar shell.

The path led us on past Brownhart Law, Greystone Brae, Black Halls, Wedder Hill and Rushy Fell until the mountain refuge hut finally came into view at the foot of the steep climb up Lamb Hill. We were roughly half way into our sixteen mile day and I was beginning, to my surprise and disappointment, to find the going difficult, not due to my controlled limp, but as a general fatigue gradually set in, the culmination of the traumas of the previous days and inadequate rations. I'd stopped for my lunch rest, then overtaken Janet and Keith as they did likewise, but couldn't face the assault ahead, after another pause, whilst they caught me, so I pressed on alone, acknowledging the first walkers so far, a couple on a local hike who were relaxing in the shelter.

My erstwhile walking companions were coping better, especially on the exhausting uphill sections, and they'd soon enough catch up, with me clinging on as the path continued its switchback progress. My intention was to get Lambs Hill under my belt, then relax and enjoy the splendid views over the closing seven miles, but it didn't turn out as hoped. For the first time since Standedge my legs were aching, protesting at the effort of propelling me up the steep hillside, despite my remembering to shorten my stride and drop my pace, at times to a feeble crawl, consciously simulating the selection of the rock bottom gear on a mountain bike.

I was concentrating not on "rushing" the mountain in an impatient attack, but a measured, slow and steady, progression, with breathing largely under control. I'd seen a TV documentary recommending this "mincing" method for difficult hill or mountain assaults, and it undoubtedly worked, Cross Fell being my definitive example. Unfortunately I was simply, not to put too fine a point on it, a bit knackered. I was also unimpressed, having given the contours on my map a cursory glance, that although The Pennine Way consistently claimed the higher ground (as it generally aspires throughout its

202

journey) it only maintained it by dropping sharply down, then back up, to crest each of the consecutive rolling hills.

I somehow dragged myself up onto Lambs Hill, which was followed, a mile later, by the higher summit of Beefstand Hill, then another mile, down and back up to Mozie Law, before a two mile slog, up, down, and up, to the summit of Windy Gyle (as opposed to "Windy" Gail, who's a good friend of my ex-work colleague Bev), today's highest point at 2,034 feet. I was really struggling, and after Janet and Keith caught me I fell behind on the final climb, my old enemy, thirst, sapping my morale.

I could last for miles on easy ground, or on most terrain given normal walking conditions, but throw in a succession of sweat-soaked climbs in hot sun and I was gasping for water every few hundred yards, only too aware that without accessible streams today's supplies would be gone (despite carrying additional bottles), and so it proved, the notoriously "dry" upper slopes of the Cheviots providing no respite. I grimly hauled myself upwards in stop-start pre-determined bursts, fixing my next objective – maybe a distinctive rock or a dog-leg in the path – where I'd pause to recover and draw strength from the height gained since my last halt.

It was the worst I'd felt in terms of overall fitness since climbing Jacob's Ladder, barely out of Edale, unfit and unattuned to the rigours ahead, and I had a "wobble" some quarter of a mile short of Windy Gyle when I wondered if I could go on – not that there was much alternative, the other option being to re-trace my steps, all thirteen miles of them. I was absolutely shattered, and my heels were on fire again. Janet and Keith were a couple of hundred yards ahead, but we'd agreed to walk in tandem from Windy Gyle, so I had no fear of being left to my own devices, just the physical effort of getting to that summit, and the additional fear, once I did, of being an embarrassing snail-pace liability over the final three miles to our B & B.

My en-route rations had been less than usual as I'd failed to take advantage of Keith's offer to bring me some sandwiches back when he nipped to the petrol station in Byrness first thing, only realising afterwards that I'd got just a couple of cereal bars and a banana left, compounded by my foolishly turning down a "Full English" and opting for my usual two boiled eggs and toast to complement my cornflakes. I was seriously under-fuelled – even the last of my Dextrose Energy tablets had gone – my only such mistake on the entire walk, and undoubtedly the result of a lazy and naïve complacency borne of the assumption that having kept my injury in check I was practically home and dry.

Instead, I was a few hundred feet below the trig point on Windy Gyle, as my colleagues plodded stoically on, feeling nauseous and shaky, sweating profusely and desperate for a drink. I waited for maybe a minute, more conscious than ever, as I surveyed the miles of nothing-ness, of my isolation and vulnerability, before pursuing my only option, that nightmare ascent. "Bloody hell, come on, Richard." That was my very worst Pennine Way moment, inclusive of injury pains, heat, melting tarmac, getting lost, being nearly blown off Pen-y-Ghent, even the terrifying clegs, but as the ground levelled out and I realised that I'd somehow battled to the top, spurred by my "get a grip" self-admonishment, my legs stopped shaking and my pounding chest eased.

I re-joined my colleagues for a five minute breather, and the gentle – in terms of gradient – traverse of the ridge and down to where the path, about a mile and a half on, broke sharp right off The Pennine Way to drop towards Uswayford Farm. My bedtime notes briefly summarised the day as "Heel problems developed again big-time and not enough food and drink – water ran out. Windy Gyle crippler, don't know how I made it". "Windy" was also a misnomer, along with Windy Crag and Windy Rigg, but at least it wasn't oppressively hot up there, and I surprised myself with my powers of recovery, feeling relatively comfortable again after our rest, and with no debilitating ascents to come.

I've heard of runners hitting the proverbial "wall" when they're on the edge of collapse, all reserves apparently exhausted, only to battle through with grim determination by drawing on hidden resources and breaking through the barrier in a "second wind". The slog up Windy Gyle was my "wall" and I'd got my second wind as we walked on towards that farm turning. This time tomorrow we'd be on our final stage, with Kirk Yetholm in our sights.

The Pennine Way shadows the Scottish border for most of the Cheviots crossing, evidenced by "Scotsman's Knowe" near The Cheviot itself, and my first – and only – sighting, unfortunately missed by Janet and Keith, of a wild haggis as it scuttled away quickly into the heather. I was so excited that I texted my mate Bob. His three word response suggested a hint of disbelief. "You are hallucinating." All three of us wondered if we were, as we descended towards dense forest – a rare plantation amongst the generally barren hills – down the path showing "Uswayford Farm 1.5 miles". Maybe we had been, as ten minutes later, approaching the trees, there was another sign "Uswayford Farm 1.5 miles".

It put me in mind of my early cycling epics, including a five country tour of Europe with two friends, and an impromptu decision by my brother and me to ride from Nottingham, on minor roads, to Newquay in Cornwall. We'd enter a village and there'd be a sign announcing "Zeal Monachorum", or some such mangle-worzeling backwater, "ten miles". We'd cycle along for a few minutes to the other end of the linear settlement, to find another sign, "Zeal Monachorum ten miles". It was irritating, to put it mildly, but clearly they'd taken the mean average distance, village to village, and stuck it on all the signs, however sparsely distributed. As for our Pennine Way experience, I can only put it down to a local idiosyncrasy.

We followed the path, which seemed to go on forever, down through dense conifers, cutting at right angles across a couple of forestry tracks, dropping steeply away through the trees, back onto open ground, then finally swinging round the hillside to crest a ridge, and reveal Uswayford Farm tucked away in splendid isolation in the valley below. In fact it was so well tucked away that three veteran Way-sters couldn't work out how to get there, unsure of the correct path. After some deliberation we chose to follow what proved in all probability to be a sheep track, as it led us high above, and beyond – were we to keep going – the farm settlement, across the shoulder of the hill.

We had another collective scratching of heads, and I spotted a gate, way down below us, giving access to the track behind the farm buildings, and thus we scrambled down, through the gate, and forded the little River Usway (hence the farm name), round the back of the outbuildings, and knocked on the door. Mrs Nancy Buglass greeted us – or rather, me, so I completed the introductions. "This is Janet and Keith." "I'm expecting you, but not you two." Keith looked puzzled. "We booked it weeks ago – it was all confirmed." "Yes, and you rang a couple of days ago to cancel, had to give up due to heat stroke."

It transpired that "Janet" had called, and the wrong booking had been cancelled. It explained why there'd been no sighting of the Wigan two, (as mentioned previously, any news would be welcome) but not why she expected no-one other than me, as both couples were originally due to stay that night. Regardless, it didn't matter, as I was the only anticipated arrival. "Well, I've got a room anyway", ventured Mrs Buglass, as if inviting Janet and Keith to confirm that they still wanted it (as opposed to retracing their steps and dossing in the forest).

Our landlady seemed distant and cold, and had few words, directing us brusquely upstairs to our rooms. I had to ask if we could have drinks - mine being the usual iced orange and lemonade in a pint glass, followed by no less than three full re-fills of cold tap water - and saying nothing of the pre-arranged evening meal, which was announced sharply - "Dinner's ready!" - by a shout upstairs a couple of hours later as we rested in our respective rooms. It was her first communication since our arrival. We had a shared bathroom, which Janet and Keith kindly insisted I use first, before I retreated into my spacious, light and airy accommodation, with its choice of three (or was it four?) unboarded beds, where I was surprised to find the bonus of a TV, dozing to the background of the Open Golf.

I don't profess to be a student of the human condition, but I'd instantly felt a sadness in our landlady's aloofness, which Keith exposed by an innocent question as she served our excellent evening meal, accompanied by three large lagers and the friendly attentions of two appealing (unless you're a rat or a rabbit) Border Terriers. It opened up a warm and moving discussion, which led on to a relaxed conversation revealing, amongst other things, that she kept prize goats, and that their sheep were breeding stock subsequently sold on for fattening on richer pastures down the valley.

Uswayford Farm is officially recognised as England's remotest Bed and Breakfast, and it's twenty one miles by vehicle, down a track then onto a minor road into the Coquet Valley, to the nearest shop, so it's bad news if you forget the milk, and of course they've had many an experience of being totally cut off in winter and spring snows. Water is drawn from an underground supply that has so far never failed. I think the location might just sneak into the definition of "rural".

If it ever closes its doors to guests then The Pennine Way has a problem.

~

Day Twenty. Uswayford Farm to Kirk Yetholm.

"Stepping down the glory road"

Final day! I discovered, after Mrs Buglass enquired about my limp, that her husband, who sat discreetly in the back kitchen and exchanged a brief "Good morning", had similar problems with heel damage, the not particularly good news being that he'd found it a painful and debilitating long-term condition. Walking was not recommended, but animal wool was (wonder where they got their supplies from?), and she was surprised when I showed her the wads ready for stuffing into my boots.

Breakfast over, only sixteen miles lay ahead, including the haul back to re-join the Way, and the three of us levered our feet into our boots for the last time in Pennine Way action before bidding our landlady a fond farewell. As we set out, intent on following a route that would thread us correctly back up the hillside and through the forest, Mr Buglass zoomed up the steep slope of the opposing moor on his quad bike, one of the dogs perched precariously behind him, barking furiously. It's difficult to imagine farms without dogs, and given the isolated nature of this undervalued occupation – which unsurprisingly possesses one of the highest suicide rates – their company must sometimes be a lifesaver. It's an environment that pairs man plus best friend in a timeless relationship.

Despite following instructions and crossing the Usway further up by the little footbridge, rather than paddling across at the ford, we still had to zig-zag, eyes peeled, up the steep slope before re-claiming the defined path, albeit not where we should have, that climbed between the trees and beyond, onto the open ridge. Uswayford Farm, in addition to being the remotest B & B, also has the distinction of being the most difficult to get into and away from, our head-scratching approach last night matched by similar confusion as we tried to retrace our steps.

Having eventually done so, we found ourselves back, at a surprisingly early 9 a.m., on The Pennine Way where we'd left it, but not as we'd last seen it. Two small tents were pitched, with quad bikes parked outside. I shouted a "Morning!" through the canvas (or its modern equivalent) and got a muffled "Morning" in response. The assumption, and hope, was that they were up there on Forestry Commission or other legitimate activities but if they were merely thrill seekers I wish a plague of clegs on them, their homes and their first-born. Not that there were any in evidence, which was a slight disappointment, as I would have liked a very small-scale intrusion just to show the ignorant and repellent (in terms of horsefly attraction) Janet and Keith exactly how I came by my itchy red lumps.

Still, there was the glorious open scenery as compensation which, buoyed by my food and rest, and the excitement of our final day, I was appreciating to the full. Northumberland is one of England's finest counties, possibly my favourite. I've walked the magnificent Simonside Hills whilst on holiday in Rothbury, explored most of the wonderful, wild, coastline, including a visit to The Farne Islands, with its seal colonies and spectacular bird life – the horizontally whizzing exocet missiles known as Puffins, the aggressive but attractive Arctic Terns (earlier comment refers!) and the stunningly beautiful, wave-hugging, Gannets, to name but three examples.

I stayed in the lovely town of Alnwick barely a week after finishing my walk, where I was a privileged visitor in order to twice see my Estonian nieces Eva and Anneli, plus Eva's husband Toomas, with their choir from little Elva (near Tartu) perform to great acclaim at The Alnwick International Music Festival. I also attended a Northumbrian night and reflected on this region's tradition of folk music, dance, dialect and poetry, in which respect it's retained a common heritage with its Celtic and Scandinavian neighbours and relatives. Long may it endure, and all credit to those who, like Runrig in terms of their Gaelic legacy, take legitimate pride in passing down and enriching and evolving their cultural roots. Unfortunately, I don't think an evening of traditional Nottinghamshire folk music, clog dancing, fiddle and accordion playing would have much of a legacy to draw on!

The weather forecast (wrong again) had predicted cloud and heavy thundery showers by early afternoon, but we were treated to a perfect summer's day, in the high twenties, and a glorious still evening, with scarcely a cloud from first to last. Butt Roads quickly came and went, followed by King's Seat and Score Head, and not for the first time I wondered at the origin of these names, often whimsical and eccentric, for seemingly featureless and irrelevant areas of hillside or moorland. Where exactly did Butt Roads become White Knowe, and why? They were presumably relevant to territorial possessions or grazing rights, as well as the self-explanatory landmarks, for example Windy Gyle, recorded and "codified" in deeds and by early cartographers, to be subsequently formalised in perpetuity by Ordnance and similarly authoritative mapsters. There are thousands of bits of uninhabited Britain with an assortment of weird and wonderful names.

We passed Mallie Side to our left, but The Pennine Way then led us slightly right, and steeply uphill, to Cairn Hill (west top) which at 2,438 feet was to be the highest point on our traverse of The Cheviots. An optional spur broke away for a mile (and the same mile back) to take in The Cheviot itself, at 2,676 feet, but it's not considered a mandatory part of the Way, and the general consensus is that despite its height it's a fairly uninspiring and featureless summit, so we opted out. The Pennine Way takes a sharp left at this point, losing just 56 feet in its gentle descent to Auchope Cairn, at 2,382 feet, and what for me was the most spectacular and memorable section of the entire Cheviots, the deep "V" shaped valley, down below to our right, known as Hen Hole.

That section of just under a mile from the Cairn to the second mountain refuge hut was breathtaking, although I was glad we were heading north as it's probably the steepest part of the Cheviot journey, and I was more than usually grateful for my stick and trouble-free knees on the jarring descent. It would be a severe early test heading south from Kirk Yetholm. We rested briefly, inscribing our names in the visitors book at the little wooden shelter, and chatting to a foreign accented lady (I forget where, she may have said

Czech, or Swiss) with a dog, who was about to tackle that fierce ascent on a day's hike.

There was a palpable feeling, as we moved off again, of last day euphoria. School's out, or would be tomorrow, and today's lessons were an exercise in coasting to the afternoon bell, or in our case The Border Hotel, Kirk Yetholm, the official finish (or start) of The Pennine Way. My total distance, I reckoned, amounted to 280 miles, an exact and fairly modest sounding 14 miles per day overall, or 15.135 in actual walking time, taking out my rest day and the half day to Cowling, but I was still feeling proud of myself, all things considered, as we faced the one remaining significant ascent, up onto the locally well known viewpoint of The Schill, at 1,985 feet.

As we started our climb, somewhere near the very slightly Scottish sounding – although we were still just in English territory – Birnie Brae, we met that rarest of species, a southbound Way-ster. He was bursting to tell us of his experience up on The Schill. The chap himself, similar age to me, was clearly an experienced walker, fit and lean, had already walked The Pennine Way northbound and was now trying it in the opposite direction, as you do – or at least as he did.

He'd engaged a family in conversation, to find, to his amazement, that they were also southbound Way-sters, fresh out of Kirk Yetholm, but to all intents and purposes they seemed clueless. Overweight, over-packed, and with almost no reserves of water – he reckoned about one desultory litre between three of them – they were ambling along and videoing the proceedings, with enough equipment, including batteries, to sustain a film set. He'd set off after them, and was already, only five miles out, a full mile ahead. He was incredulous when they told him that they were heading not for Uswayford Farm – which itself seemed, on the available evidence, mission impossible – but the entire crossing of The Cheviots to Byrness.

Whether he tried, politely, to dissuade them, or at least enlighten them with a helpful warning, he didn't say, but he was still shaking his head in disbelief as we parted, with mutual best wishes, and his congratulations on our imminent success. We wondered if he'd maybe exaggerated a little. He hadn't. They were still there when we

211

reached The Schill, sticking out like the proverbial sore thumb. We'd chosen to take our final relaxing break there, enjoying, for once, the hot sunshine now that the metaphorical heat had gone out of our challenge, with the wonderful feeling that only four and a half miles of easy descent (apart from a sneaky hill just before the finish) lay ahead, but we automatically kept our distance from the trio and flopped down further on.

I think I exchanged a brief nod. They just exuded "different planet". Dad, maybe in his forties, was busy filming mum and teenage son with the bulky camera. Mum was reposing on a rock. Son was lying flat out on a ledge, stripped to the waist facing the sun, and trying to set a Pennine Way record by getting heat stroke within the opening five miles. Both parents carried excess baggage of their own, not counting their recording gear and huge packs, which were enough to challenge Pickfords. They were giggling and carrying on like schoolkids.

Janet reckoned that if they set off immediately (which didn't look likely) and maintained a good average walking speed (which looked impossible) they still wouldn't make Byrness by 10 p.m., but a more realistic assessment was 2.00 or 3.00 a.m. I suggested that as a qualified GP she should go over to them and forbid it on medical grounds. I've no idea what became of them, and they may have defied our superficial misgivings, although I doubt it, and their apparent lack of respect for the challenge ahead and, by implication, the rescue services, was in sharp contrast to the attitude of everyone else we met along the Way.

We descended from The Schill, around the shoulder of Black Hag, to a point where a choice of route met us. My guide stated: "for those with surplus energy an alternative route (roughly the same distance but more climbing) exists over Steer Rig and White Law. Lesser mortals will branch left at this point to drop straight down to the valley below." I'd already made my decision ("lesser mortal") based partly on my previous experiences on The Bowes Loop, and shortly after Bellingham, of "alternative routes", plus increasing fatigue and thirst which mitigated against any unnecessary climbing.

Keith favoured the higher route, his guide notes extolling its scenic virtues, and Janet was more or less neutral, although I think she had a slight preference for the official route. I was not to be dissuaded, so we agreed amicably to take separate paths and meet up again three miles on where the Way became one again at a track meeting the metalled road into Kirk Yetholm, and walk together over the final two thirds of a mile.

Quite literally, "You take the High Road ......", and I probably was in Scotland before them, if only because I was a few paces ahead near Black Hag, where Scottish soil appears to be claimed, albeit that there's no visible evidence, and strangely it never even crossed my mind until the last 200 yards when I asked Keith if we were officially in Scotland yet. I can't vouch for the High Road (although Janet and Keith enjoyed the views) but I was well impressed with my choice as an easy path wound its way down between the mountains into the valley, with stunning views, a fitting reward for all my endeavours and trials.

Past Old Halterburnhead, then Halterburnhead, with its handful of cottages, and civilisation reclaimed, with decidedly mixed feelings, as the path met a farm track - and two lads on motorbikes - that soon became the tarmac home. I saw a large bird of prey, probably a buzzard judging from its serrated wings, but I couldn't be sure, as it floated lazily on the warm air currents above a patch of wooded hillside. I watched it for several minutes before it dropped into the trees, and out of sight. The aptly named Sunnyside Hill came and went, then Janet and Keith came into view, high on the ridge to my right, dropping down the steep hillside to met me where the official and alternative routes converged. Perfect timing.

That last little bit, on sticky tarmac and in hot sunshine, was surprisingly taxing, as the little lane cut sharply up and across the side of Staerough Hill. Even Keith expressed dismay, before Kirk Yetholm finally showed itself immediately ahead as we crested the brow. A short descent, past the Kirk Yetholm sign, and there was The Border Hotel, official finish of The Pennine Way. It stands at the far right-hand end of the green, which is the centrepiece of this attractive village, with its cottages clustered around its periphery, but before tracing those final few triumphant paces I had one pre-determined task to perform.

I plonked my rucsac down, rummaged into its deeper recesses where lay my fleece, shorts and waterproof trousers, and extracted my almost pristine, only worn once since purchase, (for my evening meal at The Langdon Beck Hotel) Nottingham Forest Away shirt, in fetching Brazilian yellow – which is something of a misnomer given Forest's current status. Its moment of glory had arrived. I peeled off my blue insect-repellent top and claimed the final twenty yards of The Pennine Way in my Forest shirt, posing for photographs, courtesy of Keith, outside the Border Hotel, preceded by congratulatory handshakes and hugs. Well done to all!

Into the shade of The Border, and I sunk a desperately needed pint of orange and lemonade before the landlady asked for our names for presentation of our personalised Pennine Way certificates, which was a nice surprise. Complimentary drinks also arrived, in my case a cider for a change, but as I remarked, "It's a bloody long way for a free half!" We chatted with another southbound Way-ster – there was a mini glut of them on this July Saturday – expressing surprise at his mid-afternoon assault on the Cheviots, but he was relaxed and confident. An experienced walker, he intended to take advantage of the cooler evening to press on, and simply pitch his tent at a suitable spot when he'd had enough – quite a comforting thought, provided you've enough rations of food and water. Overnight camping whilst parched would be a recipe for disaster. I wonder what he was to make of the Schill family when he caught them, probably at the first mountain refuge hut.

There'd been a fire at the hotel, evidenced by the plastic sheeting over the roof of the accommodation block, as re-construction proceeded, but the restaurant was open, so we booked a celebratory evening meal before adjoining to our replacement accommodation at The Mill, and what accommodation! We'd saved the best till last, which is no mean tribute as I'd enjoyed some excellent digs and only been disappointed on a couple of occasions. The Mill, at the far end of the village past the imposing and unusual church, stood, unsurprisingly, alongside the little river, and was exceptional.

A very recent and high standard conversion, it provided top quality facilities and friendly service to rival a luxury four star hotel, to such an extent that we inspected each other's rooms, mine having as its centrepiece an impressive chandelier, which might sound pretentious, but was a perfect complement to the tasteful furnishings and décor. The large en-suite was immaculate, all fancy taps, marble tiles and indulgent extras, and I felt a bit over-cosseted as I crammed my stinkies into their carrier bag, for shoving into the bottom of my dusty rucsac, and propped my stick carefully in a convenient corner.

I had a choice of two double beds, with their precisely scattered pretty cushions (gathering them up and putting them in a tidy pile, as I had at Hawes – just what else exactly are you supposed to do with them?) and selected the bed directly facing the TV cabinet, where I half dozed and half watched more Open Golf, as Tiger Woods cruised, despite another full day's play remaining, to what seemed inevitable victory.

My own victory tasted pretty sweet, although I was limping heavily again. I hope I haven't left myself with permanent damage, as, several months later, and with the whiff of another walk in my nostrils – maybe even a Pennine Way repeat, but on a different schedule – I'm still struggling. I'll give it until the lighter evenings return, then the reluctant last resort of an appointment with my GP, whose advice I studiously ignored before I set off from Edale. I'm glad I did though, and whilst my little jaunt may not be exceptional in terms of outdoor challenges I'm proud of my achievements. I've scratched my 36 year itch and met some good friends and companions, of whom I'm especially grateful to Janet and Keith.

They were off to Berwick-upon-Tweed by taxi first thing Sunday morning for a direct early train to Derby, where they'd left the car with family, who'd taken them up to Edale that first morning. Their arrangements would have suited me, with an easy connection from Derby to Nottingham, but I declined their offer of sharing as I intended to enjoy a lie-in and "savour the moment" in Kirk Yetholm before getting the local bus to Berwick, where I'd find a B & B and spend a lazy afternoon and evening before the Derby train on Monday morning - which is exactly what I did. As my rucsac spent most of the journey on luggage racks, as opposed to my back, I even wore my Forest shirt, relishing the odd hostile look as I waited for my connection at Derby station.

In the meantime, there was that little matter of our dinner appointment at The Border Hotel, and the unanimous verdict was that it matched our accommodation. I originally passed on a starter, opting for an orange juice in anticipation of a large main course, but the arrival of Keith's Haggis and Field Mushrooms broke my resistance, and the waiter brought another one for my exclusive attention. It was delicious, as were our respective main courses, but we still found room for dessert.

Keith ordered Sticky Toffee Pudding.

~

Comhlan Ceilteach na H-Albainn

Play Gaelic
The Highland Connection
Recovery
Heartland
The Cutter and The Clan
Once in a Lifetime
Searchlight
The Big Wheel
Amazing Things
Transmitting Live
Mara
Long Distance
The Gaelic Collection
In Search of Angels
Live at Celtic Connections
The Stamping Ground
Proterra
Day of Days
Runrig – The Best
Summer 2007 – to be released

Moran taing!!

~